W9-CYT-097

MEXICO

WITHDRAWN

Help Us Keep This Guide Up to Date

Every effort has been made by the authors and editors to make this guide as accurate and useful as possible. However, many things can change after a guide is published—establishments close, phone numbers change, facilities come under new management, housing costs fluctuate, and so on.

We would love to hear from you concerning your experiences with this guide and how you feel it could be made better and be kept up to date. While we may not be able to respond to all comments and suggestions, we'll take them to heart and we'll make certain to share them with the authors. Please send your comments and suggestions to the following address:

The Globe Pequot Press
Reader Response/Editorial Department
P.O. Box 480
Guilford, CT 06437

Or you may e-mail us at:

editorial@globe-pequot.com

Thanks for your input, and happy travels!

Choose Retirement Series

CHOOSE MEXICO

Travel, Investment, and Living Opportunities for Every Budget

Eighth Edition

JOHN HOWELLS AND DON MERWIN

The Globe Pequot Press

GUILFORD, CONNECTICUT

Text design by Laura Augustine
Maps by Lisa Reneson © The Globe Pequot Press

ISBN 0-7627-2603-2

Manufactured in the United States of America
Eighth Edition/First Printing

CONTENTS

Authors' Preface to the Eighth Edition

Ageless, timeless Mexico—the crash of surf on a deserted Pacific beach, the clop of burros' hooves along the cobblestone streets of a serene mountain village, the rhythmic slap of a woman's hands as she shapes her family's daily tortillas—some things never change. But others do, some too rapidly and too often for any book to keep up with: the daily fluctuation of the exchange rate (the number of pesos you will get for your dollar), the price of a bottle of beer, the cost of an airline ticket to Guadalajara. What we do our best to reflect in each successive revision of this book (this is the eighth edition) is the great middle range of things that change from year to year: the laws governing permanent residence in Mexico, the overall trend of inflation, the communities currently most attractive to prospective retirees, the best sources of up-to-date information on those things that change from day to day.

The task of keeping informed is made easier for us by the tremendous amount of information on the World Wide Web and our ability to keep in touch with our sources all over Mexico by e-mail. But nothing can substitute for the feel about life south of the border that we get from our frequent trips there, especially those extended stays when we shop for our food in Mexican markets, get our hair cut by Mexican barbers, and talk directly with native-born and foreign residents.

The growing popularity of cable and direct-by-satellite TV is one of the newer facts of life in Mexico. Turning on the set in our apartment or hotel and seeing the latest stock prices or baseball scores may break the spell of that wonderful feeling of being a million miles from home so prized by many vacationers. But together with the ease of daily "conversation" with friends and family back home via e-mail, it does provide the sense of connectedness that is an essential for the comfort of many who have chosen to live in a foreign country.

The increasing presence of American companies and products is another new fact of life. A walk through one of Mexico's rapidly proliferating shopping centers could almost (but not quite) convince you that you never left home. Many of our observations in previous editions about the scarcity of familiar items and brands are no longer valid. It is no longer likely that you will have to ask visitors from the United States to bring you a half-dozen tubes of your favorite toothpaste.

The good news is that the new and the old seem able to exist side by side in today's Mexico. A short stroll away from the center of most towns will bring you to neighborhoods largely untouched by American commerce and the lifestyles of the twenty-first century. However, to get to the full richness of Old Mexico, you may want to try one of the retirement sites we have characterized as "For the More Adventurous." There you won't find a K-Mart, a boutique, or an English-language newspaper. You won't hear English spoken, either—brush up on your Spanish if you are thinking about moving to one of these out-of-the-way places. But count on it: The people there, like most Mexicans and North Americans who have chosen to live in Mexico, will be welcoming, friendly, and eager to share their beautiful country with you.

Introduction

What kind of retirement do you want? Many people are content to spend the years after work glued to an easy chair in front of the TV. Perhaps they'll play an occasional round of golf when the weather permits. If that's what they want, the idea of moving to Mexico will probably seem ridiculous to them.

But there are others who look forward to retirement as an exciting change in lifestyle, not just a break from the workaday world. They want a complete change, perhaps in an exotic setting. (If you're reading this book, you probably fall into this category.) Most people dream of a warm, temperate climate, surrounded by natural beauty and friendly people. For them life is uncomplicated, easy, yet never boring. Somewhere in the background, music plays and delicious food is close by. From the picture window in the living room or from a tree-shaded patio, picturesque mountains form a hazy green backdrop—or is it the gentle swell of the ocean's surf? Or maybe the view is of wide boulevards and handsome buildings of a cosmopolitan city. We don't all have precisely the same dreams.

Unfortunately, for most people the reality of retirement will bear little resemblance to this ideal. Fantasies are free, but comfortable living normally requires greater means than that available from Social Security or other retirement benefits, given the high cost of living in the United States or Canada today.

Warm, tropical countries abound elsewhere in the world, that's true, but most of them are not places you would want to try on for retirement. For a country to be a practical place for most North Americans to live, in addition to a nice climate, it should meet five conditions:

1. It should be affordable.
2. It should be easily accessible, so you can visit your family and friends occasionally, and they can visit you once in a while. (It goes without saying that it should be a place where they want to visit.)
3. It should be a safe place to live, a place where local people like and respect North Americans.
4. It should offer access to good medical care.

5. It should have large numbers of English-speaking residents—preferably fellow North Americans—and a well-developed society that welcomes newcomers with warmth and genuine friendliness. This last item is perhaps the most important of all. For many retirees, without an extensive and friendly population of English-speaking compatriots, life would be boring.

Clearly Mexico fulfills all these requirements. It is affordable. This is a point we will discuss in greater detail. It is accessible by air, by bus, and by car. Mexico isn't crime free, but retirees there uniformly report that they feel at least as safe as in the United States. Mexico's doctors, many of them trained in the United States, provide top-quality health care. And Mexico offers living situations ranging from some where there are great numbers of North American retirees with a well-developed network of community organizations and activities, to others where you see compatriots only when you want to.

Because Mexico is "next door," just a few days' drive from most places in the United States or Canada, trying it out as a place to live doesn't involve a major commitment. You needn't bother with complicated visa requirements; a simple tourist card allows you a six-month trial visit. Should you decide you like Mexico as a place to live, it's a relatively simple matter to convert your tourist card into a long-term visa. On the other hand, should you discover that you hate Mexico, it's a simple matter to pack up and return home for another look at your retirement menu.

The close proximity of Mexico is yet another advantage for those who want to experience foreign retirement. Most North Americans tell us they feel a need to renew their contact with home once in a while. They miss friends and relatives; they need a "culture fix." This is easy when living in Mexico, because home is just a few hours away. With your tastefully decorated house in Mexico as an attraction, family and friends will be tempted to visit, and you will have frequent opportunities to play the gracious host. If you lived in Europe, on the other hand, visitors would be few and far between.

A Different Mexico

The Mexico we describe in this book is not the country experienced by tourists on a two-week vacation. It isn't the Mexico visited by affluent vacationers who move from one luxury hotel to another, seldom coming in contact with the local people. We present you with the Mexico known by residents who live in the *real* Mexico. It is the Mexico enjoyed by North Americans—particularly those of middle age and beyond—who savor the experience and adventure of exploring a Mexican-Spanish culture, making new friends, and beginning a new chapter of their lives. These newcomers want affordable, comfortable places to live, a healthy and enjoyable climate, reliable medical care, and, above all, activities that define the difference between stagnation and vitality.

Many changes have taken place since the original publication of *Choose Mexico* some eighteen years ago. The transportation system, already good in 1985, is even better today. Luxury buses run on many principal routes, and there are faster, newer, more comfortable, and better-maintained roads throughout the country. The construction of a modern network of high-speed toll roads has dramatically changed intercity automobile travel. Today drivers no longer need to worry about finding unleaded gasoline. It's now available almost everywhere. The frequent and unpredictable shortages of consumer items that were common in the mid-eighties appear to be a thing of the past. Branches of all the familiar U.S. discount "megastores" are springing up in all the larger cities. In many respects, Mexico is becoming less quirky. If, as we do, you prize Mexico's distinctiveness, you can only hope as we do that it doesn't become too predictable and modern.

Mexico Is Not Just for Retirees

In many respects the new generation nearing retirement age in this new millennium is very different from previous waves of retirees. For one thing, many people today opt for retirement at a younger age. More people retire in their fifties, some even earlier as they are "downsized" from their professions. It's no surprise that this more youthful group is active and vigorous and demands a lifestyle that doesn't involve sitting on the front porch or passively watching hours of television. "Retirement" isn't precisely what they have in mind. They seek a "new beginning," whether this means starting a business or finding an interesting job in a new field.

Since the advent of NAFTA (the North American Free Trade Agreement), many barriers to going into business in Mexico have been removed. North Americans are experimenting with various enterprises, applying their experience from their business lives, looking for a satisfying niche in an exotic foreign location. Many international corporations have located in Mexico since NAFTA made this practical. The job market for skilled workers has opened windows of opportunities for those who want to work and live in Mexico. The bigger towns and cities have large numbers of North Americans employed in offices, factories, and research labs. Mexico City, Guadalajara, Puebla, and other cities are hosting thousands of expatriate workers. Working papers are required, but the corporations have little trouble acquiring permission for employees to live in Mexico.

Living in Mexico Part of the Year

More and more people are discovering that Mexico is an ideal place for part-time living. Uncounted thousands spend pleasant winters there and return to their homes north of the border every spring. When we first started writing about retiring in Mexico, we tended to underestimate this phenomenon. "Wintering" in Mexico, or anywhere else for that matter, seemed like something you read about on the society pages, something that only rich people could do. The more we travel in Mexico in winter, however, the more people we meet who are neither tourists nor full-time residents. Their homes are in Burlington, Vermont, or Duluth, Minnesota. They enjoy a month (or two, or three) in Mexico's sunshine and rejoin their neighbors, children, and grandchildren in the spring.

The opposite side of this coin is the great influx of "summer Mexicans" who flee from the heat and humidity of the southern states, especially Texas, to enjoy the moderate climate of Mexico's central plateau. Some are retirees, some are teachers, and others have jobs that leave their summers free. They, too, develop strong ties to the country, returning to the same places year after year, but their real homes continue to be up north.

Therefore, although this book was written primarily for people who are planning for retirement, we keep hearing from two other groups: (1) people who are already retired but are unhappy with their current situation and are hoping to find something better and (2) younger people, particularly those engaged in seasonal work, who find Mexico a great place to live for part of each year. Why not escape winter by relaxing on a tropical beach or enjoying a sunny mountain village? For those planning to retire "at home," a part-time retirement in Mexico is an excellent idea. Reasonable prices in Mexico make early or partial retirement possible on an income far smaller than you might imagine.

Seasonal retirement is practical for those who don't want to move away from family, friends, bridge partners, golf buddies, their gardens, their hobbies, and so on. Living part of the year in Mexico allows you to choose the best seasons in both your home base and your second home in Mexico. This is possible because of the menu of climates Mexico offers: cool mountain towns to escape Phoenix summers, warm beach towns and sunny desert towns to escape Minnesota winters.

Some part-timers rent the same place every year. They may arrange for a place to store their extra belongings so they don't have to lug them back and forth every time they visit.

Having a yearly "lease" on the same place permits you to become acquainted with the year-round neighbors. You'll feel at home in your second home, knowing the best places to shop, where to dine, and all the special things your chosen community offers.

Returning to the same town at the same time of the year also puts you into social contact with others who have similar patterns, and you'll make many new friends, who will greet you with joyous homecomings, parties, dinners, etc. Thus you have two sets of friends: those in your home-base town and those in your seasonal home. These second friends have a way of expanding your social connections in the States (or Canada) with visits back and forth while at home.

Obviously retirement in Mexico isn't for everyone. (Thank goodness for that, or the country would soon be overrun with North Americans.) Most retirees decide not to move away for retirement or, if they do move, stay in their own country. Others feel that a total change of scenery is called for. For them, the chance to start a totally new life with new friends and experiences can be an adventure in itself. Still others need to move away from the high-cost areas where they presently live and are looking for someplace more affordable. Fortunately Mexico is an alternative for both full-time and part-time retirement that doesn't involve a total severing of ties.

An Affordable Cost of Living

Over the years Mexico's low cost of living has enabled expatriates to enjoy a fascinating life with a gracious lifestyle far beyond what a similar budget would allow back home. Prices for goods and services, rents, and other living expenses vary from very low to moderate—depending upon the particular curve of the currency exchange cycle the country is going through. This is what happens: The value of the peso gradually rises against the dollar, which results in inflation from the standpoint of the person using dollars. Then a sudden drop in the value of the peso brings prices down dramatically, starting a new cycle. The last time the sudden drop occurred was December 1994, when the value of the peso fell from about three to the dollar to about ten to the dollar. Prices remained the same in pesos, but because expatriates received more than twice as many pesos for the dollar, actual prices were more than cut in half. Then the cycle started all over again.

However, the cycle can never zoom high enough to make Mexico as expensive a place to live as the United States. Why? Because of the differences in labor costs, utilities, and locally produced food. When your maid and gardener are happy to work for $1.00 an hour, when locally grown foods cost a fraction of what they cost on the other side of the border, and when you needn't spend a fortune to heat your Mexican home in the winter or air-condition it in the summer, your budget should never stretch to the breaking point. At the time this edition of *Choose Mexico* was written, most costs were about two-thirds of those in the United States and the dollar had started to climb in value against the peso.

Not everything in Mexico is bargain priced. Some items cost as much as in the United States. Airfare, gasoline, highway tolls, imported foods, and long-distance calls are no bargains. Yet these costs aren't critical in a country where good public transportation abounds, domestically processed foods are varied and delicious, and e-mail substitutes for the lost art of letter writing and for long-distance telephone calls. Room rates in luxury hotels, particularly in resort areas, are pegged to the international, not Mexican, economy. Yet we've found clean, comfortable hotel rooms for as little as $25 per night, and nowhere on our most recent trip did we pay more than $50. We ate in good restaurants, paying a maximum of $10 per person for a full-course dinner with beverages. (These prices are not uniform throughout the country and vary depending on the region. Baja California, for example, is a bit more pricey than the mainland, and rents in a small village will be much less expensive than those in a large resort town.)

Living in Mexico can be inexpensive, depending upon your lifestyle, yet we must emphasize that the biggest attraction here is not cheap living. As we've stated many times in previous editions of *Choose Mexico*, we do not encourage those with extremely limited funds to move to Mexico. You'll find no "safety net" here—no welfare, no food stamps, no one to take care of you—and the expatriate community resents having indigents descend upon them. Furthermore, full-time residency requires a minimum income or else a tedious and expensive return to the border every six months to renew visas. (Even this latter option may not be available forever.) Always make sure you have some money as a backup, because someday you may want to return to your former home. Consider Mexico's affordable cost of living as the icing on the cake, not the only reason to live here.

Singles

Although our examples of living in Mexico are framed in terms of couples, there is no community of retirees in Mexico that does not include a large number of singles, both men and women. Single men can and do go anywhere in Mexico that their fancies take them, depending upon their level of adventure. Single women, however, seem to feel more comfortable where there is a concentration of their compatriots.

Of course, much has to do with the level of personal safety in any given town. Suzanne Kelly—who moved to Ajijic a few years ago and who publishes an on-line retiree newsletter called *Mexico Mama*—said in a recent interview: "I have no problem living in Mexico as a single woman; in fact, I find my Mexican neighbors keep an eye on me. And, there is about as much crime here as anywhere else I've lived—about the same as in the California college town I came from. As far as romance goes, there are few available men in Ajijic of my age, in their forties, so ladies, if you're shopping for a man, you could find the 'pickin's' slim. Though I keep myself plenty busy with video projects and my newsletter, I do wish I had more English-speaking friends my age."

Judy King, who sells real estate in the Guadalajara area, says, "I moved here single and feel that is an advantage. I made this choice for me, without trying to coordinate my desires with a mate's wants and needs. I have seen a few marriages split up because one wanted to go back and the other wanted to stay here—so they did! I never am afraid for my personal safety in this country. I have driven from the border alone several times; I walk in the villages at any time of day or night; I live alone. But in Mexico, unlike in the United States, I am always surrounded by families. My homes have been the villages on the North Shore of Lake Chapala, closely surrounded by the homes of my Mexican neighbors. Families are always walking on the sidewalks, people sitting on their stoops, or just inside their doorways, with their families. Even when in downtown Guadalajara, a city of ten to twelve million persons, I feel comfortable walking alone at 10:00 or 11:00 at night, because of the family groups moving about the city."

Note: Unless otherwise stated, all telephone and fax numbers in this book are in Mexico and require that you dial the proper international access, country, and city codes to reach. These numbers are listed under international calling in many U.S. directories; an international operator can help if you have trouble.

WHY CHOOSE MEXICO?

The People

In the course of gathering information for the first edition of this book, we mailed a questionnaire to hundreds of retired Americans living in Mexico. One of the questions we asked was, "What do you like best about Mexico?" To our surprise and delight, the answer most frequently at the top of the list was "the people." What is it about the Mexican people that appeals so strongly to North Americans? What qualities transcend the barriers of language, class, ethnicity, and culture to evoke this response so universally? First, it's their friendliness. Mexicans routinely treat strangers with warmth and curiosity. The fact that you are a foreigner as well as a stranger seems to be incidental. Second, it's their happiness. It may be anomalous, but poverty in Mexico is much more common than misery. The people there seem to have the ability to enjoy life, no matter how difficult its circumstances. It is a gift that as a people, we in the United States do not appear to possess.

Related to their friendliness, but separate from it, is their helpfulness. Mexicans are almost always willing to stop whatever they are doing to be of assistance to a friend, a neighbor, or a stranger. They even seem to welcome the opportunity to be helpful (or perhaps to stop what they are doing). Another related quality Mexicans possess is courtesy. Politeness is not enough to make an individual or a people good, and, perhaps as a reaction to our belated recognition of that fact, we in the United States have given up politeness altogether. Mexicans, however, are too deeply steeped in a tradition of courtesy centuries old to have acquired the knack for rudeness. Most people still ask to be excused when they must squeeze by you in a crowd, and they still preface every request or order with *por favor* (please).

Then there's the love the Mexicans so obviously feel for their children. Much has been said and written about *machismo*, but there is no more common sight in Mexico than a father carrying and caring for his baby or young child. A sensitive observer of the Mexican scene has noted that North Americans are often distressed by the callousness with which the Mexicans treat animals, but that Mexicans are equally scandalized by the verbal brutality North American parents visit on their children. Perhaps if Mexican children were not so extremely well behaved, the sight of a parent screaming at his offspring might be more common, but as it is, we've never seen it.

As you spend more time in Mexico and learn more Spanish, your understanding of Mexicans is likely to undergo many changes. It will become clear, for instance, that easy friendliness will not often evolve into deeper friendship. Despite this contradiction of the Mexican character, the appeal of the people remains the uppermost reason for choosing Mexico.

The Beauty

Gorgeous beaches flank both sides of the country, some crowded with sun-drenched tourists happy to escape from northern winters, some silently inviting you to explore miles of untracked sand. From the picturesque desert panorama of Baja California to the tropical jungles of the Yucatán, the country abounds in breathtaking scenery. This draws a multitude of Canadians and Americans who spend billions every year taking in the beauty of Mexico.

Cities with modern buildings and elegant restaurants flowing with excitement thrill many North Americans, whereas others prefer villages with cobblestoned streets and concerts in the town square. Each part of Mexico has its particular character. Each city and village is distinct, its personality differing dramatically from all others. This uniqueness is not found in North America, where so many towns are carbon copies of each other, down to identical restaurants, signs, and mass-produced architecture.

We've heard people state that they think Mexico is ugly, because they've visited Tijuana or some other border town and weren't impressed. This judgment is about as fair as one made by a European visitor who, after flying into the middle of Nevada, claimed that the United States was a desert, with almost no one living there! (As you might suspect, we don't particularly recommend border towns as choice places to retire.)

Something that impressed the Spanish conquistadores was the inhabitants' love of flowers. There was something almost religious about blossoms, and they were to be found everywhere: in gardens, along roads, painted on walls. Almost 500 years later the Mexican people's use of flowers continues to impress newcomers to the country. No home is complete without some tenderly cared for potted plants in the windows and perhaps bougainvilleas blooming over the door. In fact Mexicans don't take this floral beauty for granted. So much of it, provided by nature, is all around them, and what requires a pot, some earth, some seeds, or a brush and some paint is considered as much a necessity as food and shelter.

The Climate

Many people whose experience with Mexico is limited to brief visits to towns on the United States border, or whose picture of the country was formed from cartoons and Westerns, think of Mexico as a hot, dry place with endless vistas of treeless desert, spotted with cactus and cattle skeletons bleaching in the sun. Of course Mexico has its share of places that are unbearably hot, bone-chillingly cold, too humid, or too dry. However, the good news is that Mexico presents newcomers with a menu of magnificent climates. The country is a checkerboard of valleys and plateaus, often with different climates in neighboring sections. In the tropics, for every 300-foot increase in altitude, the temperature drops one degree Fahrenheit. While the Gulf Coast cities like Villahermosa and Veracruz might swelter at ninety-five degrees, Mexico City enjoys temperatures of seventy to seventy-five degrees. There is also a difference in climate between the Pacific Coast and the Gulf Coast. The constant sea breeze blowing across the Pacific keeps summer and winter temperatures pleasant, whereas the Gulf Coast can suffocate in the summer and catch chilly northern winds that whip down from Canada in winter. Not by coincidence, the places where most Americans (and Mexicans) choose to live are either at high enough altitudes to enjoy "eternal spring" or on the Pacific Coast where the temperatures are higher but tempered by continual ocean breezes.

Living in a Foreign Country

Canada and the United States have too many similarities in language, worldviews, and customs to be considered "foreign." Therefore, for millions of North Americans, Mexico may be the only foreign country they will ever visit.

Mexico appreciates these visitors, for they pour billions of dollars into the economy. (The Mexican government refers to tourism as its "green pipeline.") Tourists carry away good memories of a vacation well spent— along with uncounted tons of curios, weavings, pottery, and a host of other items as presents for their friends back home. They enjoy the beaches, mountains, and interesting countryside and cities, yet they often miss the most charming part of Mexico: its unique culture. Underlying the tourist traps, American-style restaurants, and curio shops is a truly interesting country.

When we talk of foreign travel, we often think of Europe. To be sure, Mexico has European roots, beginning with the Spanish conquistadores. Yet behind this background is a rich tapestry of customs and beliefs that dates back to the Aztecs, the Mayas, and even earlier civilizations. Folk beliefs, legends, manners, and other cultural artifacts are colored by this heritage. This blended culture is neither European nor Indian; it is Mexican. Once you begin to understand the country and its people, you discover an exciting new world.

Historical Background

At first glance, it doesn't stand to reason that Mexico should be so different from the United States or Canada. After all, the only thing that separates the countries is an artificial line called a "border." Sometimes a high fence or deep ditch—more often just a shallow river or an imaginary boundary that can only be plotted on a surveyor's map—the border is nevertheless real. Once you step across that line, you enter a different world. In some respects you step backward in time half a century or more.

To understand why Mexico is so different from the rest of North America, we need to take a quick glance at history. Beginning in the late 1700s, the United States and Canada experienced heavy waves of immigration, which increased in volume for about a century. For the most part early immigrants were laborers, farmers, and others who longed for the abundant land in America and sought a new start in life. They knew how to till the land, how to build houses, how to work in factories. They brought the technology of the industrial revolution, which was sweeping Europe at that time.

The immigrants discovered that the choice lands were occupied by native tribes. The newcomers, determined to have the natives' land, either slaughtered the original owners or forcibly moved them ever westward. Small, family-operated farms soon sprang up across the continent. In the towns small mercantile or manufacturing enterprises arose. The United States and Canada thus began as working-class and middle-class societies, and they have more or less retained these traditions through the centuries.

But Mexico was settled much earlier, in the 1500s. This was long before the industrial revolution wrought its changes upon the world. The original Spanish settlers in Mexico were *hidalgos*, the minor nobility and warrior class of Spain, which after several centuries of fighting had just defeated the Moors. Eager for adventure, the *hidalgos* leaped at the chance of conquering new territories, of becoming lords in a new world.

These soldiers brought with them the ideas of feudalistic Spain with its notions of nobility. The *hidalgos'* ideas of farming weren't small farms, but huge estates operated by serfs, just as was the custom of nobility in Spain.

The conquerors came as an army, without women. But instead of killing off the natives, the early Spanish married Indian women. From the Spanish point of view, it would have been detrimental to exterminate the natives; they were needed to operate the huge farms, or *haciendas*. Indian tenant farmers simply shifted from serving Aztec overlords to the new Spanish ones. The Indians thus went on tilling the same lands their ancestors had for centuries.

As Indians intermarried with the Spanish, a new race, called *mestizo*, was created. The *mestizos,* with their darker skins and slightly Indian features, became the racial cornerstone of Mexico. As the races blended, so did the customs, traditions, and folklore to create a new, uniquely Mexican culture.

With the conquest of Mexico, Spain quickly divided the country's land among the nobility, and within a few decades the entire country was solidly under the control of the new owners. So unlike the British colonies of North America, Mexico was colonized rather swiftly. Then immigration slowed to a trickle. Modern European traditions were slow in reaching Mexico. While the United States and Europe were undergoing industrialization and modernization, Mexico remained an agricultural country with worldviews formed by feudal Spaniards of the 1500s.

Many Different Mexicos

As you travel about the United States and Canada, you'll find remarkable similarities between one section and another. To be sure, the scenery in Maine is different from Alabama or Nevada, but many, many things are the same. Meals served in Denny's or IHOP are indistinguishable, for example. People read the same books, watch the same TV shows, discuss the same current events, and generally speak the same dialects of English, using common slang words and sharing common humor, likes, and dislikes.

Mexico is not so homogeneous, and its diversity is part of its charm. It is divided into many physical segments, each separated by geography and history. Each section has its own traditions, cuisine, climate, and, often, even its own language.

If you take a look at a map of Mexico, you'll begin to see why these differences exist. You'll notice a long, narrow country, with several mountain chains that run north and south, splitting the country and forming barriers against east-west communication. In pre-Columbian times, trails across these sierras were few in number and difficult to travel. Tribes living in the valleys developed unique languages and different civilizations. You'll also notice that today most highways and railroads run north and south. This is not only because of the mountain barriers, but also because most of the highways and railroads were built years ago by U.S. manufacturing and mining interests that wanted to ship raw materials out of Mexico to feed northern factories, then ship finished goods back to Mexico.

Furthermore, the country is laterally sliced by rivers and canyons, sometimes thousands of feet deep, that made north-south communication difficult in olden days. It's still not easy today. Each of these sections, over thousands of years of settlement, developed its own variants of culture, food, housing, and style. Today, even though TV and radio have bridged many of the gaps, these differences persist and are a source of local pride. Almost any Mexican you meet will inform you that his or her particular section of the republic is universally recognized as the very best place in the whole world!

Cultural Diversity

The resident or retiree can choose from an amazing variety of individual cultures as well as climates, each one distinct and a delight to discover. Each is a microcosm with its own cooking techniques, styles of dress, and accents. When you get away from the big towns, you often hear people conversing in Nahuatl or Quechua, the languages of the ancient Aztecs and Mayas. The Mexicans themselves often look physically different from region to region. Because geographical barriers kept them apart for thousands of years, individuals tended to marry within tribes, keeping bloodlines relatively pure. At least forty distinct racial and language groups are represented in Mexico.

On the eastern coast around Veracruz, home of the Huastecan tribes, typical clothing is tropical white, with the men wearing shallow straw hats. The women love bright embroidered trim on their dresses. On the west coast around Tehuantepec, where the temperature is equally tropical, women tend to wear ankle-length skirts. A bit farther north around the Costa Chica area, the Indian women wear long woven skirts of cochineal-dyed yarn and used to go topless. The early missionaries weren't able to completely wipe out the custom, although they did convince most women to wear a white, flouncy overblouse. This outfit is worn by most today. (The younger set long ago instituted blue jeans and designer blouses as fashion staples instead of traditional dress.)

In the Yucatán women prefer to wear a loose dress of light cotton (a *huipil*), and the men often work bare chested, wearing lightweight, white muslin trousers. Because temperatures and humidity can be oppressive, this kind of dress is very practical. On the other hand, the northern part of Mexico is influenced by the "western" clothing of Texas and Arizona. There the climate is similar to Texas, Arizona, and New Mexico, so it isn't surprising that clothing styles should be influenced by fashion in those states.

In the southern part of Mexico, nearby Guatemalan tribes affect styles with bright, colorfully woven garments. Depending upon the particular tribe, men may wear woolen skirts or knee-length trousers. The patterns of the weavings denote which village the wearer is from, and the colors of the ribbons in the hair indicate whether the person is married or single.

Although each section of the country has its own clothing styles, styles from New York, London, Paris, and Mexico City invade the fashions of young Mexicans, particularly in the larger, more cosmopolitan cities. The smaller the town or village, the more likely you are to find older, more traditional dress.

Different Diets

Mexican food varieties are another joy to the authors of this book. Each section of the country is proud of its own kind of dishes and its own style of cooking. Part of the fun of traveling in Mexico is sampling dishes from different parts of the country.

Most tourists think of Mexican food in terms of tacos, burritos, and chili con carne. This is understandable, because these dishes are just about all that's served in most Mexican restaurants in the United States. Similarly most foreigners believe that typical American cuisine consists of hamburgers and hot dogs. Just as you can find hamburgers in the United States, you can find your fill of tacos in Mexico, if that's your dish. Most restaurants that cater to Americans include tacos on the menu, but a really good Mexican restaurant would no more offer tacos and burritos than would a gourmet restaurant in the United States offer hamburgers and hot dogs. There is so much more to Mexican cooking!

In the Yucatán you'll discover such treats as venison cooked with a vinegar-cream sauce, or smoked *jabalí* (wild peccary) or *cochinito pibil* (roast suckling pig, cooked in a pit with a delicious sauce). In the mountains you'll find succulent quail, delicately flavored with herbs and grilled over a charcoal fire, or eggs cooked with a dry cheese that transforms them into a delightfully textured breakfast. Mexican seafood is fabulous. Some of our favorite dishes are *huachinango al mojo de ajo* (grilled red snapper with garlic-butter sauce), *langostinos* (charbroiled freshwater lobsters), and a bewildering number of shellfish dishes. As an example of menu variety, one favorite Mazatlán restaurant offers almost twenty shrimp dishes. One of the authors even tried iguana stew on a recent trip to Mexico. It tasted a little like chicken but was very bony and had little meat. It's not recommended unless you're truly hungry.

One of the delights of living in Mexico is being able to cook some of these regional dishes at home, to experiment and learn. A trip through a typical market, with its variety of fresh fruits, vegetables, and meats, makes shopping and menu planning a pleasant adventure rather than a chore. With its tropical climate many parts of Mexico have year-round growing seasons for produce that is seasonally unavailable in the north. Just about any time of the year is good for incredibly sweet strawberries and luscious melons. Tropical fruits such as mangoes, pineapples, avocados, and bananas are picked for the Mexican market when they are ripe, not days or weeks ahead to allow for ripening en route, as they must be when destined for the United States and Canada.

Shopping is also fun because foods are not only fresh but also available in a profusion and quality that most of us barely remember. In time Mexican agriculture may become sufficiently mechanized and chemical fertilizers may become cheap enough to mass produce the tasteless fruits and vegetables that we have learned to settle for in the United States. But for now Mexican fruits, vegetables, eggs, chicken, and pork burst with flavor and enliven any dish in which one chooses to use them.

Retirement Choices

The difficulty of choosing the right retirement or long-term living spot is finding the section of Mexico that is just right for you. This is where this book should be of help. You can choose a tropical climate to escape winter, or you might want a dry, pleasant summer season. Like cool evenings and warm days? Balmy to warm evenings? Many people select the best of all worlds by living near the beaches in the winter, then, when humidity and temperatures begin to rise, moving to their favorite village high in the mountains.

The nice thing about making a search for the right place is that it's fun to do, and you can do it simply by using your tourist card privileges. You can travel about, live a few weeks here or there, and make comparisons. You can see what kind of North American neighbors you would have and get their opinions on living there. One thing you'll find out: There is no one place that can suit everyone. Your needs and desires are unique, so only you can decide.

Two Mexicos

Many people find it hard to believe that living in Mexico can be economical. "Why, we paid $300 a day for our condominium in Cancun," said one indignant couple, "so how could you possibly live there on a small budget?" Admittedly this was an extra-luxurious, three-bedroom condo with a balcony overlooking the beach. Yet numerous tourists report paying $100 a day or more for rooms.

For tourists Mexico is a real mecca. On a two-week vacation, they can escape the snow and ice of New York or Chicago and do it in real style. In Mexico the beaches are marvelous, and restaurants offer great service, with white-jacketed waiters and menus that are as good as any at a Sheraton or Hilton in the United States. For only two weeks, what difference does it make if you pay $100, maybe $150, a day for a room? One Acapulco hotel charges $300 a day, but this includes your own private swimming pool and a car. If it's -20 degrees back home, you may decide you've earned a little luxury in your life. Besides, a $100-a-day room in Mexico is a marvel compared with a $100 room in New York. But with prices like this, how can you possibly expect to live or travel in Mexico on a modest income?

Two Realities

The answer is that Mexico is divided into two realities: one for tourists and one for residents. Tourists pay different rates, often for the same items. Tourists make their reservations with travel agents, who earn their living from 10 percent commissions. They aren't likely to even have the $30 rooms among their listings. But most North Americans who live in Mexico would think it absurd to lay out that kind of money, not when a $30 room is more than adequate. They can't afford to pay $200 a day for a condo, not when $300 a month can rent a small apartment. People who live in Mexico consider it ludicrous to go to a high-priced hotel restaurant and dine on Holiday Inn cuisine, especially when so many marvelous local restaurants offer tasty specialties at a fraction of the cost.

One of the most important changes we've observed in the eighteen years since the first edition of *Choose Mexico* was published is the increased difference between the tourist and resident economies. It seems that Mexican entrepreneurs (and the international ones who run the fancy hotels and restaurants) have learned that tourists are willing to pay much higher prices than are common in Mexico.

Is the secret of inexpensive living to stay away from luxury resorts, like Acapulco, Cancun, or Puerto Vallarta? Not necessarily. Acapulco, for example, can be one of the cheapest places to live in Mexico. From its initial marketing as a beautiful place for beautiful people, Acapulco has consistently overbuilt hotels and apartments. As soon as one high-rise is completed and half full, another is started. There are plenty of $30-a-day hotel rooms and occasionally $300-a-month apartments. The bargains are to be found away from the beach, sometimes on hillsides with gorgeous views of the Pacific. Twenty-five years ago, these were top-of-the-line accommodations, but in order to compete, the owners of these properties had to continually lower their rents. When you save $100 a day, so what if you have to walk 5 blocks to the beach? If you're going to be a resident, this type of bargain is what you look for.

One thing to keep in mind about living expenses in Mexico is that foreign tourists make up but a tiny part of the population. The vast majority of tourists are Mexican wage earners who can't possibly afford to spend like the foreigners. A $30 hotel room represents about a week's wages for many Mexican workers. Ninety percent of the people in a resort town work there. Well-paid workers average only $200 a month in wages, so they can't afford to pay much for rent or groceries. Most of the housing market is aimed at them, so rents and prices are scaled accordingly. You're either a rich tourist or a resident.

As a potential resident or retiree, you must make this a do-it-yourself project. Might as well start out traveling like a resident from the beginning! At your bookstore or library, pick up one of the low-cost travel guides to Mexico—the "Mexico on a Budget" type. They tend to be accurate about inexpensive hotels and travel tips. Except for the Christmas holidays and Easter week, you will seldom have problems booking the hotel of your choice.

Don't bother with a travel agent, because the kind of hotels that budget books recommend usually don't pay travel agents' commissions and therefore aren't on their computers. In forty years of traveling in Mexico, we've never had problems finding an inexpensive hotel. Cab drivers are helpful, but often they get a tip from the hotels for bringing guests, so naturally they want to take you to their special hotel. Take with a grain of salt anything a cab driver tells you. Don't be persuaded to deviate from your original choice, even if the cabby tells you the hotel is closed or that he knows one that is cheaper. See it for yourself first. The guidebooks are pretty accurate; cab drivers are not.

Once you arrive and are safely entrenched in an economical hotel, you can start searching for an apartment or a house to rent. If you're in a place where there are a lot of North Americans, you'll usually find listings and announcements posted on a bulletin board in the favorite gringo supermarket. Sometimes you'll see FOR RENT signs in windows or advertised in the local English-language newspaper. But the best way to find rentals is to ask other foreign residents. They always seem to know what is vacant or what is about to be vacated.

Often your hotel will have an apartment or suite for rent. This is a great way to test the town for its potential without getting involved in long-term rental agreements. (Few landlords are willing to rent for less than two or three months.) A hotel rents by the day, week, or month, and often charges only a little more for an apartment than for an ordinary room. We've rented some nice apartments for between $15 and $20 a day. Particularly common are hotel "efficiencies" in resort places like Acapulco and Puerto Vallarta.

Like most furnished apartments hotel kitchens come equipped with dishes, silverware, pots and pans, five-gallon jugs of purified water, and even dish towels. The bonus is that every day a brace of efficient maids scours the tile floors, changes the linen, and brings in fresh water, exactly as in a hotel. In addition they do your breakfast dishes and put them away in the cupboard. We usually leave a small tip every day, and it's greatly appreciated.

In some areas, such as Guadalajara and Lake Chapala, many apartments are owned by North Americans. It seems that every time a gringo couple decides to retire in the mellow climate of Lake Chapala or Ajijic, they think about building a house. It then occurs to them to build a few rental units for supplementary income. The result is a predictable oversupply of rental units. Rents are forced to a low level to keep the apartments full. The only drawback to renting one of these units is that you will probably have to wash your own breakfast dishes and sweep out the place yourself or hire a maid to do it for you. The going price is about $15 to have someone come in two days a week to clean and do the laundry. Can you handle that?

Our recommendation to nontourists is to take a hotel-apartment that rents by the day or week, even if it costs a little more than an ordinary hotel room and even if you have no intention of cooking many meals. There is nothing like starting off the day by having breakfast on your patio or balcony. Planning the day's adventures while you relax in pajamas is infinitely more fun than spending half the morning getting dressed, then waiting for someone to bring you a second cup of coffee.

For the finicky or those worried about the dreaded "tourist disease," you have the satisfaction of preparing your own meals, using purified water, and taking other hygienic precautions. Your food is as safe as if it were cooked in Omaha.

A few tips about apartment-hopping in Mexico:

- Invariably, you won't find a can opener in the kitchen. Don't ask why; just bring or buy one.
- Be sure you have matches for lighting the stove and candles for candlelight dining on the balcony (and for frequent power outages in some areas).
- When freezing ice cubes for drinks, use bottled water, not tap water, which may or may not be drinkable. (As an aside, we note that many tourists religiously avoid drinking tap water, then brush their teeth with it. And they wonder why they get sick!) Bottled or boiled water in any form is the only kind that should enter your mouth.
- It isn't necessary to avoid fresh fruits and salads. Just wash everything in a solution of bottled water and water purification pills, which can be purchased at any drugstore for pennies a box. (Doing this won't spoil the taste.)

The "Tourist Disease"

Why do they call it the "tourist disease"? Many people believe that only tourists are affected, that natives "build up an immunity." In fact no one, including local residents, builds up an immunity to the most serious of these disorders, amoebic dysentery. By observing some simple rules of hygiene, residents avoid getting sick. When they don't follow these rules, they get sick just as the tourists. We know of many people who have been scared off by an unhappy experience with *turista* or have heard of others who suffered through their whole two-week vacation in Mexico. It doesn't have to be that way. Ask anyone who lives there.

Everyone has bacteria in their digestive systems; they are necessary for good health. But a phenomenon common to anyone who travels from one place to another is encountering a new strain of bacteria. The resident bacteria fight the intruders, and the intestines finally get tired of all the fuss and decide to produce a little diarrhea. This is a mild form of the "tourist disease" and is nothing to worry about. It's the bad-guy amoebas you must worry about. But common sense can avert problems. Most expatriates who live in Mexico report that they seldom if ever have "tourist problems."

As a potential resident, you must relearn a few basic habits. These will distinguish you from the two-week tourist and keep you from a lot of misery. Before long these rules become automatic, and you won't even have to think about them.

Of course don't drink the water in any form other than boiled or bottled. By the way, you don't have to boil it for hours and hours. Because no organism can survive at temperatures higher than 150 degrees Fahrenheit, just bringing it to a boil is sufficient. Some water systems are all right, but we recommend boiled or purified water anyway; make it one of your automatic habits. Always soak salad vegetables (lettuce, tomatoes—anything that isn't going to be cooked or peeled) in a solution of water and purification tablets for twenty minutes.

Finally, one of the most valuable pieces of advice this book can give you about avoiding dysentery: When selecting a restaurant, don't be impressed by the nicely dressed waiters, immaculate linen, and sparkling silverware; check out the clientele. Notice if local people eat there. If local people don't patronize a place, there's one of three explanations: The food is overpriced, poorly prepared, or not fit to eat.

Too often a "tourist" restaurant is owned by absentee owners and operated by low-paid employees who really don't care if you get sick or not. They know you won't be back again anyway, and you eat in so many places you won't know where you got the "bug." But a family-operated restaurant, one that caters to local people, can't afford to have anyone get sick. When word gets around, the place is out of business. One of this book's authors as a youth lived in Mexico for many years and has traveled extensively throughout the country for the past forty years. Only twice has he caught the curse. Both times he ignored his own advice and patronized a spiffy, tourist-only restaurant where no Mexicans ate!

Why all this fuss about boiled or bottled water? Isn't any Mexican water fit to drink? If not, why not? The answer is that some water is probably okay, particularly that either coming from desert areas, where the water is pumped from deep wells, or flowing from the high mountains, where few people are around to pollute it. The problem is that Mexico has many priorities well ahead of the construction of modern sewage disposal plants. The costs would be astronomical, and the money is simply not there. Even where there are facilities for modern disposal, expanding home and hotel construction means that sewage production exceeds the capacity of these plants. So most of the sewage goes into septic tanks and eventually seeps into the groundwater. Where there is a high water table, such as you find at the coastal resorts, some sewage, with its amoebas and bacteria, inevitably finds its way into the water system. Wherever water is drawn from shallow wells, you can have problems. A further complication in Mexico City is that the water and sewage pipes are often damaged by earthquake activity, and they leak—not much, but enough to sometimes make you sick. One trend, at least in the expatriate neighborhoods, is the installation of state-of-the-art water purification systems in homes, complete with filters and ultraviolet light treatment. One resident of Mazatlán says, "We and our guests have been drinking directly from the tap for more than six years without incident. Some friends took a water sample back to the United States and had it compared with their tap water. Our water was much cleaner!"

To become a healthy nontourist in Mexico, you have to continually follow commonsense rules. Before long you will become so used to the drill that when you return to the United States, you will hesitate before using tap water to brush your teeth.

Two Price Systems in Mexico?

You often hear people claim, "There are two prices in Mexico, one for the Mexicans and one for the gringos." Some believe, for example, that different menus are handed to gringos and Mexicans. This simply isn't true. Most prices are fixed by government decree, and the government is serious about enforcement. When you rent a room, for example, the ceiling price is supposed to be clearly displayed at the desk and in your room.

But, as we have observed earlier, there *are* two price systems—not for Mexicans and foreigners, but for residents and tourists. You won't find different prices being charged to the two groups in the same restaurants and hotels, because menus and room rates are prominently displayed.

You will, however, find higher prices at the hotels into which tourists are booked by travel agents and the restaurants in those hotels. Ironically, the government often turns its head at violations by tourist hotels. Residents, whether Mexican or foreign, know of equally nice places that charge a fraction of the price.

Restaurants and stores, particularly the nontourist places, are anxious to have residents' repeat business, so they can't very well overcharge you, or you'll never return. However, that old game of bargaining does go on in Mexico. Some merchants feel obligated to quote an unrealistic price, and they often feel cheated out of the fun if you go ahead and pay without a little arguing.

How do you know if you're paying the resident price or the tourist price? Don't all Mexicans expect you to bargain? Should you offer one-third the asking price? These questions are relative to the product being offered and the price asked. For example, if you're in a market and the vendor wants the equivalent of a dime for a handful of onions, ask yourself: "What do I gain by arguing him down 20 percent?" A few pennies or a nickel may mean nothing to you but plenty to the vendor. Actually individual entrepreneurs face a lot of competition in the native markets, so they try to keep their prices attractive. They want to see you become a regular customer, and they usually go out of their way to make you happy.

On the other hand, if you're buying something that costs a lot of money, then a 20 percent discount would be significant. If it's big money, sometimes it's worth bargaining hard, just as you would when buying an automobile or house back home.

Bargaining is an art form that you might enjoy, but accept the fact that you will never win. Just as you never really beat an automobile salesperson at the car game, you'll never quite get the final value in Mexico. Bargaining is fun to do, and no one gets hurt feelings. Yet serious hassling over pennies doesn't mark an American as an astute bargainer; it marks him or her as a cheapskate.

It's interesting to watch the tourists bargain. As soon as they settle down on the beach, a swarm of eager vendors begins landing like flies on a lollipop. They'll offer jewelry, blankets, sweaters, you name it, and the bargaining begins in Spanish, English, and sign language. Everyone has a glorious time, and in the end, the poor merchant reluctantly agrees to drop the price of the $40 necklace to only $10. The tourist is delighted at his prowess in saving $30.00, and the vendor is discouraged that he allowed such a fine $1.00 necklace to go for only $10.00. Like the car dealers back home, the beach vendors are experts. But don't get the idea that everyone you meet is trying to scalp you. Most merchants you deal with in everyday living situations are anxious to do business with you and take pride in having a good relationship with *norteamericanos.*

If you visit a store with price tags on all items, it's pretty sure that the owners mean business, unless you're talking big money. If you're thinking about a $100 purchase or a $1,000 deal, then maybe it's worth your while to bargain against the posted price. You may not be successful, but it's worth the try to shave off 10 or 20 percent. But if the price is only $2.00, you're wasting your time haggling.

One complaint occasionally heard about *Choose Mexico* is that it is drawing more and more North Americans into the country. "They come down here, throw money around, pay big wages, leave big tips, and ruin things for the rest of us!" is the way one woman put it.

It's true that when more foreigners move into a town or village, the demand for domestic help creates a boost in wages. It's also true that foreigners tend to pay more than the going rate for lots of things. This means more money circulating in the community and slightly higher prices all around. The final result is that Americans pay a few cents more for goods and services, and the Mexicans have more money in their pockets. Because Americans are known to pay higher wages, the local people are eager to work for them. Working for an American family is prestigious, and workers try very hard to be good employees and keep their jobs.

Our stock answer to complainers: Mexico is not your private discovery. Mexico is not for the sole benefit of a few stingy gringos who want to keep the local economy depressed so they can save a few pennies. We are guests in that country, and as guests we should rejoice in any improvement in the living standard of our hosts. If you have to pay $1.00 an hour for help instead of 75 cents an hour, just remember how much you would pay back home and think of what that extra money will buy for a Mexican family.

Yes, there are two Mexicos. One is for tourists; the other is for residents. The happiest residents are those who consider themselves part of the community, and by the same token, they are the best liked by their Mexican neighbors. The unhappiest residents are those who try to change things and make Mexico into a bargain-basement copy of the United States.

Finances in Mexico

Early editions of *Choose Mexico* placed a strong emphasis on minimum budgets for living south of the border. This was due in no small measure to the authors' concern about whether they and the hundreds of thousands of other Americans at or approaching retirement age would have sufficient income to enjoy the "golden years" that had been promised them. Average Social Security benefits were not nearly large enough to provide comfortable living almost anywhere in the United States, and stories of older people struggling to make ends meet were common.

We were happy to be able to tell our readers that many of their compatriots were "making it" in Mexico on as little as $400 a month, a figure that spelled grinding poverty in the United States and Canada. Not only were they surviving on this budget in Mexico, they were enjoying a pleasant—though not affluent—lifestyle. Over the years, as successive waves of inflation (which made living more expensive) and devaluation (which made it less expensive for those with U.S. or Canadian dollars) swept over Mexico, our assessment of a minimum budget fluctuated widely. Always our figure was based on what retired people there told us they were spending, confirmed by our supermarket, real estate listings, and other on-site research. We became used to people doubting and disputing our minimum figure (including some people living in Mexico) basically because it could not provide the lifestyle they considered adequate. Our minimum budgets were literally that—they required the use of public transportation (rather than ownership of a car) and careful shopping.

Eighteen years after that first edition, things have changed both in the United States and in Mexico. American retirees are no longer impoverished. Today they probably have more disposable income than any other age group. Prices in Mexico have, at least in the short run, stabilized at about two-thirds of their United States equivalents. Depending on the fate of the Mexican economy under the country's new leadership, prices may go lower, or they may go higher. It is highly unlikely, however, that it will become more expensive to live in Mexico than in the United States or Canada.

At this time the Mexican government requires an income of about $1,000 per month for a single person and $1,500 for a couple to become legal residents. If you own a home in Mexico, the requirement is halved. (As in the past, many who cannot afford or do not want resident status live in Mexico as "tourists," making semiannual trips to the border to renew their visas. However, this could change as the immigration authorities make more use of computers, which would enable them to limit the number of renewals you could obtain in a year.)

Clearly the minimum income for resident status is more than adequate for a gracious, satisfying lifestyle, if not a luxurious one. With that income you should be able to afford a housekeeper and a gardener (at least part time), medical insurance, and a certain amount of entertainment and travel. What we cannot say with precise confidence is what the situation will be when this book is due for another revision two years from now. Much depends on inflation and the exchange rate, which we'll discuss shortly.

What does an adequate income level mean in terms of your retirement lifestyle? The following paragraph is a quote from Nadine and Henry Laxen, who live in a lovely home in an upscale neighborhood of Mazatlán.

"We go to the movies here every week, and a ticket costs $2.00, while popcorn is 80 cents. Our full-time maid [who comes in six days a week] is paid approximately $50 per week, and she is very well paid by Mexican standards. On the other hand, if you want to buy imported electronics or appliances, be prepared to pay double. A 32-inch Sony TV costs over $2,000, as does a large Whirlpool side-by-side refrigerator. All in all, I would say that you can live quite well on $1,000 per month, and live like a king, or at least a high-level prince, on $2,000 per month."

At the other extreme is John Fugate, a widower who retired to Mexico from Oak Ridge, Tennessee. His pension is generous, but he chooses to live frugally, in the village of Siqueros, 50 kilometers from Mazatlán. John is involved with the Seed Savers Exchange, a group that grows and tries to preserve heirloom nonhybrid fruits and vegetables. "I came to Sinaloa to garden and it has been successful beyond my wildest imagination," he says. "There are things I miss and things I dislike here but what I have lost in efficiency and quick service, I have gained in understanding and patience." The bottom line is that he lives on the income from growing seeds and on the crops from his orchard—on less than $400 a month. His pension and Social Security checks go directly into a mutual fund in the United States. John proves that budget living is indeed possible, with certain trade-offs, but he carefully points out that he doesn't recommend this life for everyone.

Inflation, Currency Exchange, and Devaluation

Another obstacle to quoting a budget for living in Mexico is that economic conditions are continually shifting. Variations in the dollar-to-peso exchange rate cause the value of the dollar to rise or fall from time to time. How many pesos your dollar buys obviously will affect your budget. Furthermore, inflation is always at work in Mexico, gradually pushing up costs, just as it is north of the border. However, in Mexico the inflationary curve is usually somewhat steeper, with prices rising to a point where the peso must be devalued against the dollar, which then brings prices way down for those with dollars. This adjustment can be gradual, but at times it can be dramatic.

For some reason people tend to confuse inflation rates with the rate of currency exchange against the U.S. dollar. But they are very different animals, both of which must be taken into consideration when figuring how much it will cost you to live in Mexico. The exchange rate determines how many pesos you will receive for each American (or Canadian) dollar. When that number is increasing more rapidly than the rate of inflation, it is good for anyone who has dollars. However, when inflation is running wild and outdistancing the exchange rate, the real cost of everything you buy will be increasing.

Mexican devaluation is hardly unique; it's happened over and over in the course of the past half century. Historically the peso's exchange rate and inflation move in waves. The wave goes something like this: The government arbitrarily decides what the rate will be and holds it there against the dollar despite world market pressures. Prices gradually rise while the exchange rate remains constant. This has the effect of overvaluing the peso and undervaluing the dollar. Expatriates have to cash more dollars every month to live in Mexico. That's inflation, isn't it?

Eventually the exchange rate gets way out of balance and something has to give. The government is forced to devaluate to bring the value of the peso in line with the global economy. Then a new cycle begins. The longer the government waits before devaluing, the more drastic the effect upon the economy. A spectacular devaluation occurred in 1982, with the peso spiraling downward from about twenty to the dollar, to an eventual level of 3,000 to the dollar before it was stabilized. The last major devaluation was in 1994, when the peso lost 40 percent of its value overnight. Of course, this meant that those with dollars found them worth 40 percent more!

What does devaluation mean for North Americans who live in Mexico and have bank accounts both in the United States or Canada and in Mexico? Is it something to dread? Not necessarily. Suddenly folks find that their dollar accounts back home will buy a lot more in Mexico. True, they will lose value on their peso accounts in Mexico, but when devaluation happens, the government raises interest rates to compensate to some extent.

An understanding of how inflation and devaluation work can be an important tool when handling finances. Most retirees and other foreigners in Mexico weren't affected in the 1994–1995 devaluation, for two reasons. For one thing, the U.S. government pumped billions into the Mexican economy to prevent a total meltdown. The second reason is that most foreign residents did as we so strongly recommended for years. We urged that North Americans keep the bulk of their funds at home and arrange for a monthly transfer of only as much money as was needed for living expenses. While acknowledging the lure of Mexico's attractive interest rates, we advised people to avoid the temptation to "make a killing."

What are the warning signs? When the peso becomes dramatically overvalued against the dollar, watch out. When Mexicans start shopping across the border in the United States because goods are cheaper there, you know the peso is in trouble. When wealthy people begin exchanging pesos for dollars to invest in U.S. real estate or when wealthy Mexicans start going to Europe or to the United States for vacations because Mexico is too expensive, then it's time to convert your pesos to dollar accounts in U.S. or Canadian banks (if you haven't already done so).

Fortunately for American travelers and retirees, the rate of inflation has been decreasing for the past several years and is currently holding steady. Now less than 5 percent (as compared with more than 40 percent a half dozen years ago), it is not too much higher than the rates we are used to north of the border. At the same time the exchange rate has hovered around ten pesos to the dollar for several years. This means that your dollar income continues to provide a more comfortable standard of living than in the United States or Canada.

Experience over the past few decades demonstrates that this could change, either for the better or for the worst. However, the efforts the current administration in Mexico is making to stabilize the economy give hope that no unpleasant surprises are lurking in the near future.

How Safe Are Mexican Banks?

Don't confuse the instability of the exchange rate system with the stability of Mexican banks. By and large the banks are quite safe. Bank accounts are guaranteed by the Mexican government, and it can be confidently stated that no one has lost a peso over the years. The value of those pesos is another story. Our advice is, once again, keep the bulk of your money in your hometown bank and transfer money to your Mexican bank only when you need it. And transfer only as much as you need, not more.

Of course you will open a checking account with a Mexican bank from which you will pay your bills to local merchants and your taxes, rent, and other day-to-day expenses. Be sure to get a debit card for convenient ATM withdrawals. The U.S. government won't automatically deposit your Social Security check into a Mexican bank account, so you must have it deposited to your U.S. bank account, along with your pension or investment income. In an emergency you can get cash advances at most banks using a MasterCard or VISA—if you are willing to pay a premium for this service—but a debit card is much less expensive.

Long-distance banking can be a headache for several reasons. You usually have to pay up to a 1.5-percent service charge to a Mexican bank to accept your foreign check, and you must pay an equal percentage to convert pesos into dollars. We're talking 3 percent per transaction just to use your own money! However, retirees here have discovered a couple of ways to get around these fees.

One way is to open a peso account with a reputable Mexican investment firm, such as Allen W. Lloyd. An account can be opened for less than $1,000, and current interest is paid on the investment. The interest rate varies from month to month, and the rates are always high. (That interest looks good, but you must keep your eye on the exchange rate and be prepared to switch over to a dollar account if you become leery.) Once you have an account, you can cash personal checks from your U.S. or Canadian bank without charge. Local residents typically drop into Lloyd's once a week for pesos to pay operating expenses.

We mention the Lloyd company because it has branches in the major retirement areas and because the company specializes in dealing with English-speaking investors. There may be other equally reliable investment companies, but most people seem to use this one. One retiree we interviewed said, "I keep $5,000 in my account, and I'm very pleased with the interest. I was even more pleased when it was drawing 42 percent. However, I'd advise against keeping more in the account than you can afford to lose, just in case another deflation happens." Other residents are less cautious, keeping much more money in the accounts. One single man said, "I could damn near live on the interest until it dropped to 24 percent!"

However tempting high interest may be, you would be well advised to keep your eye on the economy when investing money in Mexico. If there is the slightest chance of a devaluation, move your funds to a stateside bank *muy pronto*. Watch the inflation rate. If you receive a 16 percent interest rate when inflation is 12 percent, you are actually making only a 4 percent return on your risky investment. In that case, you are better off with a money market fund back home.

(For more information: Allen W. Lloyd, Apdo. 1-1470, Guadalajara, Jalisco, Mexico; phone 121–9050; e-mail: lloyd@lloyd.com.mx.)

A second strategy is to open a "Friendship Senior Checking Account" with the Los Angeles–based California Commerce Bank (a subsidiary of Mexico's BANAMEX, which has 700 branch offices throughout the republic). You can do this by mail or e-mail. Because it is a chartered U.S. bank, accounts in California Bank of Commerce are insured up to $100,000. These "Friendship" accounts are designed specifically for American senior citizens (fifty-five years or older) who live in Mexico.

You can then open a peso account with BANAMEX, where you can deposit or cash checks from its U.S. subsidiary without incurring a service charge. With a checking account at BANAMEX, you also receive a free credit card and an ATM card, so you can draw cash from an automatic teller instead of having to stand in line to cash a check.

Dollars on deposit in California Commerce's unique Friendship Senior Checking Program earn an extra 1 percent more than current U.S. interest rates for regular depositors, and there is no monthly service charge. To get the high current rate of Mexican interest, you need to invest about $1,500 worth of pesos (the amount varies), although it isn't necessary to do this in order to open a convenience account. You can draw up to $200 at a time from BANAMEX without any service charge.

(For more information: California Commerce Bank, 2029 Century Park East, Lost Angeles, CA 90067. Or BANAMEX, Banco Nacional de Mexico, International Department, Isabel La Catolica 43 44, 06089 Mexico. Both banks are owned by Citibank.)

Current Investment Strategy

What's the potential for investing in Mexico? (If we could predict the future, do you think we'd be writing books instead of counting our money full time?) Okay; if you insist on our unqualified opinion, we'll hazard a guess that the financial picture in Mexico will follow the familiar scenario of 1982 to 1994. That is there'll be a period of stagnation, with prices in dollars exceptionally favorable for *norteamericanos*. Then the peso will begin to rise in value. It will slowly gain against the dollar through two Mexican presidential terms, possibly three. At the end of the second or third term, the world's economists will once again express astonishment when devaluation hits. You needn't have a Ph.D. to figure this out. Just look at history. It happens over and over, yet economists always seem bewildered by it.

Now many retirees are fascinated with an interesting side effect of devaluation: bizarre interest rates. As the peso falls, interest rates soar. For example in 1995—after the initial devaluation—interest on money market accounts (in pesos) swung from a low of 30 percent to a high of 86 percent! These rates varied monthly, depending on the paranoia of the market. Unfortunately dollar accounts aren't permitted at this time, so all your investments are automatically converted to pesos. Of course there's no reason you can't convert your profits to dollars and put them into your hometown bank.

Interest rates in 2000 were considerably below those in 1999, sometimes dipping below 10 percent. Bear in mind that one swift, overnight devaluation could wipe out your profits, and then some. When the peso is riding the trough, the peso is almost sure to lose value. Therefore high interest rates must compensate for this loss of value.

Like all good gamblers, you need to know the chances you're taking, calculate your odds of making money, and most important, not gamble any more than you can afford to lose.

Mexican Stock Investments

Mexico's stock market is known as the Bolsa. It is similar in many ways to securities markets in America and Europe, but there are important differences. For one thing, the Bolsa is smaller scale. Not only are far fewer issues traded, but the daily volume is a tiny fraction of that on the New York Stock Exchange. The market is so thin—there is so little activity—for most issues that liquidity can be a very serious problem. And, of course, a sudden devaluation can wipe out a large part of your investment overnight. If Mexico's economy continues to expand, there is probably still much money to be made on the Bolsa. Some retirees—those who read the Mexican financial pages daily or who find a trusted financial adviser—may raise their standard of living to celestial heights and leave princely inheritances. But for the average person of moderate means, we strongly counsel prudence and patience. In Mexico there are many ways to enjoy oneself without being a millionaire or making financial gain the focus of one's life.

Real Estate as an Investment

At the time our first edition was published, Mexican real estate was selling at prices unthinkable in the United States or Canada. This was soon after the devaluation of 1982, when property values dropped dramatically. Early readers of *Choose Mexico* rushed down to snap up these bargains. As you can imagine when a flood of buyers waving fistfuls of dollars hit the retirement areas, housing prices shot up. They doubled, then doubled again. However, because the prices were so low in the first place, even at these quadrupled prices, the homes were bargains compared with similar homes in California or Florida. Those who bought property as the cost of living was rising did quite well on their investments.

What happened to the real estate market after the devaluation of 1994–1995? Did it suddenly crash as it did in 1982? Not this time, at least not in the same way. Those who paid their rents in pesos found their rents had dropped by 40 percent, but those who rented from other *norteamericanos* were paying in dollars, so nothing changed. Mexicans who were selling their property were forced to drop the asking price, especially when selling to other Mexicans, because they were trading in pesos, not dollars. Retirees who owned property, on the other hand, thought in terms of dollars and saw no reason to drop asking prices because the peso was worth less.

Prices on choice retirement property could possibly drop as time goes on, but our guess is that the market won't change significantly. The bottom line is that the real estate market works on the age-old principle of supply and demand. With today's conditions so favorable for retirement in Mexico, even more gringos will be going there looking for property to buy. And as long as there are buyers, prices probably won't fall very low. (This is just a guess, so please don't make any real estate decisions based on it.)

To summarize, real estate can be an excellent investment, provided you make rational decisions and bargain for a good price. Buying on the open market from Mexican sellers will undoubtedly give you an edge. Some things you ought to know before buying a home are discussed elsewhere in this section, but our principal caveat bears repeating here: Know or be advised by someone who knows a lot about the area, the laws, the real estate market, and construction.

REAL ESTATE OPPORTUNITIES

For some reason or other, we North Americans think we have to own a house. Maybe it's something left over from the Great Depression, a security blanket of sorts. It's more than that, of course; during the past decades in the United States, home ownership has been a way of keeping ahead of inflation and, in many parts of the country, achieving great appreciation of value. We write loan interest off our income before taxes, and overall we come out pretty well financially.

But things aren't necessarily the same in Mexico. For one thing, few homes are sold with bank loans (although the owners of new developments will sometimes finance through U.S. or Canadian banks). Buyers customarily pay cash for property, so you'll have no interest payments to deduct from your income. Therefore, you'll have a large investment in a home—money that otherwise would have been bringing in dividend or interest income. Also because you're retired or perhaps living on savings, you probably won't have much income tax to pay or much income to deduct from in the first place.

But doesn't property ownership protect you from inflation? Not necessarily. Get rid of the notion that during times of inflation, property is always a hedge against falling purchasing power. When you're in a country undergoing hyperinflation, property doesn't usually rise in value with the economy; instead, it can drop in value. This was clearly the case during Mexico's period of hyperinflation. Why? Because in order to keep ahead of the inflation game, people need hard currency (meaning dollars) in their hands to manipulate and invest in things that go up in value. It wasn't until inflation in terms of dollars set in that values went up; then the Mexican economy did okay.

Figure it this way: Real estate value is partially determined by how much rental income a property might bring in if rented to a tenant. However, when inflation eats into tenants' incomes, their ability to pay good rents is lessened. Property becomes a lousy investment when owners reason, "Better sell and get some dollars!" Then when everybody wants to sell and nobody wants to buy, prices tumble even faster.

This is what happened during the inflationary jump in the early 1980s. As the value of the peso plummeted, so did dollar values of real estate. In the late 1980s, however, prices stabilized and began creeping upward. In fact, within a short time, real estate prices regained the losses incurred after the initial devaluation and more. This was due to the increased demand by North Americans and the liberalized Mexican laws concerning property ownership.

Since the devaluation of 1994, real estate prices have held their own and continued to appreciate. Because much of the prime real estate is in the hands of foreigners, it holds its value regardless of what the economy or currency exchange rates do. Expatriates don't think in terms of what the peso is worth; they deal in dollars, so a devaluation or inflation doesn't affect their asking prices.

Having pointed out that property ownership is different in Mexico, we need to add that despite the drawbacks, many North Americans find great joy in buying old colonial homes and restoring them. Others want to build their own places, doing their own designing and testing their artistic abilities as architects. Fortunately, with the low cost of labor and the availability of unusual building materials such as custom-made tiles and hand-formed bricks, the cost of redoing a home is certainly reasonable.

Can Foreigners Own Property?

A common misconception is that Americans can't own property in Mexico. For years the government tried to restrict foreign ownership of land with diminishing success. The fear was that Mexican citizens would have little chance to compete with affluent foreigners; property ownership for Mexicans would be a thing of the past. In fact this is one of the fears most often expressed by Mexicans when discussing the NAFTA treaty.

Despite the Mexican government's efforts, the foreigners seem to have won. For the first time in several generations, all restrictions are off in most parts of Mexico. In most of the country, you can buy and sell property just as you might in Omaha or Ottawa. Because of this change in federal law, foreigners can hold an *escritura,* or fee-simple title deed, for the property in their own names.

Foreigners are still restricted within specified distances of the seacoast or international borders in that you can't own the property outright;

even if you have FM-2 status (see page 55 for a definition), you must go through the lease process described below.

The way it works is that you purchase the property through a bank. You establish a trust, of which you are the beneficiary, and order the bank to buy the land in the name of the trust. The bank then leases the property back to you for a period of up to fifty years, renewable in perpetuity. This is a government-approved maneuver, which, as one man put it, "is a way for the Mexican government to save face. They can sell beach property to foreigners while claiming that they aren't." Formerly the leases were for thirty years, but the thirty-year leases already in effect will be extended to fifty years.

This bank trust is known as a *fideicomiso,* and because it's renewable, the time limit doesn't really mean much except that you have to set up a new trust when it expires. In the meantime you can do anything you want with your property—live there, rent it out, whatever. The bank charges an administration fee, which varies from $250 to $1,000 a year. When you're ready to sell, the buyer pays you the money and you assign the lease to the new owner. Of course a legal immigrant with FM-2 papers can buy the property in his or her own name, without bothering with trusts.

A welcome change in the *fideicomiso* rules is the elimination of an onerous part of bank trusts. Previously a lease was valid for just thirty years and not renewable; the property had to be sold to a Mexican citizen. That is, if you bought a house with a thirty-year lease and decided to sell after ten years, a new buyer would have only the remaining twenty years of the lease. This meant that the longer you owned property, the less valuable it was for a new owner. But today leases are indefinite and can be renewed without restrictions. Also leased property can be changed over to private ownership upon payment of fees if and when you decide to go to FM-2 status.

Exactly how these laws are going to work out for foreigners remains to be seen. The laws are too recent to be sure of their application. For example we understand that if you buy a house as a tourist—with an *escritura*—you are not permitted to rent the house during your absence. If indeed this is the rule, we don't know that it's being enforced, or for that matter how it could be enforced. NAFTA can, and probably will, influence these and other restrictions; only time will tell.

When considering property in the new millennium, our continuing best advice is to consult with local expatriates, real estate experts, and a recommended lawyer to make sure of what you are getting into. Under no circumstances let any money change hands before you have assurances that everything is in order; people have been hurt by real estate salespeople who say, "We'll take care of the details *mañana*."

A major caution still is that many desirable properties, often choice oceanfront parcels, once belonged to *ejidos* (community-owned farms) that could not be sold without government permission. When those rules were in effect, many North Americans lost money by buying from someone who really didn't own the property. It wasn't always that the seller was cheating intentionally. He may have sincerely believed land that his family had farmed for generations was his to sell. The laws changed drastically during the Salinas administration, and precisely how they work today is a question you need to go over with your lawyer. If nobody knew who owned the property before, how do they know today?

Looking at Property

One thing we need to make clear: Real estate agencies do not operate under the same rules as where you came from. The United States and Canada have very strict regulations, and every broker and salesperson is held to certain ethical standards. They must undergo training and pass tests to obtain their licenses. Not so in Mexico. This is not to say that real estate people in Mexico are all crooked. Most are very ethical, but many of them are amateurs. It turns out that selling real estate to other gringos is the easiest way to get work that pays anything. And just about all that's required to deal in properties is the desire to sell something and make money. It's worth your while to make inquiries among residents as to whom they recommend for agents. The better ones gain their reputations just as the bums gain theirs.

The first thing you'll discover is that the term *multiple listing* doesn't necessarily mean the same as back home. Many real estate agencies will show you only the properties they have under contract and give you the impression that this is all there is available through all other companies. The result is that you're going to waste your time looking at a small range of properties, probably in the upper level of your price range.

The solution is to visit several real estate offices and ask to see a complete list of what they have. This is the only way you can be sure you have access to most available properties. In some of the larger areas, you'll find flyers with pictures of homes for sale and sometimes multiple-listing catalogues showing several brokers' housing inventories. But not all.

Finally, when you've found your dream home, be sure you have a reputable attorney, one who comes highly recommended by your fellow expatriates. Of utmost importance: Be sure that he or she is not the same attorney who represents the buyer. (A conflict of interest like that can't happen back home.) You want someone to represent your interests who is on your side exclusively.

Mexican Real Estate Today

As detailed in earlier sections of this book, real estate has had its ups and downs in Mexico. At the moment it seems to be a mixed bag. Gringo-owned properties are holding their price levels pretty well, but asking prices for homes in all-Mexican neighborhoods can be described as bargains. Around the Lake Chapala/Ajijic area, where most buyers and sellers are gringos, the market seems to be relatively steady, although this could change. A pleasant home of new construction, suitable for a couple, can be found starting at approximately $70,000— with the top limit depending on whether you need a swimming pool, an adjacent golf course, or a gated community (or all three). Closing costs are about $1,200, which includes drawing up a trust deed (*fideicomiso*) or a direct, fee-simple title (*escritura*). By the way, many choose to go the *fideicomiso* route, rather than buying outright, because it's slightly easier.

There are some great bargains to be found in Mexico today. This is particularly true if you want something away from the usual gringo circuit. When buying away from foreign enclaves, the kind of homes Americans typically buy are often priced higher, simply because sellers know *norteamericanos* can and will pay more. For this reason it helps to have a Mexican friend do the looking and bargaining for you. (Be sure he or she is a friend and not a commission-seeker!) And look carefully before you force your money on a seller of a truly cheap house in a

Mexican neighborhood. It can be, and probably is, very rustic, inside and out, according to our standards. The plumbing could be sluggish, inadequate, maybe even nonexistent, and the electrical wires strung around the walls and ceilings like spider webs, as if the electrician weren't serious. The inside walls will probably need plaster, and the doors and window frames new wood. The whole place will be begging to be rebuilt. That wonderful bargain could be a nightmare.

For others, remodeling a home is a project of love. Shopping for just the right tile, looking for tropical woods for the doors, and working with a contractor to rebuild a house is fun for certain people. You must know yourself before undertaking something like this. The payoff, if you decide to go ahead, is that you can build your dream home through the investment of a little money and a lot of effort.

Do You Really Need to Buy?

Before you plunk down your savings on a home in Mexico, you ought to question some of your basic beliefs about real estate—beliefs that may be valid at home but not necessarily in Mexico. Property ownership in the United States has many advantages. One is the tax break on interest payments. Often it's cheaper to own a house than to rent when everything is considered, including the almost certain annual appreciation in a home's value.

In Mexico, however, if you have to pay cash, you won't have interest to deduct from your income. And you can't count on your home's increasing in value; sometimes it does, sometimes it doesn't. Most important, you probably can rent much cheaper than you can buy. For example, a house that sells for $100,000 (a really nice one) can usually be rented for $600 a month, sometimes much less. Is it wise to tie up $100,000 of your savings for a place you could have rented for only $600 a month? It may be worth it if you're thinking of the fun you're going to have fixing it up or if you have a need to own your own place.

If cost is your primary consideration, you can't beat renting. In any event, do yourself a favor and rent for a period of time to be sure you want to live in Mexico. As we stress repeatedly, Mexico isn't for everyone, and you might be unhappy to have your life savings stuck in a house that isn't selling because of a slow market condition.

Fortunately for the renter, rentals are abundant in most areas. Prices for a small apartment or plain house can be found for as little as $350 a month, depending on the neighborhood. Many people we interviewed seem to think $500 or $600 is an ordinary rent, but of course you can pay much more, depending upon the level of luxury to which you aspire. Many prefer the ambiance of a genuine old adobe home in a rustic village setting rather than one of those modern reproductions of Old Mexico in a gated community. These people maintain that the charm of their homes more than make up for the inconveniences of slow plumbing and weak electrical connections. Lower rents are a bonus. We once received a complaint from a reader of *Choose Mexico* that our book didn't adequately reflect Mexico's "high cost of living." It turned out that he rented a four-bedroom, luxury home with a view of the ocean, complete with a swimming pool and servants' quarters.

Finding Rentals or Homes for Sale

Looking for rentals or homes to buy can be a pleasant adventure. Simply walking around town may give you some leads; a SE RENTA or SE AQUILA sign might be showing in a window here and there. Don't be put off by the outside appearance of a building. A rough adobe facade with cracked plaster could conceal a beautiful patio with delightful apartments clustered about a flower-perfumed garden. Colonial buildings tend to look inward rather than show themselves to the passerby.

You can usually find a bulletin board in the local *supermercado* (supermarket), where ads for apartment and house rentals are placed, along with ads by domestic servants looking for work. If there's an English-language newspaper or newsletter, it will also contain such information. English paperback exchanges and English-language libraries usually have bulletin boards. However, most news of rentals or homes for sale is spread by word of mouth. This is particularly true of Mexican landlords; they seldom advertise in newspapers and depend on friends and neighbors to let the word out that their house is for rent. It's okay to stop fellow *norteamericanos* on the street or in a restaurant and ask them for leads. Eventually you'll find something.

We know of at least one retiree who returned from Mexico quite disgruntled because he couldn't find suitable housing the first week he was in Guadalajara. Just as in the United States or Canada, you can't expect a "dream house" to suddenly appear the moment you step off the airplane.

You have to look, search, and bargain to find your ideal place. Temporarily rent a hotel apartment, and you won't feel pressured to take the first thing that comes along. You'll have time to explore, compare housing, and you might even have fun making decisions. Our advice is to take your time, and don't expect miracles.

Some of the best housing bargains can be in house-sitting arrangements. Many foreigners who own or lease property in Mexico like to return to the United States for three or so months every year and want other Americans to watch their homes while they're gone. They're also happy to derive a small income to help with the upkeep of the house. Keep your eyes and ears open. You might try placing your own ad in the local English-language paper or posting your availability on a bulletin board. These homes are furnished, of course, and usually come with a maid and/or gardener. (The homeowners don't want to risk losing good help while they're gone, so they pay the wages while they're away.) To be a house sitter, be prepared to furnish good references.

Leases and Rental Agreements

If you enter into a rental or lease agreement, you may find yourself signing an official-looking document complete with colorful government stamps. If it's a long-term lease, there will probably be an escalation clause that pegs the rent to the value of the dollar versus the peso. More than likely, if the property owner is a gringo, the rental terms will be in dollars rather than pesos. An item to insist upon is a clause on subleasing rights. Many landlords, particularly Mexicans, don't like the idea. Nevertheless, in case you decide to take a long vacation to visit friends and family in the United States, or you feel you've had enough of Mexico and need to get out from under the lease, you should protect yourself against liability. Furthermore, should you obtain a very long-term lease and you plan on putting money into the house to fix it up to your specifications, you'll need a way to recoup this money if you decide to move on. Be sure you have a complete understanding of the rental terms, and insist on a receipt each month as proof that you are living up to your end of the rental agreement or lease.

An important consideration in renting or buying a house or apartment is the presence or absence of a telephone. Depending on the location, it sometimes takes an inordinate amount of time to have a telephone installed in Mexico. With a phone in place, you are assured of communications, and when you decide to sell, rent, or sublease, you'll have an easier time finding clients.

A final caution about rental agreements. Should you decide to rent your Mexican home while you are back in the United States or Canada, you need to be aware of your lease agreement. As in many Latin American countries, the laws are definitely stacked on the side of the renter and against the landlord.

You must be very sure of the person to whom you rent, and you must have an iron-clad rental agreement. Once someone is living on your property and decides he or she doesn't want to leave, it can be difficult to get the person out as long as he or she pays rent. We've even heard horror stories about tenants refusing to pay rent and staying for long periods of time before they could be evicted.

You could have a similar problem when you sell your property and allow someone to move in before you receive your cash. One reader reported that he believed a buyer when he said he wanted to move in and make improvements on the house so he could receive a higher mortgage. The unfortunate seller said he had already spent $8,500 in legal fees to get the swindler out of the home, and the problem still hadn't been resolved.

CULTURAL DIFFERENCES AT HOME

Mexican kitchens are remarkably different from your kitchen back home. In the United States or Canada, the kitchen—roomy, with colorful curtains in the windows and a large kitchen table with comfortable chairs—is an important part of the household. Back home, we spend a lot of time in our kitchens; we eat most of our meals there, at least breakfast and lunch, and when company comes to call, we naturally invite them to have a cup of coffee at our kitchen table.

But middle-class Mexican families wouldn't any more dine in the kitchen than we would take our meals in the garage. In middle-class Mexican homes, the kitchen is the domain of the maid, the cook, and the gardener; the lady of the house seldom enters. Therefore, Mexican kitchens are often stark and utilitarian, with a minimum of conveniences and ugly plumbing fixtures; they look as if they belong to another house. If the kitchen has a table and chairs, they're used only by the servants to take their meals.

In some of the more luxurious homes, the kitchen is actually separated from the main part of the house by a locked door. The kitchen, along with the maid's quarters, bath, and garage, are the domain of the servants, who have their own keys that unlock their section of the house but not the owner's living quarters.

However, neither the authors nor most of the readers of this book are members of that tiny upper-class society in which the presence of domestic servants is taken for granted. In fact, many of us are uncomfortable with the very idea of having people around the house who are paid to do things we could do for ourselves. Although we love to have a housekeeper clean our place on a regular basis, we also value our privacy and hate the idea of a person living with us twenty-four hours a day, continually scurrying around the house trying to look busy. Therefore, some North Americans never consider hiring servants. They enjoy doing yard work and think washing dishes and making beds is a normal part of living.

We initially resisted the idea of employing a maid, then compromised by hiring a woman to come in just in the mornings. She arrived just after breakfast, cleaned the kitchen, scrubbed the tile floors, did the laundry, and sometimes prepared the noon meal. Gradually we became used to her, because she was so unobtrusive and careful to keep busy in some part of the house where we were not. Her not living with us left the maid's room available as a guest room or a place for a house sitter while we visited Acapulco or Mexico City.

Another reason you may not wish to hire a full-time maid and gardener is the legal obligations you have toward them as employees. They have certain rights under the law: annual vacations, severance pay, notice of dismissal, and things of that nature. People who do employ full-time servants recommend that you have your lawyer draw up a one-year contract. As one expatriate from Acapulco says, "You can't argue with the intent of the laws. These people have been taken advantage of for years, so maybe it's a good thing some laws are slanted in their favor."

Open-Air Markets and the Kitchen

Long before the Spanish arrived, the *tianguis* (open-air market) was a prominent feature of Mexican life. A few tables shaded by awnings, farmers with something to sell, and townspeople with money or items to trade were all that were needed. From Mexico City to the smallest villages, that tradition is still alive today and continues to be much more than just a commercial institution.

Outdoor markets are common throughout the world. Even in the United States, where they seemed to be disappearing, they are staging a comeback in the form of farmers' markets (in big cities), garage sales, and flea markets (just about everywhere).

In few places, however, are open-air markets as prominent or as important to the life of the community as they are in Mexico, where on one or more days of the week, a whole neighborhood will be transformed into a sprawling marketplace with most of the residents drawn into its transactions.

For the North American resident or visitor, these markets are an opportunity not only to buy everything from produce to machine parts at substantial savings but also to observe closely the inner workings of Mexico. One thing that fascinates us is the juxtaposition of items as traditional as tethered chickens and trussed-up (live) pigs with other articles as contemporary as radios and cassette tapes.

In addition to these informal, weekly outdoor markets, every city and town has one or more permanent *mercados,* usually under public auspices. Usually these markets are housed in great tin-roofed sheds but spill out into the surrounding streets. They, too, are operated by a collection of entrepreneurs, each offering his or her own specialty—fruits or vegetables, meat, even clothing and hardware. At first you might feel intimidated by this seemingly disorderly hive of vendors vigorously hawking their wares, but remember they cluster according to the products being offered. Thus, for vegetables, you wander about the section where stand after stand of produce—tomatoes, onions, avocados, and potatoes—is displayed in attractive arrangements. Wander a few steps away, and you might find yourself in a profusion of clothes, or birds in cages, or perhaps stands where cassettes and CDs are sold, with boom boxes blaring at top volume. If you live near the ocean, look for the area where fish is wholesaled. Fishermen bring their catch to sell to the wholesalers, who in turn sell it to the stores. By going directly to the fishermen, you not only save money, but you buy the freshest possible catch.

Many Other Shops

Not everything in the *mercado* will appeal to you, at least not until you are used to the system. Those stalls where sides of beef, dotted with flies, hang in the open can be passed by in favor of meat markets with sanitation and refrigeration. Modern meat markets can usually be found inside the *mercados* or at least nearby.

Melons and other displayed fruits are often cut and sliced. These are best enjoyed for their aesthetics. Be sure the melon you buy is whole; when you get home, you can slice it with the assurance that it hasn't been a parade ground for flies. Any fruit that can be peeled is perfectly safe to eat on the spot. With fruits and vegetables that need washing, better wait until you can purify them in your kitchen.

Before you begin to worry that you're going to have to do all your buying from street vendors, rest assured that the *supermercado* has arrived in Mexico. Even smaller towns have miniature versions of the U.S. supermarket. Although you could do all your shopping there, you would not only miss one of the delights of Mexican living but also severely limit your choices. Like its counterpart in the United States, the *supermercado* is a convenient, usually economical place to buy packaged foods, domestic paper goods, laundry soap, beer, and liquor. For fresh fruit and vegetables, meats and poultry, and baked goods, go to the *mercado*, or community market.

Fruits and Vegetables

Because most fruits and vegetables sold locally are grown in small family plots, without the aid of U.S. mass-production techniques and not force-fed with chemical fertilizers, they taste great. The variety of oranges (which have seeds) is amazing. Their juice is sweet and refreshing. Avocados are an adventure. There are at least a hundred different kinds, each with a slightly different flavor and texture. The bland U.S. varieties pale in comparison. Carrots are often small, but they are so sweet and tasty that you could make a meal on them alone. Asparagus, broccoli, and swiss chard are so flavorful that you wonder if they're the same varieties as we get up north. Indeed they may not be. This is not the produce that Mexican agribusiness ships to the north. Like its U.S. counterpart, it concentrates on a few varieties of produce—generally those that will survive the long journey. In the *mercado*, however, you are buying from small farmers who raise the same crops their fathers planted. The emphasis is on flavor, not convenience or uniformity.

Meat

Cattle are seldom grain-fed in Mexico, which means it takes longer—six months to a year longer—to raise them for market. This extra maturity accounts for the rich flavor of Mexican beef. Of course range-fed beef is tough and stringy, which for some folks counterbalances the tasty flavor. Beef can be aged in your refrigerator, and it can be cooked in ways to compensate for toughness. At better meat markets you can purchase grain-fed beef if you prefer an extra-tender steak. Most good restaurants serve tender beef—well, tender for Mexico.

Pork is another story. Most pork sold in the markets does not come from pig farms, where animals are penned so tightly they can't move and fed garbage until they pack on enough weight to go to market. In Mexico, pigs wander loose around farmhouses and in small villages, almost as if they were family pets. They exercise and run free until they are ready for market. The result is a lean, red-meat pork, sometimes with the consistency of steak. The flavor can be incredible. If you cook this pork until it's well done, it's perfectly safe.

Outside the *mercado* you'll find many other food shops, bakeries, and small markets. Those that cater to foreign residents have higher prices. Yet food prices are so low in Mexico that it's difficult to be concerned that the dozen eggs that cost the equivalent of $1.00 in the *mercado* are selling for 25 cents more in the shop where the proprietor speaks English.

Food Prices

For a time, before the peso's recent devaluations, food prices in Mexico were approaching those in the United States and Canada. Then prices on most food items fell to a level far below what you would pay north of the border. Thus, one of the more expensive cost-of-living categories became cheaper for those with dollar incomes. Our impression, after many hours of comparing prices during our latest visit, was that overall food is at least 30 percent less expensive in Mexico than in the United States.

One difference between food shopping in the United States and in Mexico is the frequency with which one needs to shop. You can buy food so fresh in Mexico that it seems a shame to let it sit for several days in the refrigerator. In addition, going to the *mercado* is fun. People who normally shop once a week at the U.S. supermarkets quickly fall into the Mexican habit of shopping daily. They discover the fun of planning a menu around what looks enticing in the market, rather than what's available in the freezer. Shopping is an engaging form of social interaction and a fine way to practice Spanish. The standkeepers quickly recognize you and often, as a token of goodwill, put something extra in your bag after you've paid. Once, when we bought a cut-up chicken at our favorite poultry stand, the owner placed an extra neck and two gizzards into our basket. When we indicated that we really had no use for the extras, he nodded his head in understanding and replaced the neck and gizzards with three large, yellow chicken feet.

You can bargain in most markets, but it's hardly worthwhile because of the low prices. You will quickly learn to identify those who take advantage of your relative wealth by jacking up their prices. In this case, rather than waste time bargaining, simply avoid those stands and deal with friendly merchants who give you the right price and who show you they appreciate your patronage.

Outside of a few convenience foods, most items that Americans are used to are available in Mexico. Food packaging of local products, however, tends to be several years behind. Maybe this is because people prefer fresh foods to prepackaged mixes or frozen TV dinners. Bacon, for instance, is usually sliced to order rather than prepackaged in transparent material. Sometimes seemingly arbitrary little shortages can be annoying if you allow them to be. Once, for several weeks, we searched for oatmeal that was not presweetened, although it had been available a month earlier and was available again later. Some things are sold in different base quantities. For example, eggs can be bought by the dozen but are cheaper by the kilo. Oranges, though available by the kilo, are cheaper when bought by number. Go figure. When you shop every day, getting your purchases home is not a serious problem, even if you don't have a car. All over Mexico, Americans and Mexicans can be seen carrying groceries in locally produced straw bags. In some parts of the country, the bags have straps that go over your shoulders; in others, straps that you hold in your hand. (If you get tired of walking, taxis are affordable.)

Wherever you are the straw bag filled with groceries proclaims that you are not a tourist, but someone really living in Mexico. Lately, however, plastic shopping bags have been pushing aside the woven ones. Although they're cheaper and can be thrown away, they will never be quite the same as the straw bags.

Mexican Cooking

Once you get those delicious meats, fruits, and vegetables home, what you make them into will be up to you. There are Americans in Mexico whose menus seldom stray from those of their former neighbors still living in Dubuque or Toronto. (We think they're missing something.) On the other hand, if you want to experiment with the varied cuisines of Mexico, your kitchen is an excellent place to do so. You are in control and can adapt seasoning to suit your taste.

Diana Kennedy's *My Mexico: A Culinary Odyssey* (Clarkson/Potter Publishers, 1998) is an excellent English-language cookbook for

Americans who want to share what Mexico's many peoples have to offer. You can use this book as a source of recipes, as a guide to ordering in restaurants where menus aren't in English, or as a source of answers to your maid's questions about what you'd like for dinner. Don't expect your maid to be able to prepare all the dishes in the book; however, if you speak Spanish well enough, or are skillful at teaching by example, you may have your maid cooking Mexican food of which the neighbors have never heard.

A pleasant though not essential part of your preparation for retirement in Mexico might be studying Mexican cookbooks and trying some dishes. Even if the ingredients are not all readily available, you will find some recipes you can make with what is at hand.

As we've asserted several times in this book, Mexican cuisine is rich and varied and by no means limited to chiles, beans, and tortillas. Nevertheless, were it not for the creative use of maize (corn) tortillas, beans, chiles, and cheese, there would be many more people suffering from hunger and malnutrition in Mexico. These inexpensive ingredients formed the foundation of the pre-Cortez diet and are staples of Mexican cooking today. Meat, poultry, and fish are used sparingly, almost as one would use a seasoning. The result is comparable to much Asian cooking: delicious, inexpensive food that is actually more healthful than the standard American diet, which emphasizes red meat.

Years ago nutritionists wondered why Mexicans seem to thrive on a combination of foods that violate many of the basic nutritional values held by most Americans. They discovered that the nutrients, particularly the proteins, in the daily Mexican fare fit together in an almost perfect balance. Most of the U.S. scientific community now believes that fats, not carbohydrates, are the cause of America's endemic obesity and the resulting heart and circulatory problems. Also the Mexican custom is to eat the principal meal, *la comida*, in the middle of the day. Traditionally this is a leisurely meal that is eaten during the long siesta hours and that might include a nap afterward. Mexicans tend to limit *la cena*, or evening meal, to a light snack. Elaborate evening meals, if eaten at all, are eaten very late. In Mexico City, for example, many restaurants don't even open their doors until nine o'clock and are still serving meals at midnight. Enjoying the main meal during the siesta is ideal for the retiree. The maid will be there to prepare it, and you can make your own supper from the leftovers or enjoy *la cena* in a restaurant with your friends. In addition it is healthier and more comfortable, particularly as you grow older, to avoid heavy meals late in the day.

Domestic Help

Most Americans of moderate means have had no experience with servants, or perhaps they have had a cleaning woman come in once or twice a week. During the past forty years, even in homes affluent enough to afford hired help, the trend has been to substitute "labor-saving" devices for human assistance. The middle-class homemaker spends more time in the kitchen and laundry or behind a vacuum cleaner than his or her counterpart of a generation ago. Not only has help become expensive, but in the United States it is a rare employer or employee who is fully comfortable with the employer-servant relationship.

When Americans hear that domestic help is readily affordable in Mexico, they often wonder whether they would like to hire someone to cook, clean, and do laundry. They visualize someone who is a servant because he or she is unable to find other employment, someone who deeply resents his or her situation and feels demeaned by having to take orders and work in someone else's home.

In Mexico, as we've said, domestic service is considered an entirely acceptable occupation. Despite low wages, there are enough benefits to make domestic service desirable and satisfying for many. Some benefits are tangible, like the guarantee of one or more nutritious meals each day and the higher wages usually paid by foreign residents. Americans often treat their help better than local employers and are more egalitarian and generous in ways that sometimes aren't apparent. Other benefits include the status a domestic servant gains from close connection with relatively affluent foreigners. In short, domestic service is not considered a last resort as it often is up north. When American residents speak of the loyalty and good nature of their servants, they are neither being naive nor condescending. Servants can truly help increase your involvement with the country, as well as making life easier and more comfortable.

Often a person will work for more than one employer and will be happy to work for you two or three hours a day, doing the breakfast dishes, scrubbing the tile floors, as well as doing laundry. For these chores, the maid will need no English and you, no Spanish. The workers' energy and efficiency will amaze you. They evidently feel that because they are being paid by the hour, they must fill up each hour, and thus will look for things to do. With one maid we had to be careful not to lay clean clothes on the bed so we could wear them after showering, for when we were ready to put them on, they would be hanging on the line, already washed. Anything that wasn't hanging up or in a dresser was fair game for the washtub.

If you wish your employees to do anything complicated, they must be taught procedures that will be strange to them unless they have had experience working for Americans. If you want a roast chicken for lunch, you must make clear how long you want it cooked, what kinds of seasoning you want, and what, if anything, to put inside. Even something as simple as making picnic sandwiches can be a mystery to someone for whom bread is a luxury, seldom if ever used in her house. If, on the other hand, you want to try *chile con queso* or *chiles rellenos*, the maid will need no instruction. Unless you're willing to take time teaching and explaining, you're better off doing the complicated American cooking yourself and letting the maid help you with shopping and cleaning up the kitchen afterward.

Handymen

Often you can hire someone who will take care of your garden and also serve as a repairman, a bartender, and a watchman. He helps the maid, runs errands, and negotiates with local business people for you. If you're going away to Acapulco for a week, often the gardener will stay in your house to watch things. Many gardeners have several clients, so it's easy to find someone who only wants to come in for an hour or two a day to water plants and make sure everything is working properly. Above all, do treat your servants with respect, and don't talk down to them. Being a domestic servant in Mexico isn't a low-status job, and you want your employees to be proud of working for you.

Do You Need to Know Spanish?

If you're going to fully enjoy Mexico, of course, you will need to learn to speak Spanish. However, you won't starve if you don't know Spanish, and you won't lack for social connections just because you are too lazy to learn more than a few phrases of the language. You'll survive. Many North Americans have lived in Mexico for years and learned just enough Spanish to ask where the bathroom is or order another round of drinks. Occasionally they enter the wrong bathroom, that's true, but rarely does a waiter misunderstand an order for more drinks. If you plan on hanging around with Americans for your entire stay in Mexico, or if you insist on living in expensive hotels and condos, then it really doesn't matter whether you learn Spanish or not.

Once you learn to communicate in Spanish, though, you suddenly find new doors open to you. Mexico becomes a totally different place. Instead of being limited to a small circle of English-speaking friends, you can venture out into the exciting world of Mexico. You can participate in everything that is going on around you instead of being puzzled and mystified by it. You will find yourself being invited to visit homes and join in festivities that before were inaccessible. You will have fun dealing with merchants, servants, and neighbors, entering into much closer relationships with them. You will no longer fear hassling with bureaucrats or arguing with the police and taxi drivers. When traveling like a resident in posh resort towns, you will be in a much better position to locate those $20 hotel rooms. In short, when you learn Spanish, you truly become a resident of Mexico who is ready to enjoy the country to the fullest.

But isn't it difficult to learn a foreign language? Yes, it is; language learning is not easy. You often hear someone say: "Oh, I won't bother studying the language now. I'll pick it up when I get there." Unless you're younger than ten years old, the chances that simply by being around Spanish speakers you will be able to "pick up" the language are less than zero.

The only way adults learn a foreign language is the old-fashioned way: through study, practice, and more practice. Studying Spanish can not only be enjoyable, it can be a rewarding activity, part of getting settled in your new home.

Even if you already speak some Spanish, we highly recommend that one of the first things you do upon arriving in Mexico is to enroll in a language class. Besides polishing your command of the language, you'll find classrooms excellent places to meet people and enlarge your circle of friends. Your fellow students will form their own social groups, which hold parties and get-togethers—any excuse they can find to practice Spanish.

LIVING WITH MEXICAN LAWS

Your Legal Status

We are often asked, "Do I have to give up my citizenship if I retire permanently in Mexico?" Of course not. Very few North Americans would consider Mexican retirement if this were the case. Fortunately there are a number of ways to become a legal resident of Mexico, and none of them affects your citizenship in any way. The options open to you range all the way from using the tourist cards (readily available to anyone wishing to visit Mexico) to *inmigrado* status, which gives you all the rights of a Mexican citizen, except the right to vote.

It seems as if the rules for becoming a resident of Mexico are continually undergoing changes. Following are the latest regulations for the four basic types of resident visas, but realize that more changes are always possible. One pleasant change in the recent past is that it is no longer necessary to be older than fifty-five to become a resident. As long as you meet the financial requirements, any age will do. Another welcome change is that it is easier to meet the financial requirements (more about this later).

Tourist Visa (FM-T)

As its name suggests, the tourist visa is essentially for people vacationing in Mexico. All that is required is proof of citizenship. If you cross the border in a car, you can request a 180-day visa. This allows you one six-month stay in any one-year period. If you travel by air, there's a ninety-day maximum, although it can be renewed for an additional ninety days at any Mexican immigration office. Many North Americans live long term in Mexico by renewing their FM-T every six months.

Advantages of a tourist visa (FM-T): No income requirement. No need for legal help to obtain visa.

Disadvantages: Must be renewed every six months by making a trip to the border. Does not allow you to import your household goods and appliances duty-free. You cannot work when you have a tourist visa. Your automobile is allowed only one six-month entry permit. There's a possibility that the government could crack down on multiple, back-to-back visits on tourist visas and insist that you apply for FM-3 status.

Visitante Rentista (FM-3)

A *visitante rentista* is a one-year visa designed for those who want to live at least part-time in Mexico but may not want make the move permanent. You can come and go if you wish, but do not have to leave the country every six months. You are entitled to a one-time, tax-free import of a reasonable amount of household goods and a car within three months of securing the FM-3 status. This document must be renewed each year for five years, after which you can either upgrade to an FM-2 or simply continue with the FM-3. Income requirement is currently about $1,000 a month for the head of a family, plus $500 per dependent. (The current required amount is tied to a multiplier of the minimum wage and fluctuates with changes in the exchange rate and the minimum wage.) If you own property, your income requirements are reduced by 50 percent.

In the past the income requirements were strict, with the applicant being required to produce evidence of pensions, bank trusts, or other guaranteed monthly income. Nowadays you just have to produce bank statements for the previous three months to show that at least $1,500 for a couple or $1,000 for a single has been deposited to your account each month. (These figures are approximate; they vary with the peso-dollar exchange rate.) We understand that some consulates have requested proof of pensions, but we've been assured that this should not be the case. Try a different consulate. This simple way of proving income makes it much easier for someone younger than the age of retirement to qualify for residency in Mexico.

Advantages of a visitante rentista *(FM-3):* Applications processed routinely. Cheapest (when you figure in cost of trips to the border to renew tourist cards) and easiest way to reside in Mexico. May bring in household goods tax-free. Your automobile is legal as long as your FM-3 is valid.

Disadvantages: Not too many; this is the route most people take when retiring in Mexico. Requires some red tape and dealing with Mexican consulates. It's possible to do it yourself, without the assistance of a lawyer.

Inmigrante Rentista (FM-2)

Inmigrante rentista status is for those who are serious about living and making their homes in Mexico. The income requirements are higher—

again based on a multiple of the minimum wage, which comes to about $1,500 for the retiree and $750 each for dependents. Again, this amount is cut in half if the applicant owns a Mexican home. This status requires renewing an FM-2 visa yearly, for five consecutive years, then applying for permanent immigrant status. Once you have *inmigrante* status, you can work at any job or endeavor you please, including a business. You will have all rights of citizenship except for voting.

Advantages of **inmigrante rentista (FM-2):** After renewal for five years, leads to *inmigrado* status.

Disadvantages: Need to show higher monthly income. Longer, more difficult process to obtain. Restricted from leaving the country for long periods of time.

Inmigrado

Once you've been in the country for five years as an *inmigrante rentista* (FM-2), you can apply for permanent residency as an *inmigrado.*

Advantages of **inmigrado status:** Those with *inmigrado* status have all the rights of a Mexican citizen except for the right to vote. You can work or operate a business without restrictions. You no longer have to prove financial capability. Of course you don't have to give up your U.S. or Canadian citizenship. The only restriction is that more than thirty-six consecutive months' absence from Mexico, or accumulated absences of five years over a ten-year period, will result in cancellation of the visa.

Disadvantages: Granted only after five years as *immigrante rentista.* Requires an attorney who is aware of the rules. Restrictions on amount of time allowed out of the country.

Which Status Is Right for You?

The process of obtaining the longer-term residential statuses is, like any dealings with the Mexican bureaucracy, complicated and exasperating. If you are blessed with the patience of a saint, you can probably do it all yourself. If not, it may be worth the additional expense to retain a Mexican lawyer. If you are going to Mexico for relaxation, you may not want to spend your time in lines in government offices. Besides, in Mexico, even lawyers' fees are moderate.

Which status is right for you? You'll probably want to start with a 180-day tourist card before making any binding decisions. While in Mexico you will undoubtedly receive advice from longtime residents, and you'll hear more arguments than we could possibly make for or against each option. You can always upgrade to FM-3 status while you are in Mexico.

Differences between U.S. and Mexican Laws

Many Americans are concerned about the differences between the legal systems of Mexico and the United States. Some dread the possibility that they might, because of some misunderstanding, end up in a dreary Mexican jail. This fear evaporates in the Mexican sun, however. We have found no American resident there who expressed concern about the law. Of course if your retirement plans include dealing illegal drugs, this reassurance does not apply. On the other hand, we've encountered a few gringos who, for one reason or other, spent some time in a Mexican jail. From their experiences we can safely say that you don't want to do time there! Mexican law, like most European systems, is one of codified statutes. This is often referred to as Roman law or the Napoleonic Code. North American law, on the other hand, is based on English common law, in which each case may be considered unique and each decision may be based on prior decisions in other courts. Under Mexican law almost every possible violation or transgression is thoroughly codified or listed in law books, and extenuating circumstances play little role. Instead of long jury trials to determine punishment or damages, the magistrate simply looks up the law code that applies—and that's it. Awards in damage suits are usually limited to the actual proven losses.

Sentences for criminal acts are longer, and parole is not as easily available as in the United States. On the second conviction (even for relatively minor offenses), a criminal is judged to be a "habitual" criminal, and upon a third conviction is sentenced to twenty years away from society. That doesn't mean nine months in the slammer and then parole. It means twenty years. Perhaps as a result serious crime, particularly in smaller towns and cities, is much less frequent than in most places in the United States.

Bringing Your Car into Mexico

For some time Mexico has been plagued with autos entering the country and never leaving. Thousands of illegal or stolen cars are running around Mexico, evading taxes, driving tax collectors bonkers. In an effort to stem the flow, the government devised a system of bonding your car as you enter the country. When you enter Mexico on a tourist card (FM-T), you'll be able to import your car for the same period—usually 180 days. The customs authorities at the border will require:

1. The original certificate of title
2. If your car is being financed, an affidavit from the lien holder authorizing you to take the car out of the United States
3. A valid state registration
4. A valid driver's license
5. A credit card (VISA, MasterCard, American Express) in the driver's name, used to pay a $12 fee and to back up your promise to remove the car from Mexico at the end of the six months of your stay (If you don't have a credit card, you'll have to post a bond equal to the car's value.)

You should also carry a copy of a U.S. or Canadian insurance policy, effective for at least two months from the date of entry. This isn't required, but it covers some bases.

And of course you should either have a Mexican insurance policy in hand or be prepared to buy one immediately after crossing the border. Technically Mexican insurance isn't required, but if you don't have it, you're taking terrible chances. Your U.S. or Canadian policy won't help you, because Mexico does not recognize any insurance unless issued by a Mexican company.

Your car permit will be good for the six-month term of your tourist visa (FM-T). If someone other than the owner or owners will be driving (such as your husband or wife if not an owner of the car), be sure to have this noted on the car permit by the Mexican official. That will make the person an authorized driver. Any licensed person can drive the car as long as the owner is in the vehicle, but unless that person is noted on the car permit, he or she is not considered an authorized driver. Do not under any circumstances permit an unauthorized person to drive the car when the registered owner is not in the vehicle! The fine can be truly substantial. And save all the paperwork; you'll need it when you return. Caution: If your car is found in Mexico beyond the six-month term or without the proper documents, it can be confiscated. For more information contact your nearest Mexican consulate.

However, if you plan to stay in Mexico on a *visitante rentista* visa (FM-3), you will probably want to legalize the vehicle for a year at a time to match your visa. You first enter on a regular six-month car permit, and then within thirty days of receiving your FM-3 status, you apply for a one-year car permit. This permit, along with your FM-3 permit, must be renewed each subsequent year. You will have to keep up your U.S. state license in the meantime. (Many people feel it's simpler to buy a Mexican car and be done with it!)

After five years you can apply for your *inmigrante rentista* (FM-2) status, and if you elect to do so, you'll have to pay taxes and nationalize the car. FM-2 residents aren't permitted to own a foreign-registered car. Of course, you can simply renew your FM-3 status should you so choose. One word of caution: The rule is that an automobile is allowed only one six-month tourist permit per year. The old maneuver of taking your car across the border every six months and immediately returning may be outdated soon. This rule has been unenforceable in the past, but with today's computerized system, there's every reason to believe that you could be denied immediate reentry if you don't have an FM-3 visa.

As we mentioned, you should either secure a Mexican auto insurance policy before crossing the border or buy one immediately after. The reason we stress adequate car insurance is that in the event of an accident, Mexican law requires that your vehicle be held until damages are paid or until you guarantee proper payment via an insurance policy. If bodily injury is involved, police can detain you until the problem is resolved. Because courts usually grant compensation for the actual damages to the car and, in case of an injury, for a stipulated amount of damages for time off from work, an insured driver never has to worry about lawsuits. But if you don't have insurance, you could have a lot to worry about.

Mexican police are not empowered to assign fault for the accident, so whether or not it was your fault, you'd better have the appropriate proof of insurance with you; always keep the policy with you when you drive. The good news is that Mexican insurance companies are very good about helping you and making sure your auto is fixed. We've heard of them finding hotel accommodations for clients whose autos are being repaired. So drive as carefully as you do in the United States, and stop worrying.

Mexican Labor Laws

In many aspects Mexican labor laws are similar to those in the United States as they apply to the maximum workday and workweek and the employment of minors. There are, however, some special rules regarding vacations, bonuses, and termination of employment that have particular relevance to those of you who plan on hiring a maid or a gardener.

Workers with more than one year's service are entitled to an annual vacation of at least six workdays. This increases at the rate of two workdays a year for the next three years (to a total of twelve days' vacation a year). In subsequent years, two workdays of vacation are added for each five years of employment. Thus, if someone worked for you for nineteen years, he or she would be entitled to a vacation of eighteen workdays, or three six-day weeks.

After one year of employment, workers are also entitled to an annual bonus equal to fifteen days of wages (paid before December 20). Those who have not been employed for a full year get a bonus prorated for the time they have worked.

There are a number of grounds for which an employee can be dismissed for cause (including more than three unauthorized absences from work within a twenty-eight-day period). The rules and their enforcement vary from one locality to another. Check with your neighbors as to the guidelines in effect for hiring help. In general the labor laws do a good job of protecting workers without unduly burdening employers.To avoid having a terminated employee bring a case to the State Labor Board, an employer should insist that the employee sign a form in front of witnesses, then file it with the authorities. Again, check with neighbors or aquaintances as to what form this document should take in your area.

Employee Benefits

Remember: If you have full-time employees, you are liable for more than just their wages. The national labor code stipulates a number of benefits that you must pay by law, not just out of the goodness of your heart. In addition to holiday and vacation pay, you must provide Social Security, a Christmas or New Year's bonus (called an *aquinaldo*), and severance pay. Check with your neighbors to find out where to sign up and pay.

Some people think that by paying much more than minimum wage, their generosity negates their obligations. Not so. The benefits are due and payable no matter how much extra you pay. Some feel it's better to pay minimum wage and the benefits based on that salary, then give the employee a monthly bonus or regular gifts.

Police in Mexico

Police officers in the United States and Canada are generally thought of as highly trained and professional. Taking bribes is considered sleazy in the extreme; we are horrified when a cop is "on the take." Although not exactly highly paid, most U.S. police officers earn from $30,000 to $50,000 a year, and more with overtime and bonuses. American taxpayers consider this a good investment; they feel they get what they pay for.

But Mexico is reluctant to pay public employees decent wages, sometimes even living wages. Therefore, many government employees, including police, feel they should be compensated by the public for any services they perform. North Americans have difficulty accepting this practice; they harshly refer to it as bribery and corruption. However, Mexicans choose a softer term, *la mordida* (the bite), and take a more tolerant attitude. They consider these payments tips, just as one might tip a waiter for his services.

In contrast with the adequately paid and professional U.S. police officer, police in Mexico come from the lower socioeconomic classes, have little or no training, and are pitifully underpaid. Many Mexican police earn the minimum wage. From this meager amount they must pay a *mordida* to their superiors for the "privilege" of holding this low-paying job.

Now nobody could possibly expect a police officer to feed and clothe a family on minimum wage, not even in Mexico. Therefore, he is expected to supplement his salary by "collecting fines" or taking *mordidas*. Officially, this is frowned on, but the officials who frown disapprovingly over the practice fully expect the collection of *mordidas* to continue, and they encourage it by refusing to pay a living wage. Furthermore, higher officials routinely hold their hands out for their share of the *mordidas* collected by the cops. Again, a police officer feels that he's doing nothing wrong by collecting the fine from you. He considers it a favor to you by not issuing a traffic ticket and making you go to police headquarters to stand in line to pay your fine (while, outside, another cop is removing your license plates because you've parked in a no-parking zone).

If you ask Mexican taxpayers why they don't pay police a living wage, you'll hear: "What? Spend my taxes to pay a cop to chase speeders? Let the foolish speeder pay the cop's wages, not me. If and when I get caught speeding, I'll pay. Not before!"

This is not to say that all Mexican police lack professionalism and pride or that they cannot be honest, competent, and conscientious. (Again, they don't consider taking *mordidas* to be dishonest.) They can be very tough on real criminals. As a matter of government policy, when it comes to minor indiscretions, police are far more tolerant with foreigners than with Mexican citizens. We've seen North Americans get away with offenses (such as public drunkenness) that would land an ordinary citizen in jail for three days. Treating tourists or foreign residents roughly or unfairly is a serious matter, which can cause repercussions throughout a department. Should you have an unpleasant experience, you are obligated to report it by calling the Ministry of Tourism's twenty-four-hour hot line (in Mexico City) at 5–250–0123.

In Mexico City you'll encounter "tourist police" who speak English and whose job is to see that the tourists are assisted. They have a tendency for overkill, however, and will attack you with friendliness, practically insisting that you visit the places they think you should. They'll flag down a cab, push you inside, and send you off to the tourist market before you know what's happening. (While this may seem very friendly, you must realize that the cab driver is probably the cop's brother-in-law, and they split the commission for delivering you to the tourist market.)

Mexicans Are Serious about Their Laws

Many laws in Mexico seem to be honored in their violation, which sometimes gives an American the wrong impression. For example, the largest piles of trash and garbage are invariably found stacked around signs that proclaim, DO NOT THROW GARBAGE HERE! Speed limit signs have no relation to the speed of the traffic. Stop signs seem to be invisible to most drivers, and stern prohibitions are simply a challenge. The foreigner residing in Mexico, however, would be wise to consider himself or herself a guest. Obeying laws should be no more an imposition than it would be in the United States. If you park in a no-parking zone, you might find your license plates impounded. To get them back, you must first go to a bank where you get a receipt for the fine you must pay, then to the central office where confiscated plates are held.

Some legal matters are taken more seriously in Mexico than back home, especially business relationships. If you break a lease, for example, you may discover that the landlord has impounded your belongings, and the judge agrees with him. The law might come down very heavily on you if you cheat someone out of money or refuse to pay a legitimate bill. As we've noted above, there are special rules for hiring employees, such as your maid or a gardener. Trying to get away with something on a real estate deal can be expensive, as many an American who tried to circumvent the laws against buying *ejido* property and lost all his or her investment can attest. (New laws have all but eliminated the *ejido* problem; some of these properties can now be legally sold.)

One way to ensure an extremely unpleasant stay in a Mexican jail is to be illegally in possession of firearms in Mexico. As attached as you may be to your trusty rifle, shotgun, or handgun at home, don't try to sneak it past the customs officers at the border. Even if you succeed, chances are very good that the police at your destination will find out about it and will not treat it as a minor matter. There are several North Americans in jail at this moment because they brought a gun across the border.

A North American who normally obeys the laws in his own country can expect no more trouble in Mexico than he would at home—probably less, because he usually behaves as a guest in a foreign country. But those who think that the law applies only to others, those with contempt for the customs of their host country, or those who feel that the law shouldn't apply to Americans as it does to Mexicans are likely to be quickly disabused of these attitudes.

STAYING HEALTHY SOUTH
OF THE BORDER

Far too much of the discussion of whether Mexico is good for your health boils down to the question "Can you drink the water?" The short answer to that question is, "Yes, but not water from the tap." We'll cover that in detail a little further on, and we hope that we can persuade you that it is a relatively trivial concern. Far more important is the fact that the vigor and happiness of the typical U.S. retiree in Mexico points to the ways in which the country is indeed a very healthy place for older people.

There are both physical and emotional reasons for their well-being. The climate in most places where retirees have chosen to live is healthier in several ways than in the communities they have come from. For one thing, it is drier. For generations the attractions of a low-humidity climate have been bringing people who suffer from respiratory and rheumatic diseases to the American Southwest. With the exception of its coastal areas, Mexico is blessed with a climate that is at least as dry. In addition Mexico possesses something the southwestern states do not: It has (again, in the communities favored by retirees) temperatures that are moderate year-round.

Some people avoid Mexico because they fear for their health. They have heard that no one escapes *turista*, or "Montezuma's revenge," and imagine a stay made miserable, if not dangerous, by gastrointestinal woes. Some Mexican water supplies are indeed contaminated, but clean, safe water is available everywhere. Furthermore, the contaminated water can be purified easily, as can vegetables and fruits that have come into contact with that water. As we've noted, every prudent Mexican and foreigner recognizes the importance of guarding against the hazards of impure water and untreated raw fruit and vegetables. The necessary steps are incorporated into his or her life so that these precautions become as natural as washing one's hands before meals. (This practice is a very good idea in Mexico as elsewhere. Some studies report that one's hands are likely to be a major source of the bacteria that get into one's mouth.)

Water is safe after being boiled for a few minutes. Treating it with chlorine tablets or a reliable filtration device also takes care of bacteria or amoebic problems. If you have a maid, she will make sure you always have an ample supply of purified water both in the kitchen and in the bathroom so that you will not be tempted to brush your teeth or swallow a pill with tap water. Fruit and vegetables fresh from the market are stored separately from those that have been made safe by a brief soaking in purified water to which some chlorine tablets have been added (available inexpensively at any drugstore).

Ice must be made with purified water and, like fruit and vegetables, should be consumed only in places where you can be confident that the necessary precautions have been taken. The law in Mexico is that ice cubes must be made from purified water. That requirement, however, does not extend to bulk ice. Almost always restaurants and stores will use purified water for ice cubes; because it is so inexpensive, there is no reason not to. If a restaurant doesn't follow the law, cheating by using tainted water, its customers will soon know about it and will no longer patronize the place. Bad restaurants don't remain in business for long. In the beginning you'll have to rely on the knowledge of the local Americans about which restaurants to avoid. In time you'll develop your own sound instincts.

Some travelers, worried about gastrointestinal illness, dose themselves with antibiotics, which are readily available in Mexican pharmacies. However, this is a bad practice; these medications have dangerous side effects. Recently the fad has been to take hefty dosages of Pepto Bismol as a preventative. Carl Franz (in *The People's Guide to Mexico*) swears by the efficacy of Pepto Bismol and confirms that it works. This is fine for travelers, but if you're going to be living in Mexico, you don't want to spend the rest of your days pouring that pink stuff into your stomach. Once you've settled into your new life, you'll find these kinds of self-medication unnecessary.

Good health, however, is more than avoiding unfriendly bugs. It involves your total physical and mental well-being and your whole outlook. If Mexico is the right place for you, you can be healthier there than you could be anywhere else. Almost everything that can make you happy—the climate, the good food, the constant activity— will also make you healthy. These elements, in addition to the commonsense principles of sanitation discussed above, are the essential prescriptions for good health. If you have a chronic illness, your doctor will have some additional rules and perhaps some medications for you, but you should find them no more onerous in Mexico than in your hometown.

Health Care

Americans living in most parts of Mexico report the availability of competent English-speaking doctors and dentists. The questionnaires we mailed to retired Americans devoted special attention to the quality of medical and dental care, access to hospitals, and the availability of medications. We emphasized these areas because books written a couple of decades ago treated health care, at least outside the biggest cities, as a problem. We are gratified to report, however, that today (according to responses received from retirees in every part of Mexico) there are good doctors and dentists in most cities of any size. Quality hospitals are within easy traveling distance, and most of the commonly prescribed medications are stocked by Mexican pharmacies.

A few of our respondents stated that they might go to Mexico City or to the United States for an unusual or extremely serious illness, but most indicated that they thought that they could find sophisticated facilities and personnel in the nearest big city. Because we know of people who, if they became ill in Miami or Los Angeles, would go to hospitals and doctors in New York, we are inclined to conclude that the needs catered to by air evacuation services are more emotional than medical.

Doctors

Many doctors in the United States are Mexican trained. As the number of qualified students seeking entrance to U.S. medical schools exceeded their capacity, many young Americans went abroad for their medical educations. Mexico was one of the countries in which they found training facilities of top quality. In short there is no more reason to be concerned about the qualification of a reputable Mexican doctor than there is to be about an American one. Two nice things about Mexican doctors: They still make house calls, and office visits are usually not much more than $20. Specialists, of course, are more expensive.

Although not every town is blessed with a first-rate hospital, few are far from one. Few drugs require prescriptions in Mexico, and those that do can be filled at any pharmacy. If, however, you need some special or unusual medication, it would be wise to bring a supply with you on your initial visit to Mexico and, if you find it is unavailable there, to confer with your physician when you return to the United States. He or she can tell you what may be substituted. If there is no substitute available in Mexico, receiving a regular supply from the United States, though a nuisance, should pose no problem. Incidentally, in Mexico many prescription and over-the-counter drugs cost less than 40 percent of their U.S. price.

Dentists

Quality dentistry is available in Mexico at exceptionally low prices, and many Europeans as well as North Americans travel here to have work done. Often patients save enough to pay for most of their vacation expenses. For those who live in Mexico, the low cost of dentistry is part of the low cost of living. Prices will vary between locations and the type of practice a dentist maintains. That is, one who specializes in wealthy, Mexico City patients will, of course, be more expensive than a dentist in a small village. Very likely the quality of care will vary as well; ask for recommendations from friends and neighbors before choosing a dentist.

A recent "dental vacationer" reports that a crown cost about one-tenth of the U.S. price.

Medicare

As we've said, routine and emergency medical care of high quality is available in many places in Mexico. Nevertheless, those retirees who are eligible for Medicare (which does not pay for care or treatment received in Mexico) or who have a trusted physician in the United States will wish to return there if they become seriously ill. If they're not well enough to travel by routine means, there is a commercial "air evacuation" service that provides emergency air transport to destinations north of the border. For a monthly fee one can arrange to have this service available when needed. Air transport of casualties, which was first employed in Korea and came into its own in Vietnam, has been adopted in civilian medicine and without question has saved many lives. How appropriate this air service is (except to enjoy the financial benefits of Medicare) may be a moot point. If nothing else, it gives Americans in Mexico the emotional security of knowing that in the event of serious illness, within a few hours they can be under the care of American doctors in an American hospital.

On the other hand, we've interviewed retirees living in Mexico who are convinced that medical care there is as good as back home. One man claimed that hospitals in Mexico don't have a "factory" mentality, where doctors worry more about about malpractice lawyers than they do about patients. Also physicians in Mexico are willing to prescribe medication for pain, which the doctors in the United States will only do "if you are screaming and threatening bodily harm." To this add the practice of doctors making house calls instead of requiring you to travel back to the hospital for postoperative follow-ups.

Of course you must recognize that not every town in Mexico will offer top-quality care; some clinics—especially rural ones—are quite rustic at best. You'll need to check out facilities and make your own decisions.

Health Insurance

Of course many Americans retiring in Mexico are too young to qualify for Medicare and have to rely on other health insurance to pay major medical expenses. Some U.S. insurance companies cover you wherever you travel or live. Certain carriers pay a slightly smaller percentage of the total when you are out of your home area, but because health care in Mexico is so inexpensive relative to U.S. costs, that won't be a problem. Most Blue Cross plans will pay for your hospital stays while in Mexico but usually require that you pay for your hospitalization at the time of service and wait for reimbursement. We advise that you check with your insurance broker to determine the extent of your coverage while in Mexico and to discuss any adjustments necessary to maximize your protection at minimum expense. In Guadalajara the American Society offers low-cost health insurance to its members.

Another option available to North Americans in Mexico is low-cost medical coverage by the national health system. Twice a year there are open enrollment periods when you can join. The cost is about $300 a year for full coverage. This plan covers medical, hospital, prescription drugs, even dental care and eye examinations. We believe this is something to investigate after you have been here a while and have had the opportunity to check out the quality of the hospitals and physicians in the community in which you decide to live. Our understanding is that there is no age limit; we know of a woman who joined the plan when she turned eighty-six years old.

Several folks we interviewed stated that although they had insurance coverage back home, they rarely used it. One man said, "I have a major medical plan that covers everything over $15,000. But when I went to the local hospital here for emergency treatment, the bill came to less than $2,500! This covered several doctors for separate opinions, surgeons, an anesthesiologist, hospital stay, laboratory work, X-rays, electrocardiograms, sonograms, prescription drugs, and follow-up care for three months following surgery." He added, "A friend of mine paid more than $2,500 for just one night in a Las Vegas hospital!"

Other Health Considerations

Many of our readers have inquired about the provisions Mexico makes for people with physical handicaps. From what we have observed and been told by people who face the problem, Mexico is still far behind the United States in dealing with accessibility. On the positive side the gentle climate does make getting around somewhat easier, and the low pay scale enables people who need help to afford it more readily. Also on recent visits we noted more curb cuts, particularly in the larger cities. Most airports and many bus terminals have wheelchair access. Each airline, domestic or foreign, can give you information on the arrangements it can make for wheelchairs or other assistance.

For the tourist traveling in Mexico and eating in restaurants, adhering to a special diet—perhaps one low in sodium, sugar, or fats—could be difficult, though clearly not impossible. For someone who lives there and prepares his own food (or has it prepared by a servant), there is no real problem. One of the delights of living in Mexico is the abundance of fresh fruits, vegetables, and poultry all year. In many places fresh fish is always available. Most diet convenience foods are now available in Mexico, and with reasonable inventiveness, almost any dietary prescription can be followed.

Mexican cuisine is discussed in greater detail elsewhere in this book. But we add a brief reassurance here for those potential retirees who may feel intimidated by the food's notorious spiciness: You could live in Mexico for years without ever being forced to eat anything the least bit *picante,* even if all your dining were in restaurants. Any town is likely to have several restaurants where the food is "continental" rather than Mexican, and not all dishes in thoroughly Mexican restaurants are highly spiced. In the more elegant restaurants, the dishes are not spicy at all, but with an emphasis on French sauces, they are not guaranteed to be low calorie.

Volumes have been written about the role of lethargy and stress as aggravating factors in chronic conditions that are common in people past middle age. Lethargy comes from inactivity, from boredom and fatigue. Perhaps because of the stimulation of the unfamiliar or because of the vibrancy of Mexican culture—its sights, sounds, and smells—one encounters few bored and unhappy retirees there. Visitors to Mexico, almost without exception, comment on the lack of stress and the relaxed atmosphere there. So maybe it is the absence of many negative and unnecessary forms of stress that makes so many expatriates consider Mexico a healthful place to live.

GETTING AROUND MEXICO

One big advantage to living in Mexico is the opportunity for travel. You have the entire country to choose from, with many interesting locations just a few miles from anywhere you decide to live. At your leisure you can afford to visit little-known or out-of-the-way places that ordinary tourists seldom see. You can lope on down to Acapulco for a weekend as casually as you might visit the local lake or seashore back home. All of those exotic beach towns you've read about are just a bus ride away: dream places like Mazatlán, Puerto Vallarta, Cancun, plus dozens of hidden beaches and fascinating villages no one outside Mexico has ever heard of. You'll probably discover your own personal hideaway.

Mountain gems such as Zacatecas, San Cristóbal de las Casas, and Taxco beckon to you, and for a welcome change of pace, the cosmopolitan atmosphere of Mexico City invites shopping and elegant dining. Fortunately travel in Mexico costs far less than it does in the United States. Most people find they can take regular excursions and still stay within the boundaries of their basic budget. With abundant hotel rooms for less than $30 a night, how can you miss?

Because Mexican culture—cuisine, handicrafts, music, and architecture—is, like the climate and scenery, intensely regional, travel within the country offers the stimulation that people living in the United States and Canada often have to go abroad to find. Another advantage of traveling and living in Mexico is that when, in your travels, you come across the unusual piece of pottery or furniture you just can't resist, getting it home is easy—there are no shipping and customs problems caused by crossing an international border. Many North American retirees' homes in Mexico look like miniature museums, because their owners are so carried away by the beauty, variety, and inexpensiveness of the handicrafts they encounter on their trips around the country.

Bus Travel

The mainstay of the Mexican travel system is the nation's vast network of buses. Bus travel in the United States, where one company has a virtual monopoly on interstate service, is neither particularly inexpensive nor enjoyable. In Mexico it's a different story. Many companies, each one eager to take you anywhere you can possibly wish to go, compete for your business. You get the feeling that your business is important to them. The government is building new terminals—central depots where all bus lines meet—as quickly as possible in each town. There's little waiting time because buses for most destinations depart every few minutes. Yet the cost of a ticket is a fraction of the price charged by intercity, monopoly bus lines in the United States. The latest thing in Mexican bus travel is the "executive" bus, which is equipped with an amazing bump-free suspension; a rest room; the latest-release films shown on closed-circuit TV; and a friendly attendant who serves coffee, tea, and soft drinks, hands out pillows, and generally assists the passengers on the trip. By the way, all seats are reserved on first-class service in Mexico.

The best part about the Mexican bus system is that rural areas are not devoid of bus lines as they are in the United States. We've traveled in some of the most remote areas in Mexico—to high mountain villages, through jungle country, and across desert terrain—but no matter how isolated the area might seem, before long a bus comes rumbling and bouncing along, carrying passengers from one village to another.

Mexico offers several levels of bus service, and not all buses operate with the newest equipment. Sometimes the vehicles are ancient, dented, and in need of paint, but sometimes the equipment is the latest in air-conditioned luxury. Officially, there are three types of service—first, second, and executive class—but these terms don't necessarily describe the equipment. The main difference between first and second class is that first-class buses take reservations and can sell only as many tickets as there are seats. Executive class is just a bus company term for a step higher than first class. There could be meals or drinks available or maybe a TV movie shown. Second-class buses are permitted to crowd on as many passengers as possible, allowing people to stand in the aisle. Additionally second-class buses are slower because they make many more stops, sometimes stopping to pick up passengers whenever anyone waves a hand at the driver. Also some second-class buses traveling through truly isolated rural areas permit passengers to carry produce, chickens, and piglets to market. This adds immensely to the adventure of bus riding in Mexico. Your living adventure in Mexico isn't complete without at least one ride on a second-class bus with a squealing pig in the aisle!

Most North Americans choose first-class service. However, if you'd like to see Mexico on a different level than other tourists and you speak some Spanish, second-class travel may be an adventure you'd enjoy. Second-class buses are usually older and always slower. They turn off the pavement at every opportunity and bump their way over unpaved roads to visit any number of picturesque villages. While the bus takes on passengers and disposes of cargo, you often have fifteen or twenty minutes to wander about the square, inspect the inevitable church, or order a bowl of steaming chicken *caldo*. If you were driving, it would never occur to you to detour off the busy highway. The other passengers take pride in pointing out landmarks as you go along; they seldom have the chance to talk with a real *norteamericano*.

Mexican Railroads

For more than a century Mexico's government-subsidized passenger train services linked isolated communities scattered across the country's rugged terrain. The rail network provided a much-needed transport system that allowed farmers, workers, and merchants as well as adventurous tourists an exceedingly cheap way to travel. Train fares were much lower than bus fares. Passenger service provided trains connecting Nogales and Nuevo Laredo on the U.S. border with Merida in the Yucatán and Oaxaca in southern Mexico. Traveling in swaying old coaches right out of the 1920s, sometimes in ornate drawing rooms or tiny sleeping cabins, a special breed of travel buff was drawn to Mexican train travel.

Since the railroads were privatized, profit has become more important than convenience and service. Despite protests from poor families and farmers who cannot afford automobile travel or relatively expensive interstate bus service, the government is withdrawing support for all but a few lines. Eventually only passenger service to the Copper Canyon and the Tarahumara Sierra will be supported. This is because of the extremes of the terrain and the difficulty of building roads there for alternate transport. With much nostalgia we announce the end of an era.

Automobile Travel

Chances are wherever you live in the United States or Canada, existing without an automobile is next to impossible. Our society has forsaken public transportation to the point that it's almost nonexistent. We depend on our cars just as cowboys depended on their horses back in the Wild West days. Without an auto even the simplest shopping errands are all but out of the question. Fortunately Mexico hasn't "modernized" itself to the point of phasing out public transportation. Taxis are cheap and plentiful, and buses are everywhere. Just stand still, and before long, one will come along to take you where you want to go. Because public transportation is so convenient there, many retirees elect not to have a car in Mexico, particularly if they're trying to live on a budget. Nevertheless, there are times when a car comes in handy. You might want to show visitors the sights or drive to the next town to do some heavy shopping. Car rentals are readily available for these special occasions. A daily rate as low as $45 includes insurance and unlimited mileage. By renting a car whenever you need to make a jaunt to Acapulco or Guadalajara, you can enjoy motoring without the expense of maintaining an automobile.

But many North Americans are so automobile dependent they can't visualize life without a car. They either bring one with them or buy one in Mexico.

The requirements for bringing cars into Mexico are constantly being revised. At one time you couldn't keep a U.S. car there for more than six months. This rule has been changed several times, and we suggest you get the most recent regulations just before you move. If you enter the country on a tourist visa good for a six-month stay, be sure to get an auto permit of the same duration. Otherwise, you will have to drive to the border after three months to get a new permit.

Any current driver's license from the United States or Canada is valid in Mexico. You need no other. However, you must have Mexican automobile insurance, which can be bought at the border and renewed in most places in Mexico. This is just about the most important advice you'll find in this book. The law doesn't mandate that you have insurance, but common sense does. Also bring proof of your U.S. or Canadian insurance. (We've never been asked for it, but everybody seems to think it's necessary.)

We've heard several horror stories about Americans who drove without insurance in Mexico. Even in the case of a noninjury accident, the police must, by law, arrest anyone who doesn't have insurance—at least until they can prove financial responsibility. You can't blame them for this; a gringo would be sorely tempted to abandon his wrecked auto and return home if the damages might be more than his car is worth.

To make another point: It's important not only to have insurance, but also to carry the name and phone number of an insurance agent and lawyer with you at all times. Lately there's been a disturbing trend in the way the police handle accidents. When a traffic accident occurs, the police have the right to impound your vehicle. They don't always do this, but they can. When this happens, you need to have an insurance adjuster or an attorney come to your defense.

An injury accident, however, is considered more serious; police may hold a driver for up to three days to be sure there is no criminal fault. Usually, when it's pretty clear what happened and criminal intent doesn't enter into the picture, they won't. But they can. So be sure your insurance policy provides for the services of a lawyer in the event of an accident. For example, if someone is injured and it's your fault, you could be held financially responsible not only for damages to the car of and medical expenses for the injured party, but also for supporting the victim's dependents until he or she recovers. The insurance company should be liable for these expenses, but it takes an attorney to keep you out of the fray.

We've heard many heartwarming stories of insured motorists who were given excellent treatment by their Mexican insurance companies. Typically, the insurance agent found them a place to stay and had someone watch over the vehicle to supervise repairs and make sure the work was done satisfactorily.

Another tip on insurance: Report accidents as soon as possible. If you wait until you return to the United States to make your report, there's a good chance you've lost your claim. You must report the accident where it happens. And, if you are driving a rental car, you must report an accident within six hours of its occurrence, or the insurance company won't pay. Too often the driver of a rental car simply leaves the car where it was damaged, thinking it is the rental agency's problem and that the insurance will cover it. Days later, by the time the rental agency appears on the scene, the car may have been vandalized or stripped to the frame. Again it's your liability if not reported within six hours, and the insurance company will refuse to pay.

Buying Insurance

Insurance rates for daily coverage in Mexico are set by the government, so there is very little difference between companies. However, when buying policies for six months or more, you can save a bundle by shopping. Some companies sell only by the day, so a one-year policy would be astronomical, as much as $2,500. But insuring by the year might cost $600 with another company. It used to be that the only way to save money on insurance was to go through an RV travel club or special brokers. However, at least one U.S. company, Sanborn's, also offers Mexican long-term insurance at discounts. One insurance strategy is to purchase enough daily insurance coverage to get you to the region where you want to settle, then ask local residents which insurance agents they recommend. They'll have the up-to-date information on rates and coverages.

A typical policy on a recent model car should cover collision, upset, and glass breakage, with $100 deductible; fire, "total theft," wind, hail, flood, and earthquake, with no deductible. People often decline full coverage on older cars; auto repair in Mexico is cheap, so they're willing to gamble. It would have to be a serious accident to cost more to repair an old car than the cost of an extended, full-coverage policy. While you might gamble on collision, property and bodily injury insurance are essential—no matter what you're driving. Only a fool would drive in Mexico without liability insurance. On the other hand, it's unnecessary to overinsure; because insurance awards in Mexico are usually limited to actual damages, it isn't necessary to insure more than $25,000 for property damage and $30,000 per person bodily injury.

Although these amounts are adequate under Mexican law, there's always the possibility of having an accident involving a U.S. citizen, with subsequent litigation in U.S. courts. Therefore, some people feel better with higher liability insurance.

Buying an Auto in Mexico

Many residents avoid the problem of importing an auto by simply buying one in Mexico. For our money, the most practical and economical car in Mexico is the good old VW "Bug." This reliable machine is still being manufactured in Mexico by the Volkswagen people.

The old-fashioned VW sedan sells for around $7,500 new in Mexico. (Used cars are proportionately priced.) Automobiles are taxed on their age, with the highest percentage of taxes the first year, declining every year for ten years, until it reaches a level of zero. That's why many people prefer to own older cars, say ten years old, when taxes are nil. Because auto repair is inexpensive, the local mechanic can keep the old Beetles in good running condition. An older VW in good shape, about ten years old, routinely sells for between $2,000 and $3,000.

With VWs so popular, you'll find mechanics all over who are expert in VW repair. One bit of advice: Don't think about buying a new VW and bringing it back to the United States. It won't pass the rigid U.S. specifications for items like smog, safety glass, etc.

Gas Station Smarts

Gasoline comes in two flavors. There's the old-fashioned leaded gas, which is used in older cars and some economy cars like the VW. This gasoline is called *regular,* or *Nova;* it's about 30 percent cheaper than the higher-octane, no-lead *Magna-sin.* Important: Regular gas comes from the blue pumps, no-lead from the silver pumps, and diesel from the red pumps. Watch which kind goes into your car. Filling your gas tank with diesel will cause no end of trouble. Occasionally those working around *gasolineras* know very little about autos, other than how to pump gas into your tank. Don't let anyone tell you that the red pump is gasoline!

Beware of kids who come running to start pumping gas into your car before you have a chance to think. Some of them have a scam where they clown around and get your eyes off the pump so you don't know how much gasoline has been put in. They then quickly set the meter back to zero, quote you an outrageous amount, and pocket the difference. In addition, if a pump isn't brought back to zero before starting, you'll pay for fuel you haven't received. Keeping your gas cap locked until you are ready to stand by and watch will ensure that they can't play games.

Here's a little more advice, which, if followed, will prevent you from ever being taken at a gas station. Before you pull into the station, make a close estimate of how many liters you will need. (There are 3.64 liters to a gallon.) Then multiply the number of liters by the price, which is standard at all stations. Round this figure off to the nearest even amount, and try to have the exact change ready. Next get out of your car and carefully watch the whole proceedings. Check that the pump has been turned back to zero; don't let anyone distract you from this mission. Always have a calculator in your hand. This makes the person pumping gas think you know what you're doing (even if you don't). Then ask for the exact amount of pesos you want to spend, rather than the number of liters, for example, *"Cien pesos, por favor."* (Or write it on paper: "100 pesos.") This way, you only have to watch the pesos meter on the pump. If you have exact change or ask for an even amount, you cannot be shortchanged. If you hand the attendant bills larger than the amount on the pump, carefully count it out to him; a favorite trick is for him to innocently say, "But señor, you handed me a 50 peso bill, not a 100!" (The bills look enough alike that you can feel you've made a mistake.)

When a boy wants to clean your windshield (this service is never provided by gas stations), remember that he's doing it for tips. We usually say yes, even if the windshield doesn't need cleaning, because it's probably the boy's only way to earn a peso. The spare change isn't going to make a difference to us; it will to the boy. If a herd of kids comes around, choose one youngster and wave the rest away, or you'll have a forest of hands seeking tips. Once a little entrepreneur (about five years old) pounded all four of our tires with a chunk of wood, then seriously announced that he had checked the air in the tires and that they seemed to be full. We gave him the customary coin plus an old tennis ball for his services. His look of delight told us that he will be pounding on tourists' tires for some time to come.

Rules of the Road

As in all countries there are special customs and rules for driving in Mexico. When you're on the road, you need to know these rules in order to understand what's going on around you. These customs vary from region to region. For example, in the northern desert, where you might expect lots of high-speed driving, you'll find that some Mexican drivers refuse to drive faster than 30 miles an hour in the belief that slow driving prolongs the life of the car. They're probably right—you'll find a plethora of 1970-vintage cars still creeping along the highways. They aren't driven fast enough to wear out.

Slow driving may be interesting, but it's also dangerous for the American who whips along at 60 miles an hour while others cruise at 30. A good rule is to drive as if there were a 25-mile-an-hour car around every curve, and be prepared to slow down. On the other hand, in Mexico City, where congestion can be appalling, drivers go as fast as they can. Sixty miles an hour seems perfectly reasonable to a cab driver in the capital; after all, he's getting paid by the mile, not by the time.

We try to avoid driving in Mexico City. If possible, we enter early Sunday morning, when traffic is lightest, park the car, and take buses or taxis for the rest of our stay. Anywhere else in Mexico is a piece of cake, but Mexico City turns many a macho driver into a trembling wimp.

Turn Signals and Right-of-Way

In the United States, our system of turn signals seems self-evident. When the left signal is blinking, it means, "Be careful, I'm going to turn left!" However, in Mexico, a blinking signal could mean any number of things, depending on what the driver wishes it to mean. Often a left signal doesn't mean a left turn at all. It means, "It's okay to pass if you want; I don't see anyone coming in the opposite direction, but if I do, I'll pull over to let you get by safely." On the other hand, it could mean the driver is actually planning on turning left. If there's any possible left turn ahead, better wait. A flashing right blinker usually signals a right turn— but not always. Sometimes the driver is saying, "Don't pass," or he may just be blinking for the hell of it. You never know. A flashing of both lights at once seems to say, "Look out, I'm going to do something silly, so stay clear!"

All of this makes sense of some sort when you consider that, under Mexican law, the vehicle in front has the right-of-way. If the guy in front of you decides to make a left turn, make a right turn, swerve into the next lane, or suddenly stop and ask directions, you have to be prepared to avoid him, and the people in back of you give you the same courtesy. Well, usually they do.

At first this system of right-of-way can be puzzling for the tourist, especially in heavy city traffic, with cars swerving from lane to lane in front of you. What you must realize is that you have the right-of-way over all those behind you. Therefore, instead of worrying as you must in the United States about all the cars on the road, you can concentrate on trying to outguess the idiot in front of you. Whatever lane changes you make are cool, because those behind you are watching you very carefully. You'll find that when you cut in front of people, they will obligingly drop back and give you room, instead of honking their horns and waving their fists as gringo drivers might. Actually we consider it a fairly good system, and most drivers, once used to it, find it rather easy to get around in Mexico (except in Mexico City). The smaller the town, the lighter the traffic, and the slower people drive. Again, remember that the guy in front is always right. If you're in front, that guy is you. Having said all of this, we urge you not to totally give up worrying about the driver behind you who could be a gringo who doesn't understand the system!

One exception to this rule is when someone is passing you; then you must concede the right-of-way. Always be prepared to help him get safely around you. Even if the other driver is breaking the law by passing on a hill or curve, you're equally guilty if you don't drop back and let him pass.

Highways and Byways

During the oil bonanza of a few years ago, Mexico embarked upon an ambitious road-building project. The emphasis was on constructing new highways to reach areas that were previously accessible only by dirt or gravel roads. So you'll find miles of fine highways that lead you to some great places, areas where you can drive all day on new roads and seldom see another vehicle. Because of a lack of funds, though, many other highways, the busy ones, haven't been maintained, and they tend to disintegrate rapidly.

North American drivers aren't used to watching out for road hazards. We take it for granted that manhole covers will be in place and that a sign will give adequate warning when a bridge is out ahead. We assume that shoulders are safe to park on in an emergency and that farmers will keep their livestock off a busy highway. But in Mexico the motto is "Driver beware!"

What does this mean for the novice driver in Mexico? Simply that you must slow down and drive cautiously, just like most of the Mexican drivers. So you take an extra twenty minutes for your trip because you drive 50 miles an hour instead of 70. You'll find that you'll see more of the country and arrive a lot more relaxed.

The most important motoring advice we can give is never attempt to drive the highways at night. There are several good reasons for this. One is that livestock roam freely throughout the country. It can be somewhat distracting to be driving along at 70 miles per hour on black asphalt and suddenly come across an almost invisible black bull sleeping on the road. Animals love to bed down on the pavement at night, because it holds the daytime heat and makes a cozy place to sleep. A 1,000-pound animal can neatly remove the wheels from your car if you collide with it at high speed. Even worse is clipping a burro. This cute little animal also finds the warm asphalt a great place to stand and snooze. When a driver zooms around a curve and cuffs a burro with his bumper, he finds that the animal is just the right height to flip up in the air and glide across the hood at 50 miles an hour. Burros stop looking cute when 200 pounds of bone, hide, and muscle come crashing through your windshield.

Another hazard of night driving is suddenly finding the lane blocked by a line of large rocks. "What the devil are rocks doing across the road?" you may well ask. I once heard a nervous American speculate that maybe *bandidos* had placed the rocks as a roadblock. No, no. No *bandidos!* The rocks are actually placed there by truck drivers. Here's what happens: Truckers prefer traveling at night because the traffic is much lighter and they make better time. When a truck breaks down (a frequent occurrence), the driver has no choice but to stop in the right-hand lane (there's rarely a roadside shoulder). But he doesn't want to crawl under the truck to make repairs if it means taking a chance that another driver will not see him and will crash into the back of his truck. So he first goes back 50 yards and places rocks—the biggest rocks he can carry—across that lane to warn other truckers and motorists. Oncoming drivers are thus alerted that something is wrong up ahead and will have time to stop or swerve. If the oncoming driver doesn't see the rocks, his vehicle will tangle with a barrier of 50-pound boulders, and the trucker will be safe. Usually, when the repair job is finished, the trucker rolls the rocks off the road. But not always; the driver is anxious to get on his way.

A related problem occurs when a truck has to stop on a hill for any reason. Once he's ready to get started again, the driver finds it a hassle trying to work clutch, brake, and accelerator at the same time. So he puts a heavy rock behind each rear wheel to prevent the truck from rolling backward. With the truck wheels braced against the rocks, it's much easier to get going. The rocks remain on the road, waiting for you as you round a curve. You can imagine the damage they cause. Rocks are easy to avoid in the daylight, but not at night.

Another hazard about night driving is that some Mexican drivers routinely turn their lights off, to see if anyone is coming, when passing on a curve. Guess what happens when the car coming the other way also has its lights out? Also, some older cars don't have working taillights. Occasionally a car won't even have headlights; its driver is content to drive along simply using the moonlight for illumination.

Do you now understand why you don't want to drive at night? We have to admit that we violate these warnings from time to time, when we have a schedule to maintain and driving after dark is the only way to do it. We've never had an accident, but the tension level involved tells us it just isn't worth it.

The speed limit on good highways is usually 100 kilometers (60 miles) an hour; the posted limit is much lower in towns. Sometimes that limit is ridiculously low, and you'll notice that few people observe the signs unless a cop is in sight (which is rare). Without many police around to enforce the rules, your chances are excellent for getting away with driving 50 kilometers an hour in a 30-kilometer zone. Yet why take the chance? Drive slowly and safely in Mexico, and you'll never get into trouble.

Traffic Tickets

If you are stopped for a violation such as speeding or failing to observe a stop sign, the police officer will probably hint that you can save a lot of time if you pay the fine directly to him. That way, he won't have to take your driver's license and license plates to ensure that you'll show up at the station tomorrow to pay the fine.

Now don't get upset and accuse the officer of being a crook. In the unofficial system of Mexican traffic rules, a traffic cop can accept a cash donation in lieu of a ticket and keep the money as part of his salary. Most officers are paid minimum wage or less, so they're expected to catch speeders to earn enough money to live on. Technically they aren't supposed to do this, but in practice, almost all of them do take payoffs, or *mordidas*. For the police officer it's sort of like working on commission. Even with low prices in Mexico, a person can't feed his family very well on the minimum wage, so most Mexicans expect the police to take the money.

If you've actually violated the law, you have no cause to complain; just negotiate the fine and pay it. The police officer is actually doing you a favor by not taking your license plates. You either pay the cop, or you waste a day by going to the police station to pay. Haggling over the amount of the fine is usual, and the money is traditionally folded and passed surreptitiously. We keep a couple of dollars worth of pesos folded behind our drivers' licenses and simply hand it over when we're caught doing something wrong. You can expect the cop to lecture you as to how dangerous it is to be going the wrong way on a one-way street, or whatever, then apologize for stopping you, and that's that.

What's the safeguard against a cop's stopping you for something you didn't do? Simple: Insist on taking the ticket. That way he's wasted his time by stopping you, because he gets nothing if you pay at the police station. For that reason a cop seldom hassles motorists unless he can convince them they've broken a law. So if you're innocent, say so, and don't even discuss paying a fine. It will be an inconvenience for you, but it will make it easier on the next driver. If you're guilty, just pay up; that's the system in Mexico. Until Mexican taxpayers agree to pay police decent salaries, as we do in the United States, the system of *mordidas* will continue. You don't have to like the system, but don't try to change it single-handedly, or you may make an enemy of the police. We've often been criticized by people who point out that the practice is morally wrong for suggesting that drivers pay *mordidas* to cops. But we have to tell it like it is, and not how we'd like it to be.

Help on the Road

Don't be discouraged about driving in Mexico. If you take normal precautions and understand what's happening around you, it's perfectly safe. (John Howells has driven many thousands of miles in Mexico, with only two minor accidents. Don Merwin has never had an accident in Mexico but admits to having driven far fewer miles.) What if your car breaks down on the road? Chances are one of the first cars along will stop to help if you are stranded on the highway. You'll quickly find that mechanics are everywhere: men who've spent their lives keeping their old machines running with innovative, creative repairs.

If you sit long enough, you might see a Green Angel (*Angeles Verdes*) coming to the rescue. What's a Green Angel? To promote tourism and to help motorists in general, the Mexican government has a fleet of repair trucks that cruise the highways, looking for cars in trouble. These Green Angel trucks (painted green, of course) patrol the major routes and try to cover each highway at least once a day and occasionally twice a day or more. The trucks are loaded with gasoline, oil, spare parts of all descriptions, plus two trained mechanics. Usually one of them speaks English. If you're in trouble, it's their duty to stop and make the necessary repairs. You pay the cost of parts, gasoline, and oil, but the labor is courtesy of the government. Lately some of the Green Angels' funding has been reduced, but the workers are still trying to cover their routes once every day.

You might want to take note of this phone number—it's the twenty-four-hour hot line for the Green Angels: 520–0123. You can call from anywhere in the country (assuming you have access to a telephone), and the dispatcher will get in touch with a Green Angel by radio. If you park by the side of the road and raise the hood, someone will surely stop to help. At the next town this good Samaritan will phone the Green Angels for you or notify the police, who can call the hot line.

Also, during peak tourist times, the Mexican army is utilized for tourist assistance. As you drive, you'll see olive-drab jeeps and trucks with soldiers sitting alongside the road or patrolling the countryside. The jeeps sometimes carry signs that read ASISTENCIA TURISTICA. Although it's doubtful that the soldiers could repair a car, they have radios in their jeeps and can call a mechanic or the Green Angels quite quickly. These troops are generally used on the least traveled routes, where the Green Angels don't patrol, but they can sometimes be seen on major highways.

If you drive very much in Mexico, you will from time to time come across random customs inspections on the highway. Officials—sometimes military, sometimes civilian—stop traffic and check for contraband. The main items they are looking for are drugs, guns, and ammunition. Please, don't carry any guns or ammo unless you have the proper permits, or you can really get into trouble—big trouble—jail!

Often a tourist misunderstands and feels threatened by these inspections. This misunderstanding, we fear, has given rise to stories of *bandidos* or shakedowns. We've heard of people nervously thrusting money into the inspectors' hands, thinking that's what they want. These stories would be funny if they weren't so damaging to tourism. The inspectors aren't interested in tourists other than to make sure they are really tourists and not loaded down with illegal contraband or .30-caliber ammunition. They want nothing other than your cooperation in letting them look in your trunk or under the hood. But if you are going to force money upon them, most will gratefully accept it.

One-Way Streets

Perhaps a word or two about a few other traffic customs are in order here. The system of one-way streets puzzles some American drivers. Because the streets in most older towns were designed for horse traffic, they are often quite narrow and, by necessity, one way. The direction is indicated not (as you find back in Buffalo) by a large sign on the street corner, but by small arrows high up on the corners of the buildings.

These signs also control traffic in a unique and commonsense manner. The arrows come in three colors: red, green, and black. If the arrow you can see on the building is green, that means you're on a major street and have the right-of-way over any car coming along the cross street. A red arrow means you must yield. Black means it's first come, first served. But remember that the first one there always has the right-of-way. Actually this system works rather well and keeps traffic flowing along the narrow streets with a minimum of congestion or accidents. Of course just because you have a green arrow doesn't necessarily mean you can charge ahead with confidence. Always slow down and look both ways; you might run into a tourist who doesn't know the system.

Please don't let any of these cautions frighten you. Driving is an excellent way of seeing the country. You can amble along at your own pace and stop where you like to explore villages or have a picnic on a country lane. The pace of driving is slow in Mexico, but it matches the pace of living. Above all, don't worry about getting off the road and into remote areas. Just as in the United States and Canada, the more rural the countryside, the more simple and friendly the people. Farmers and other Mexican villagers are every bit as hospitable as farmers in Tennessee or Iowa, maybe more so.

New Toll Roads

Built by private enterprise with government help, these 75-mph divided highways are miracles in safe, high-speed travel. Because these new roads charge tolls, most cars and slow trucks prefer to use the free roads. At first the tolls were exorbitant, as the builders were eager to recoup their expenses and make a profit. But then the construction/management company went bankrupt, and the government took over the system and lowered the tolls considerably. It's still expensive, but very convenient, taking you to your destination in less than half the time you'd spend on the free roads. The downside to toll road travel is that all you see is countryside, cattle, and an occasional farmhouse. You miss the interesting (and crowded) towns and cities of Mexico.

RV Travel in Mexico

The first thing some people do when they retire is buy a motor home or a travel trailer. They envision themselves living the carefree life of bohemian vagabonds, following the pleasant weather and enjoying the good life.

A few actually do this; they become "full-timers," as RV people call folks who live year-round in their rigs. But most end up using their RVs for temporary quarters, driving or dragging their portable homes to winter quarters in Florida or Arizona.

Given Mexico's variety of climates and interesting places to stay, it's only natural that many RV retirees are interested in Mexico as a place for full- or part-time retirement. As it turns out, RV travel in Mexico is quite popular, with untold thousands returning year after year. From our perspective there are severe drawbacks to using RVs for retirement in Mexico, although we admit there are some positive aspects of *seasonal* RV living there.

First let's dispense with the idea of mobile homes in Mexico. With few exceptions dragging one of those monsters into Mexico for retirement living is highly impractical. By the time you purchase a mobile home, struggle to move it to your location, set it up, and make the connections, you could have built a quality home and saved money in the bargain. The exceptions we've found are in Baja California, just a short distance from the U.S. border. Because mobile homes contain wiring and plumbing, all set up and ready to use, they have the advantage of being able to be installed on a lot—ready for immediate occupancy. Getting them to some sites in northern Baja is relatively easy because of an excellent four-lane highway that extends as far south as Ensenada. However, according to Mexican law, anything longer than 40 feet long or 8 feet wide requires special permits, which could mean yards of red tape. There's good reason for this law: Mexican highways are simply not designed for 12-foot-wide packages. When you try to haul that clumsy box through towns where the narrow 400-year-old streets were laid out for horses and carriages, you could learn the full meaning of the word *impossible.*

Recreation vehicles—whether motor homes, travel trailers, or pickups with campers—are fine for vacationing and part-time travel in Mexico. However, living *full time* in a tin box in Mexico leaves a lot to be desired. First of all, in most charming Mexican towns and villages, RV facilities aren't all that great. In most places RV parks are nonexistent. As a rule trailer parks are located on the outskirts of town, so you end up living where the trailer park is rather where you'd like to stay.

This leads to our second objection to long-term RV living in Mexico: It separates you from the everyday life of the community. You'll be staying in an enclave of North American RV travelers and will have few, if any, Mexican neighbors with whom to interact. You'll be insulated from the traditional neighborhoods and the everyday events that make life in Mexico so fascinating. Instead of living near the *zócalo*—where you can stroll around in the evening, socialize with friends, or lounge on a bench while reading the morning papers—you'll be parked out in the boondocks. You'll have to make a special effort to get into town. You might as well be camped in an RV park in Kansas for all the indigenous Mexican culture you'll be experiencing.

Having said these negative things about RV living in Mexico, let's examine the positive side for a minute. Many RV people regularly travel to Mexico for winter retirement and wouldn't consider any other style of living here. They counter our objections by pointing out that they enjoy living in a closed, gringo-style community. "We don't want to learn a foreign language," one woman emphasized, "and we didn't come here to absorb another culture. We simply want to spend a pleasant winter with our friends and return home when the weather thaws out back home." One couple we know drives to Ensenada every winter, parks their rig in the enclave, and, for the entire season, rarely set foot outside the protected walls of the trailer park. That behavior is a little extreme, but it makes them happy. For those who are somewhat paranoid about Mexican food, having their own kitchen is very comforting. They can prepare their own meals and feel safe. "Yes, RV people do eat out occasionally," said one woman, "but most of the time, we prefer to eat the same kind of meals as we do back home."

Others disagree that you necessarily have to be isolated from the Mexican community. One woman told of a Halloween party held in San Carlos Bay: "We informed a few taxi drivers that we were having a 'trick or treat' party for kids, and could they find some kids to attend. Come Halloween night, the taxi drivers brought over 250 children to the party! Most were dressed in costumes, and we gave out 150 pounds of candies and treats. What a wonderful night!" Halloween has become an annual event, looked forward to eagerly by the gringo and Mexican adults as well as by the kids of San Carlos Bay.

Where Do RVers Go in Mexico?

RV people tend to return to the same Mexican RV parks every year for their "winter retirement," just as they do in the United States. They eagerly look forward to meeting their friends of last season. Many long-term friend-ships have been forged in Mexican RV parks. The seasonal residents orga-nize and plan activities, from potlucks to dances. RV owners probably aren't any more friendly than other travelers in Mexico, but because they are quar-tered so close together, they have more opportunities to be friendly. Before long, everyone knows everybody else.

The most popular places for winter retirement are in Baja California and along the mainland side of the Sea of Cortez. At last count more than a hundred RV parks in Baja catered exclusively to North American snow-birds. From the border down to Ensenada, throughout the *zona libre* (free zone), where some entry laws are less restrictive than elsewhere in Mexico, many thousands of "winter Mexicans" (temporary retirees) settle in each year. Unlike most parts of Baja, year-round RV retirement is feasible here, because the climate is pleasant: high temperatures range from sixty-six degrees in January to seventy-seven degrees in August.

The accepted way of life here in the *zona libre* is to reside in commercial trailer parks, although some retirees purchase lots and set up their trailers on a permanent basis. But farther south, on the shores of the Sea of Cortez—where the population is almost nil—there's a different way of RVing. It's called "boondocking"—parking for free or almost free for months on end. In fact, boondocking is the only way to enjoy some of these beaches. Because of the absence of fresh water, there are no hotels or tourist accommodations of any sort. Unless you camp, no matter how rich you are, you can only glimpse these beautiful sights as you drive past beaches and scenery that money can't buy. For RV residents a weekly trip to the nearest town to replenish the drinking water and stock up on groceries is all that's needed for a winter's stay. (Almost nobody stays for summers; it becomes a furnace here!)

The mainland side of the Sea of Cortez—particularly places such Puerto Peñasco, Bahía Kino, and San Carlos Bay—also draws large number of win-ter visitors. The climate is about the same as in most of Baja: pleasant win-ters and horribly hot summers. Some intrepid travelers go farther down Mexico's west coast, as far as Mazatlán, San Blas, and Puerto Vallarta. When you get this far south, RV facilities aren't as plentiful. Summers are tolera-ble, but fewer RVs are on the road then, and parks are practically empty.

WHERE NORTH AMERICANS LIVE

Our discussion of specific Mexican communities that you might want to make your retirement home is divided into two groupings. The first deals with the most popular locations, those with a substantial North American presence and a long history of welcoming retirees. Without doubt, these places will be the choices of most of our readers. However, because the most popular places are not the most economical and because we know that some of you crave adventure, we discuss a number of other locations in a second grouping. These places have few year-round foreign residents and are, occasionally, harder to get to than the communities in the first group. When there are few North American residents, some communities are likely to offer a lonely life for those who do not speak enough Spanish for meaningful communication with their Mexican neighbors. At the same time any town that has electricity is within range of satellite televison, and any house with a telephone can be hooked into the Internet. So maybe isolation is a thing of the past.

Rather than weigh down our discussion of Mexico's off-the-beaten-track retirement possibilities, we will repeat what we feel is the most important caveat for anyone considering retiring abroad: If you feel a place might be right for you, before you make any important decisions, go there and spend some time seeing what *living* there would be like.

The Guadalajara/Lake Chapala Area

No part of Mexico attracts more North American retirees than Guadalajara and neighboring towns around Lake Chapala. Estimates of the U.S. and Canadian expatriate population hereabouts range between 25,000 and 30,000, with about 8,000 living by the lake. An unusually large percentage of the expatriates here are Canadians. Longtime residents say the ratio of newcomers from Canada to U.S. citizens has changed from a ratio of one to four to about one to one. We assume these figures are correct, although we cannot explain the shift in the immigration pattern.

When you ask why so many choose to live in the Guadalajara area, the list of reasons typically starts off with "climate." The weather here,

North American residents brag, is the finest in the world, and statistics consistently confirm this opinion. The Guadalajara area experiences an average of only one day completely without sunshine per month. The average daily temperatures are in the high sixties in the winter and in the high seventies to mid-eighties in the summer. Most rain falls on summer evenings (actually, May through September) after a day of basking sunshine. Guadalajara's claim to being the site of "perpetual spring" obviously has some basis in fact. Should you crave the heat of a tropical sun and the crashing of waves on a sandy beach, a three-hour drive takes you to Pacific beach resorts where you can escape those "frigid" spells of sixty-degree weather that occur during January.

One reason we would recommend Guadalajara or Lake Chapala as excellent places to start your quest for a retirement home is the large number of expatriates already there. By acting as a support group, they can ease the tension of your transition into a new lifestyle. Helping each other is an unwritten expatriate rule. This can make for an easy introduction to living in a foreign country. That's not to say that you will be living in an exclusively gringo compound, isolated from your Mexican neighbors. On the contrary: The vast majority of U.S. and Canadian citizens here live in homes and apartments interspersed throughout several attractive Guadalajara neighborhoods or in villages along the shores of Lake Chapala. If your next-door neighbors turn out to be fellow *norteamericanos*, it's usually a coincidence. Almost all of the retired residents with whom we talked reported wonderful relations with their Mexican neighbors.

In Guadalajara a variety of neighborhoods in and around the city are popular with expatriates. These neighborhoods come in all degrees of prices and elegance. According to residents some of the nicer locations are Lomas del Valle, Colonias de San Javier, Rancho Contento, Club de Golf Santa Anita, Providencia, Ciudád Buganbilias, and Barrancas de Oblatos. Housing prices in general, although fairly typical for Mexico as a whole, are somewhat lower here than in Mexico City and in some popular resort areas.

Understand that these are not gringo enclaves; these are the neighborhoods where most middle-class and wealthy Mexicans live. In fact, the general affluence of Guadalajara is one of its hallmarks: The city is one that has truly benefited from NAFTA. With large companies like IBM and Motorola operating factories here, large payrolls stimulate the economy.

Medical care in Guadalajara is tops, with two medical schools, excellent hospitals, twenty-four-hour emergency pharmacies, and other medical care services. A new hospital affiliated with a high-tech facility in California recently opened, bringing the latest in medical treatment to the area. Through efforts of the American and Canadian expatriate associations, many U.S. health insurance companies, such as Blue Cross and Blue Shield, are accepted here, and the American Legion has a health plan that ties in with veterans' benefits from the U.S. Department of Veterans Affairs. A Guadalajara clinic, Sanatorio Americas, advertises that it not only accepts Blue Cross and Blue Shield but also charges no deductible.

Guadalajara is one of Mexico's major transportation hubs, with an international airport and high-speed tollways connecting the city to both the U.S. and Guatemalan borders as well as to other parts of the country. These facilities make it easy for your friends and family to visit you and for you to return home occasionally, whenever you need a cultural "fix."

There's Always Something Doing

One of the reasons for Guadalajara's appeal is the plethora of recreational and cultural activities available there. Only Mexico City and Cabo San Lucas offer more golf courses than Guadalajara's five. Tennis courts, swimming pools, and health clubs are plentiful. Guadalajara offers a number of movie theaters showing films in English, frequent concerts, operas, and, with the great number of social organizations serving the retiree population, no end to parties, trips, and other organized activities. There are at least two libraries with books in English and many bookstores and newsstands that sell U.S. publications. Cable and satellite television have revolutionized home entertainment, and videotapes of American films circulate freely in the retiree community. More than eighty religious, civic, philanthropic, social, and special-interest organizations serve this huge and diverse collection of individuals.

Most American cities the same size or even larger might envy Guadalajara for its cultural richness and diversity. There is hardly a day in the week when there isn't a concert, a new art exhibition, or some other event at the Institute Cultural Cabanas, the Degollado Theater, or one of the city's many other museums and concert halls. A typical weekly issue of the *Colony Reporter* lists twenty or more such

GUADALAJARA

To Zacatecas

To Lagos de Moreno

To Tepic

To Ameca

Guadalajara

To La Piedad

Ajijic

Vista del Lago

Chapala

Jocotepec

Chula Vista

San Antonio

La Floresta

Rancho del Oro

Villa Nova

San Juan Cosal

Las Fuentes

To La Piedad

Lake Chapala

To La Piedad

Cojumatian

To La Piedad

Jiquilpan

To Colima

activities. The fare is thoroughly international, and like everything else in Guadalajara, the price is right.

A striking part of Guadalajara's cultural life is the city's numerous museums. Perhaps the best known of these was made from the studio of Clemente Orozco after the artist's death. Guadalajara residents are proud of this famous native son, whose murals embellish many public places. In addition many other museums display the work of great artists of Mexico and the world. It is not without reason that Guadalajara has been described as "Mexico's Florence."

Shopping isn't the authors' favorite leisure activity, but we can't deny that it seems to be a popular one in Guadalajara. Every time we turn around, there seems to be a new and fancier shopping mall somewhere in the city or its environs. NAFTA opened the flood gates for North American merchandise, and Guadalajara has taken full advantage. The huge WalMart store here, for example, is open twenty-four hours a day and has more than fifty checkout counters to accommodate customers. You'll also find such familiar stores as Price-Costco, Sam's Club, Sears, Radio Shack, Baskin Robbins, and Ace Hardware. The most recent addition is Office Depot. These stores are joined by Mexican shopping jumbos such as Gigante, Sanborn's, and others equally modern but with less recognizable names. All of this commercialization is a far cry from the way it was when we published the first edition of *Choose Mexico;* in those days you had difficulty finding toothpaste and diet soda. Many retirees bemoan this modernization, but they shop anyway.

We doubt that anyone has ever counted the restaurants in Guadalajara, but we have no doubt that you could go to a different one every night for several years. Before you reached the last restaurant on your list, you'd have to start over so that you could try all the new ones that had opened while you were sampling the others.

If all of that shopping and restaurant-hopping sounds exhausting, there's no reason why you can't do as we do and spend a lot of time sitting in one of the many beautiful parks and plazas scattered around the city, enjoying the sunshine, the sights, the sounds, and, yes, the smells of Mexico. One of our favorite little parks is decorated with the busts of Mexicans whose heroic stature was earned in such unmilitary pursuits as poetry, philanthropy, education, and music.

The center of much retiree life in Guadalajara is the American Society of Jalisco. The American Society, known to its several thousand members as AmSoc, is headquartered in the pleasant Chapalita section of Guadalajara. The society's facility is a hive of activity, with bridge games, meetings (to plan the members' frequent and very economical outings), community service projects, and just plain companionship that spills out of the meeting rooms and library into the lobby and dining area. The society offers low-cost medical insurance to its members and in other ways too numerous to count helps them to feel secure and at home in their adopted community. The AmSoc is a wonderful source of information on just about everything you might want to know about getting comfortably settled in the Guadalajara section of Mexico.

Lake Chapala and Ajijic

The fifty-minute drive from Guadalajara brings you to the shores of Lake Chapala, where thousands of *norteamericanos* make their homes. These are folks who prefer small-town or village living to big-city Guadalajara, with its five million inhabitants. When we speak of Lake Chapala as a place to live, we actually refer to a half-dozen or so communities lining the northern shore of the lake, with the towns of Chapala and Ajijic as the focal points. Driving along the lakeshore, you'll encounter the villages in the following order: Vista del Lago, Chapala, Chula Vista, San Antonio, La Floresta, Ajijic, Rancho del Oro, Villa Nova, San Juan Cosal, Las Fuentes, and Jocotepec. North American residents are dispersed throughout these towns and villages. They live in all manner of homes, condos, and apartments, as well as in several exclusive, gated communities and on small farms in outlying areas. Three golf–country club developments with upscale housing are in place, and others are under construction.

You'll find an interesting dichotomy between those who adore the intimacy of village life and those who prefer the luxurious gated villas on the hillsides. Each group can't quite understand why the other chooses the opposite lifestyle. To be perfectly honest, we can't quite figure out which side we're on. On the one hand, during a gorgeous sunset, we love having cocktails while sitting on the elegant terrace of a tasteful hillside estate (our friends', not ours). Yet there's something to be said for the quiet exhilaration of village life: the sound of church bells in the morning, the sight of burros bearing firewood, the interaction with your Mexican neighbors, and the quaint restaurant around the corner. Each lifestyle has compensating pleasures.

The mountains that loom high above the lakeside villages not only create a panoramic backdrop but also protect the lakeshore and the villages from prevailing northerly winds. This effect contributes to the delightful climate here and explains why the southern shore is comparatively undeveloped; the mountain ridge deflects blustery winds in that direction.

The lake does something else for the climate; the large body of water acts as a climate control. Winter days in Ajijic, for example, tend to be five degrees warmer than in nearby Guadalajara, and summer days can be five to ten degrees cooler in Ajijic. People who live around the lake are quick to point this out. This fact is ammunition in the ongoing feud over which place, Guadalajara or Lake Chapala, is the best place to live. It's entertaining to listen to each camp ridicule the other's choice of living arrangements. The feud extends to the individual lakeside villages, with residents of each community maintaining they live in the best place of all. Personally we think they're all correct.

The lake itself serves as more of a scenic treasure than as a source of recreation. Few people swim there, and fishing isn't great—it never has been. From time to time, the water level drops drastically. In *Village in the Sun,* the charming 1945 book that popularized Lake Chapala and started the immigration of North Americans to the area, Dan Chandos described the lake:

> It is an unusual lake. Its waters, heavy with silt, are never transparent, and reflect colors in curious half-tones that can turn a vulgar Wagnerian sunset into the blue-and-red fuchsia shot silk that Victorian parasols were made of.

Our observation is that sunrises, too, are just as spectacular as Lake Chapala sunsets. The lake does contain fish—several kinds of small whitefish, carp, and similar species—but not the kind sportsmen go after. Local fishermen harvest them with nets.

The center of the town of Chapala looks more like a small city than a village. In fact it boasts the only traffic signal (on the corner of Hildago and Madero Streets) on the lake. A wide boulevard is Chapala's main street, a kind of open mall with a tasteful center island of flowers, shrubs, and tropical trees. All the way to the lakeshore (which is paved with tile) businesses, restaurants, and hotels line both sides of the street. The town's centerpiece is a charming plaza, complete with a graceful bandstand, where townspeople like to congregate in the evenings. At the other end of the spectrum is the fascinating village of San Antonio Tlayacapan. With cobblestoned streets and weathered adobe buildings centered on an ancient church, San Antonio is the epitome of a Mexican village. This is the place Dan Chandos described in *Village in the Sun.* Curiously, though, the gringo population isn't very dense. This makes San Antonio Tlayacapan a place for total immersion in Mexican village living. Prices are affordable here as well, with some homes being offered, when we were last here, at what seemed like bargain prices to us.

Yet another lifestyle on Lake Chapala is the Chula Vista Country Club, five minutes west of Chapala. Chula Vista's delight is its nine-hole golf course and two lighted tennis courts for the use of residents. About 200 beautifully landscaped homes, many with lake views, surround the golf course. Chula Vista is known as the "Beverly Hills" of Lake Chapala, with home prices varying from inexpensive to expensive, from $83,000 to more than $400,000.

Chula Vista maintains an active neighborhood association, which continually strives to maintain the quality of services in this area. As a result Chula Vista is one of only two communities on the lake that enjoys pure drinking water (Villa Nova is the other). Everywhere else you must use either bottled or boiled water.

The town of Ajijic probably has the largest number of North Americans in residence, with the town of Chapala close behind. Distant Jocotepec attracts a growing number of new residents nowadays, partly because homes and land are less expensive. Most lakeside expatriates live either in the villages or on isolated acreages away from town, but several commercial subdivisions cater to North Americans and wealthy Mexicans. These residential communities vary from ordinary, low-cost places to luxurious, gated communities. Most newer developments are carefully designed to preserve the mood of a Mexican village atmosphere, featuring cobblestone streets and houses constructed to look like genuine colonial antiques.

For many residents the *only* place to live is in the village proper, where housing is typically Old Mexico. They live in apartments or houses hidden behind high walls, or in buildings with plain exteriors yielding no hint of what lies inside. Streets are typically cobblestoned, and many buildings are of adobe construction, occasionally of stone or antique brick. Real estate in the villages varies from cheap to expensive, and the interiors vary from rustic to fantastic. Again, the exteriors give few clues as to what lies inside.

An English-language monthly newspaper, *Ojo del Lago*, keeps lakeside residents aware of the latest news and area gossip. It opens its columns to residents who relish writing articles, editorials, book reviews—anything they care to share with the community. The content ranges from excellent reading to amateurish drivel, but it's always fun to read.

Ajijic serves as Lake Chapala's cultural and social center. It's where the Chapala Society (an expatriate association with 2,000 members) is headquartered. Even if you have no intention of choosing Lake Chapala as your retirement paradise, you owe it to yourself to take a look at the Chapala Association's library complex. Located in the center of the village, on a large estate with landscaped gardens and surrounded by a wall, the facility is the heartbeat of the expatriate society. This was the estate of Neill James. A fascinating woman who lived in Ajijic for several decades, she was well liked by expatriates and adored by natives of the area. She donated everything except her living quarters to the society, and on her death, at the age of ninety-nine, bequeathed these to the people of Ajijic. (By the way, it's pronounced *Aah-hee-HEEK*, with the accent on the last syllable.)

The Chapala Association's centerpiece is an extensive lending library, which includes 20,000 volumes as well as 5,000 videotapes, but that's only a part of it. The association sponsors numerous social events, fundraising activities, and special cultural offerings such as lectures, concerts, and other top-notch entertainment. The library hosts a computer club and a ham radio club with regular broadcasts and far too many activities to be listed here. The grounds have separate rooms for lectures, classes, and meetings; a snack area with tables; and quiet garden areas for reading and relaxing. Even though North Americans (you needn't be a member to participate) thoroughly enjoy the library complex as a meeting place and learning facility, one of its most important functions is public relations for the expatriate community. While local people take English lessons, their children take art classes. Over the years many successful artists received their start here, and today they donate their time to teach a new generation of artists. When we last visited during the holiday season, club members were feverishly working on a Toys for Tots program, raising money to bring Christmas joy to more than 6,000 local children. These activities go a long way toward creating a favorable image of local gringos. You sense a genuine feeling that North Americans are accepted as valued members of the community.

Another tradition here is the American Legion post. Its large membership reflects the presence of retired military personnel near Lake Chapala. Its tree-shaded clubhouse is set behind brick walls on a quiet side street. Its members take an active part in community affairs.

The large number of active civic and social groups in Ajijic makes it easy to meet people and become a part of the community. Take a look at the following list of activities and social groups in the area: Humane Society, Computer Club, Chess Club, several garden clubs, Culinary Arts Society, the Writer's Group, Genealogy Club, Duplicate and Progressive Bridge Clubs, Needle Pushers, Texas Line Dancing, Daughters of the American Revolution, Lakeside Little Theater, and two yacht clubs. This is only part of the list. All in all more than forty English-language clubs and charitable organizations keep people busy by the lakeside.

If the foregoing activities aren't enough, you can also take classes in art, handicrafts, music, computers, and Spanish (both conversational and structured). Or you can participate in tennis, golf, walking, jogging, horseback riding, boating, fishing, mountain biking, tai chi, and various exercise groups. A variety of passive pleasures are available too, such as taking in concerts, art galleries, and museums.

In summary, we feel that unless you are familiar with Mexico or have already picked out another community in which to live, the Guadalajara–Lake Chapala area is probably the place to start your search for the ideal retirement site. It may or may not end up as the place you decide to live. Nevertheless, given its convenient location and good transportation to most parts of Mexico, and given the unequaled support expatriates offer newcomers, going there first can make the choice easier and less intimidating.

San Miguel de Allende

Every time we return to San Miguel de Allende, we are afraid we will find it so crowded, so Americanized, and so filled with traffic as to destroy its legendary charm. The bad news is that it is more crowded, some parts of it are Americanized, and a few of its major streets—at least at certain times of the day and week—have more traffic than we would like. The good news is that it is still a charming and delightful place for vacationers and retirees. A few blocks from the town's center, in a prosperous commercial and residential area, we could easily believe that we were the only gringos around. True, San Miguel has a high proportion of foreign residents, perhaps 5 percent, but that fact seems irrelevant to most of its Mexican residents.

We were also worried that the relentless march of "modernization" might have destroyed San Miguel's colonial flavor. That fear, too, proved to be unfounded. The laws that require all new building to conform to the town's architectural character continue to be enforced.

On each of our visits, we find a number of new restaurants and shops to choose from (we thought there were enough already). The existence, on the outskirts of San Miguel de Allende, of a huge, modern shopping mall (including a well-stocked American-style supermarket, Gigante) may be an affront to those who would like time to stand still, but it is a huge convenience for anyone who would like to accomplish the purchase of such essentials as laundry detergent, vodka, and lawn chairs quickly and painlessly.

Other important additions to the town include a well-equipped, modern hospital operated by a private nonprofit association. Its staff includes six specialists and one general practitioner. Less vital, perhaps, but still a big plus, is the new bus terminal.

There are few places in Mexico where North Americans have been as happy as in San Miguel de Allende. A colonial city just less than four hours' drive or bus ride from Mexico City, it draws both visitors and residents from all over the world. What many of them share is an interest in the arts. These people are attracted both by the handsomeness of the town and its natural setting and by its several excellent art schools.

The 6,300-foot altitude produces a climate that is comfortable year-round, if you don't mind winter evenings that are chilly enough for a wood fire and summer afternoons that are warm enough to make swimming pool owners especially popular. San Miguel owes much of its attractiveness to three events in its history. The first, the depletion of the silver mines in Guanajuato, rendered San Miguel obsolete as a way station en route to Mexico City and left it a backwater. Consequently its fine colonial architecture was not demolished to make way for the progress that afflicted many other Mexican towns.

The second event was the arrival in 1938 of an American, Sterling Dickinson, who founded the art school that became the world-renowned Instituto Allende, which continues to draw outstanding artists and craftspeople from all over Mexico, the United States, Europe, and Asia. A second school, Mexico City's Palace of Fine Arts, affiliated with Bellas Artes, also welcomes foreign students, but it places more emphasis on the education of younger local artists. In addition to these larger institutions, there are several smaller schools and artist's studios that offer training in everything from painting and photography to weaving, stained glass, music, and dance.

The third event contributing to San Miguel's unique flavor was the Mexican government's promulgation of a law designating the entire town as a national monument. Hence, any development or construction that would change San Miguel's character or appearance must now have express permission.

Some grumble about San Miguel's narrow streets, paved with what must be the world's sharpest and most irregular cobblestones. These same people lament the government's stubborn refusal to allow the erection of gleaming aluminum and glass facades on the homes and shops facing onto the streets. But Los Angeles, Houston, and parts of Mexico City are always there to welcome anyone who cannot do without these symbols of progress.

About one out of every twenty residents of San Miguel is a foreigner. That ratio is sufficient to support an active English-speaking social and cultural life, but it's not large enough to make San Miguel a little bit of the United States in Mexico. There is no American enclave where foreigners are concentrated, and when North Americans there say that what they like best about Mexico is the people, they mean their Mexican neighbors (not just servants and shopkeepers) as well as their compatriots.

Recreation

Particularly for a town of its size, San Miguel has remarkably diverse opportunities for recreation, which ranges from golf, tennis, and riding to classes in yoga and dance. You can attend lectures, play in an amateur string quartet, and go bird-watching with the Audubon Society. Organizations you can join include a duplicate bridge club, an amateur theater group, an American Legion post, and a garden club. There is also an annual chamber music festival.

Spanish is taught at the Instituto Allende, the Academia Hispano Americana, and several smaller and more informal schools. Depending on the school, these programs range from a couple of hours a day to more than forty hours a week. There are students of all ages, and among other benefits, classes, whether in language or the arts, provide excellent opportunities for meeting people.

If the concerts, dance, and theater in San Miguel and nearby Guanajuato do not satisfy your cravings for culture, Mexico City is three and a half hours away by car or bus. Some residents wish that it were a little closer, forgetting that the distance is just about right to save San Miguel from being overrun by day-trippers and other tourists (especially because there is no airport in the town or nearby).

Within a short drive there are several hot spring resorts that are open to the public, where you can swim or just soak contentedly in the naturally heated water. We are not aware of any claims of curative powers, but we can testify to their calming effect on the spirit.

Restaurants

Because San Miguel is a magnet for North Americans and other foreigners, it is amply endowed with good restaurants. These range in ambience and cuisine, from spartan vegetarian to elegant continental. Italian, French, Argentinean, and Spanish food are all represented. So is the hamburger, but we are happy to report that the golden arches have not yet appeared. Specialty food stores feature items as exotic as Danish cheese, German sausage, Arab pita bread, and the international bagel. Although these delicacies may not be as economical as tortillas and frijoles, they are quite reasonable by U.S. standards.

San Miguel has so many groceries, drugstores, meat markets, and vegetable stands (as well as a large indoor municipal market with surrounding outdoor stalls) that each North American resident you consult is likely to give different advice about which are the most reliable and most economical. Actually quality, selection, and price tend to be similar in all stores. When you have been in San Miguel a while and acquire Mexican friends, they can tell you the best places to buy such national specialties as *carnitas, chicharones,* and *mole.*

A Most Unusual Library

San Miguel's unique public library serves a wide variety of functions. Its outstanding collection of English-language books, including many current best-sellers, is supplemented by an ample selection of classical and popular music on tape. After payment of a nominal membership fee, cassettes and books can be borrowed free of charge. (Most small or middle-sized towns in the United States do not have these extensive literary and musical resources.)

The library is in a restored colonial mansion, whose handsome inner court serves not only as a pleasant spot to sit and read but also as a place to meet friends. Concerts and lectures are often given there in the evening. Once a week *Conversaciones con Amigos* gathers there to provide English-speaking students of Spanish and Spanish-speaking students of English a chance to practice with each other. (Another weekly meeting of this group is held in the courtyard of one of the town's several language schools.)

On a recent visit to the library, we were pleased to find a well-equipped computer center where, for a modest fee, you can check your e-mail, surf the Web, balance your checkbook, or do anything else a PC can do.

In addition to the solace and stimulation the library provides to North Americans, it is also the base for an ambitious program of reading instruction and academic scholarships for underprivileged local children.

The library and its philanthropic activities are supported financially by weekly house and garden tours that allow both tourists and curious residents to see how the most affluent live. Helping with these tours is one of the many ways that retirees in San Miguel can repay the community's hospitality. Those we questioned described a number of opportunities for public service, such as helping with the school for the handicapped, working with the local humane society, contributing to

Atención (the weekly English-language newspaper), and participating in the cooperative burial society. In recent years the library has expanded into an adjacent building that once was a church and has added a pleasant cafe. One room in its original space now serves as headquarters for its computer classes. In addition it provides numerous satellite library facilities to the Spanish-speaking residents of surrounding villages. Work on behalf of the community and the demonstration of genuine concern for the people of San Miguel are two of the reasons for the excellent relationships that most North Americans there enjoy with their Mexican neighbors.

Daily Living

Because San Miguel attracts the wealthy as well as the talented from all over the world, it is entirely possible to find a house that sells for $500,000 or rents for $2,000 a month. Fortunately for the rest of us, however, residents report that you can find unfurnished two-bedroom apartments with rents beginning at about $200. Three hundred dollars a month is a good rent to figure on for a conveniently located and attractively furnished apartment. A house is likely to rent for a little more.

The monthly salary of a maid who works eight hours a day, six days a week, is reported to be about $120 a month. Gardeners (who often serve as general handymen) are paid about 85 cents an hour. Few couples report spending more than $250 a month for all their meals, including some in restaurants. It is easy to spend $20.00 for a meal in the town's most luxurious eating places, but $9.00 is more typical for a meal in a charming, moderately priced restaurant. And there are plenty of good restaurants where a full meal costs less than $4.00. Much entertainment and recreation is free, and a bus trip to Mexico City, more than 160 miles away, costs about $5.00. San Miguel, therefore, still qualifies as a town where a comfortable life is possible on a budget. It's odd that this town is considered one of Mexico's more expensive locations, outside of the seaside vacation playgrounds.

Several retirees in other Mexican communities have made the point that if you have no interest in community service or the arts, you could feel a little out of place in San Miguel. They may be right, but this town does have so much to offer that you might want to see for yourself.

Morelia

Ask a Mexican which is his country's most beautiful state and, unless pride in his birthplace triumphs over objectivity, he or she is likely to answer Michoacán. In the summer much of Michoacán's green, rolling landscape reminds the traveler alternatively of New England's Berkshire Hills or of a painting of peaceful rural China. Michoacán stretches from the Pacific almost to Mexico City.

Morelia is the capital of the state of Michoacán, and the city's colonial flavor has been maintained by ordinances that strictly control the styles of new construction. Several downtown banks, which conform to these rules, are lodged in restored mansions, which preserve the elegance of forgotten centuries while providing a place to exchange your traveler's checks for pesos.

At the heart of the city, Morelia's massive cathedral boasts two soaring towers that are said to be the tallest in Mexico. Although construction began in 1640, the towers and dome took an additional hundred years to complete. Flanking the impressive cathedral, the Plaza de Armas serves as the social and commercial center. Tourists and residents gather (in cafes under the plaza's elegant arched portals) to have coffee and chat while waiting for the *Mexico City News* to hit the newsstands. Shopping, restaurants, museums, and other attractions are within easy walking distance of the Plaza de Armas. The plaza is located a block from the city's university. Dating from 1580, it is the second oldest university in the Western Hemisphere.

Morelia supports an active cultural life—music, drama, and dance thrive there, as do the visual arts. Recent additions to the cultural scene are the spectacular Palacio del Arte, which boasts 5,000 seats and features internationally famous artists, and the even larger Pabellón Don Vasco at the fairgrounds. The city also hosts several excellent language schools—one connected with its own bed-and-breakfast and others that can arrange homestays with Mexican families. A homestay is an excellent way to get to know Morelia, meet other people studying Spanish, and make some friends among the Mexican community.

Morelia is indeed a colonial town, but it isn't all monuments, ancient homes, and narrow, cobblestoned streets. Once away from the city center, a startling modern facade contrasts with the colonial style. Such contrasts are more typical on the southern edge of the city, where many expatriates prefer to live. Perhaps because Morelia's population and prosperity have increased so rapidly in the past decade, some sectors are modern and elegant. The Plaza de las Americas shopping mall is among the largest and most luxurious malls that we have ever seen. It's as if Saks Fifth Avenue, Sears, Macy's, and K-Mart were combined with a luxury supermarket, and for good measure, packaged with marble floors and ultramodern fixtures. Costco, Suburbia, HomeMart (a Mexican version of HomeDepot), Ace Hardware, WalMart, and Office Depot have graced the mercantile landscape in recent years. Sears has undergone a complete renovation, emerging as the city's "fancy" store, carrying name brands ranging from Maytag to Lancôme. For lovers of the outdoors, another modern convenience in Morelia is a golf course.

Despite the fact that Morelia has been slow to catch on as a retirement site, we feel it could be a viable alternative to Guadalajara. Overall it is much cleaner, and the nicer sections of town are just as attractive and convenient as Guadalajara. Moreover, Morelia is only a fifth of the size of Guadalajara. A major difference between Morelia and other places of similar size is that Morelia doesn't support a well-organized expatriate group. Once a week in the Holiday Inn (formerly the Hotel Calinda), there's an informal gathering (with an unofficial chairperson), but this meeting is more of an excuse to get together and exchange news than an integrated association as you would find in Guadalajara, San Miguel de Allende, or Ajijic. One resident approved of this casual approach, saying, "All that politicking that usually marks political ascendancy in many expatriate organizations is not demanded here."

How many foreigners live in Morelia? Jennifer Rose, a long-time resident of Morelia, says, "How many? That's a good question—kind of like counting the number of angels who can sit on the head of a pin. About six or seven years ago, I sat down with some friends one evening and we wrote down the name of every single expatriate we could think of, just to get a count. We quit at around 600. Some people will claim there are only 150, but they're only counting those with whom they're acquainted." She further points out that although the loose network isn't extensive, it's nevertheless big enough to have among its population "some of those gringos you assiduously avoid!" In short the foreign colony here is large enough to support an active social life, and settling in Morelia today hardly qualifies you as a pioneer.

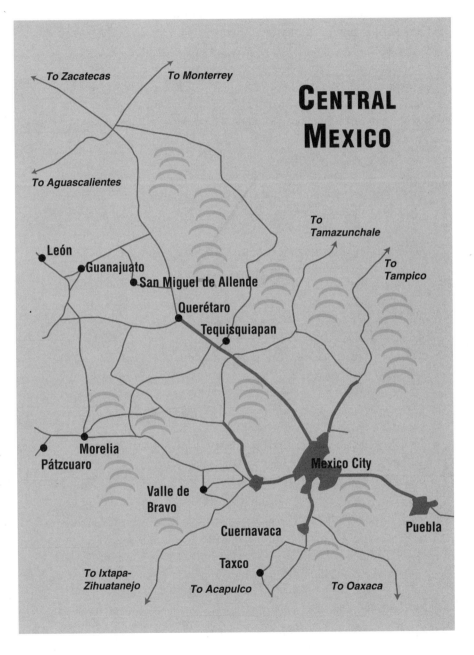

Easy outings from Morelia include Pátzcuaro and Uruapan. The latter, justly renowned for its lacquered boxes and trays, also attracts special attention for the nearby volcano, Paricutín. In 1943 the volcano suddenly erupted and spilled molten lava over the surrounding villages and countryside. Pátzcuaro owes its reputation to the loveliness of its colonial buildings and of Lake Pátzcuaro. The lake is dotted with islands, including one covered by the Tarascan Indian village of Janitzio. The island is topped by a gigantic statue of José Morelos, one of Mexico's greatest heroes and a native of the locality. The lake is also the home of the *pescado blanco*, a delicious whitefish caught by the Indians in their delicate "butterfly" nets and featured on the menus of the neighborhood's numerous restaurants. Pátzcuaro is another location that would seem ripe for retirement relocation, but so far only a handful of North Americans have taken up the invitation.

Querétaro

A couple of hours from the bustle of Mexico City, Querétaro and neighboring Tequisquiapan are traditional weekend retreats for the middle-class and wealthy families from Mexico City. Those who don't own places in Cuernavaca feel obligated to have their second home in Querétaro or "Tequis."

With brick-paved streets and ornate fountains decorating landscaped squares and shady parks, Querétaro is a textbook example of historic preservation. Mansions and public buildings dating from the seventeenth and eighteenth centuries lend an air of elegant historicism.

Exceptionally attractive, filled with authentically restored colonial buildings, and graced by tree-lined streets, Querétaro—away from the bustle of Mexico City, yet only a couple of hours distant via toll road—is the "in" place for weekend homes and retirement. The fact that Querétaro has almost as many golf courses as Acapulco (four of them) gives you an idea of the upper-class coloring of this area.

Given the cosmopolitan colonial charm of Querétaro and the village atmosphere of Tequisquiapan, it isn't surprising that a number of expatriates choose to live here. Yet, curiously, their numbers are not as high as you might expect. As best we can tell, only 150 or so North American retirees currently live here. Part of the explanation may be the area's lack of promotion as a vacation spot for Americans and Canadians. Everyone reads about Guadalajara, Acapulco, San Miguel, and all the other popular tourist places in Mexico, but we've seen little push for tourists in Querétaro. The result is that fewer people are exposed to the charms of Querétaro, so they choose other, more traditional places for relocation. This is the classic chicken-versus-egg syndrome: Large numbers of expatriates won't retire in a place where there aren't large numbers of expatriates already in place. On the other hand, there are those who don't want to live in a place crowded with gringo tourists and retirees. Querétaro may be the place for them.

Not that there aren't plenty of North Americans living here. Several multinational factories are on the outskirts of these towns, which adds greatly to the general prosperity without disturbing the tranquility and charm. However, they differ slightly from typical expatriate groups in that they tend to form friendships and social circles on the basis of their work and careers. The upper-class Mexicans who live in the Querétaro area are highly educated. Most speak English to some degree, so you won't lack people to converse with when your Spanish becomes tedious.

Tequisquiapan holds a special place in John Howells's heart because his family bought and restored a 200-year-old home there and used it as residence for almost twenty years. The Howells' house had 2-foot-thick adobe walls and a large courtyard with arched portals, which was a great place for lounging on a sleepy day. Tequis has long been famous for its hot baths and swimming pools. Just about anywhere one sunk a well, hot water was available for hot tubs or swimming pools. So it was an easy task to install a spa in the courtyard.

Tequisquiapan has changed over the years, as has every other town in Mexico. Many old cobblestoned and flagstoned streets have been paved over in the interest of speeding traffic flow through the narrow streets. Instead of lounging on the square, listening to birds, and watching wood-laden burros trot past, tourists come here to buy artwork and locally produced handicrafts. What hasn't changed is the fact that only a small number of North Americans choose to live here year-round.

We are reluctant to write off such towns as retirement possibilities just because droves of other expatriates haven't discovered Querétaro and Tequisquiapan. We realize that most of our readers will be more at ease in places like Guadalajara and San Miguel, where they have large

support groups. But some who have studied North American immigration patterns to Mexico agree that this area could be poised for a rapid
increase in expatriate population. At the very least they may be places to
take another look at after you have been in Mexico long enough to have
some command of Spanish and are ready to leave the bulk of your fellow expatriates behind.

Mexico City and Vicinity

In earlier editions of *Choose Mexico* we hesitated to unilaterally recommend Mexico City as a retirement spot. After many subsequent visits here, we still can't, but we do feel that our readers should know what
an exciting and cosmopolitan city it is. We wouldn't want to live there,
but we certainly would want to visit it frequently. Nevertheless, many
North Americans do live in Mexico City. They love it and wouldn't consider any other location.

One caveat we must emphasize: Mexico City has suffered an increase
in crime in recent years. Not long ago a wave of robberies by "pirate" taxi
drivers against passengers made headlines. It's difficult to tell just how
prevalent these incidents are. However, it doesn't hurt to repeat the common advice about taxis in Mexico City. Always travel in legitimate taxis,
the kind you'll find at taxicab stations lined up awaiting passengers.
"Pirate" taxis are those without permits; drivers roam the streets looking
for fares. Most of them are honest, but there are always a few crooks,
especially in a huge megalopolis like Mexico City.

Why do North Americans choose to live in Mexico City rather than
less hectic, less crowded cities? For the same reason some people love
New York, Paris, or London. It's difficult to explain this feeling of urban
euphoria to anyone who has never fallen in love with a large city. For
those who enjoy city life, Mexico City has it all: great restaurants, entertainment, outstanding museums, art exhibits, night clubs, and theaters.
They're all there, in one convenient, easy-to-use package. Every possible
shopping convenience, from native tapestries to WalMart and Price-
Costco, is at your fingertips. Mexico City is so different from Mexican
villages, it could belong to a different country.

Mexico City is steeped in culture; its downtown is famous for its collection of sixteenth-century colonial architectural treasures. The nucleus

of the city is a virtual museum of history and culture. Here you'll find the Americas' oldest cathedral sharing an enormous open *zócalo* with ancient, castlelike government buildings and a spectacular museum that displays artifacts from an Aztec temple, recently unearthed nearby. One of Mexico's cultural showplaces, Bellas Artes (Palace of Fine Arts), is also located in the center of town. One of the most beautiful opera houses in the world, Bellas Artes hosts internationally celebrated opera companies and symphony orchestras. The famous Ballet Folklórico, a prime tourist attraction, draws crowds weekly.

Another attraction of living in Mexico City is its cool, temperate climate. Residents here neither freeze nor swelter. This is the place for those who detest hot weather and avoid tropical sunshine; they'll wear sweaters or jackets year-round and sleep under blankets every night. Some folks—especially those with heart conditions—do find Mexico City's mile-high altitude a problem, but most people have no difficulty adjusting. After a day of taking it easy, we jump right back into the swing of things.

Of course many foreigners live in Mexico City because they work for multinational firms, which are well represented in the country. This is nothing new—for decades Mexico City has been the headquarters for foreign business enterprises. In the olden days, when this writer lived in Mexico City, we called ourselves the "British-American colony," and we numbered in the thousands. Because of this large number of expatriates living in the metropolis, you'll find a pool of social contacts among retirees and working residents' families. The large number of English speakers living in Mexico City is reflected in the scope of English-language news media. Besides a daily newspaper, the *Mexico City News*, at least one all-English FM station broadcasts network news hourly from the United States as well as daily (or more frequent) English-language features.

Members of the foreign colony tend to congregate in certain elegant neighborhoods, in homes or apartments that look out over tree-lined boulevards or quiet side streets. They live in areas such as Las Lomas, Chapultepec, and El Pedregal. A very popular neighborhood in the center of the city is the Zona Rosa ("pink zone"), a place of upscale apartments, boutiques, and fabulous restaurants. Before making decisions about retiring here, be sure to consult with residents who have lived here for some time. They can guide you to the safe neighborhoods to consider for your new home.

From this writer's viewpoint, an enormous drawback to living in Mexico City is the automobile traffic. Parking is impossible, and the city is so congested that drivers are restricted, with serious fines levied for venturing out on the wrong day of the week. A few experiences with traffic here will turn anyone into a confirmed pedestrian. Many Mexico City residents don't even own cars; they prefer to use taxis, buses, and the excellent subway system, and they rent cars for weekend jaunts around the country.

Of course you needn't live in Mexico City to enjoy its many historic and cultural attractions. Buses and trains are convenient and inexpensive from anywhere in the country. For the average person, Mexico City isn't well suited to retirement living, but if you love the city and its exhilarating atmosphere, be sure to get in contact with the Newcomers Club of Mexico City (www.newcomers.org.mx/). The group comprises almost 700 families who will welcome you to their twice-monthly meetings. The club's cultural and social calendar is extraordinarily full, beginning with welcome and orientation classes and extending to activities such as neighborhood coffees, language classes, tours of interesting places in Mexico, bridge games, and charity affairs.

Valle de Bravo

Anyone who enjoys the active life—water sports (including swimming and sailing), tennis, and golf—and has an ample retirement income should take a look at a retreat favored by those knowledgeable Mexicans who can afford it and by a small group of U.S. and Canadian retirees. Valle de Bravo is a couple of hours' drive from Mexico City, on the side of a mountain west of Toluca. It is renowned for its climate, which somehow manages to be significantly warmer than Mexico City in winter and cooler in summer. What's more, there is considerably more sunshine here, and the air is crystal clear. Despite the influx of boutiques and upscale restaurants, it still enjoys much of the serene beauty that must have characterized this country town before the construction of the huge artificial lake that has made it so popular with sports enthusiasts.

The luxuriantly wooded hills—filled with streams and waterfalls—that surround the lake would not be out of place in New England or the Upper Midwest. Rentals tend to be expensive and hard to come by, but much land is still available and building costs are low. With apologies to those of our readers whose lives, like ours, tend to be sedentary or whose budgets are too limited to consider such a trendy site, we thought we ought to let the more athletic and prosperous retirees know that such a place exists.

There are several excellent hotels in Valle de Bravo. Some of them offer moderately priced weekend packages, so you can see the town for yourself. Even if you don't or can't choose it as a retirement site, it's a wonderful place for vacations.

Oaxaca

At slightly higher than 5,000 feet, Oaxaca's climate is a bit warmer than Mexico City's and, without the latter's industrial development, it boasts much cleaner air. Oaxaca's population is passing 300,000, but its large area and the absence of steel and concrete skyscrapers and other visible hallmarks of twenty-first-century life effectively conceal that fact.

Oaxaca is easy to reach from Mexico City by air, bus, or rail. The west coast beaches of Puerto Angel, Puerto Escondido, and Huatulco are close by and are easily accessible by plane.

The great majority of residents, both of the city and of the surrounding state of which it is the capital, are Indians. They are proud of their heritage and their historical resistance to assimilation into the politically, culturally, and economically dominant cultures of the last five centuries: first Aztec, then Spanish, and now Mexican. Oaxaca was the birthplace of both Benito Juarez, "Mexico's Abraham Lincoln," and Porfirio Diaz, an ironfisted president for many years, and was the home of numerous accomplished artists. It is conscious of its colonial and Indian past and has preserved much of its architectural history. Oaxaca is as different in appearance and atmosphere from cities in northern Mexico as Tucson, Arizona, is different from Portland, Maine.

On Saturdays handicrafts flood in from neighboring villages and spill out of the huge Juarez market onto the surrounding streets. Black and green glazed pottery, innumerable baskets in a great variety of shapes and sizes, hand-loomed textiles, and many skillful copies of the Monte Albán idols and jewelry beguile even the most apathetic shopper. On other days of the week, there is a market, or *tianguis,* in one or another of the many surrounding towns. A trip to these towns can also provide the opportunity to visit the studios of the many talented artisans whose work is sold in the shops of Oaxaca.

Every Mexican town of any size has its *zócalo* or town square, but few are more sumptuous or lively than Oaxaca's twin plazas. Filled with tall, handsome trees and countless wrought-iron benches where locals and foreigners alike while away many sunny hours, and ringed by sidewalk cafes, it is the heart of Oaxaca.

There is an unusually handsome bandstand on which a variety of instrumental groups play several evenings a week. Almost the entire town turns out for these concerts, and parents sit around the *zócalo* gossiping while children play on the grassy parts of the park. The stream of peddlers whose wares include carved, painted wooden animals, bird-shaped ceramic whistles, hammocks, baskets, serapes, belts, and even elaborate carpets could become annoying after a while, were it not for the fact that a polite but firm refusal is usually sufficient to send them on their way. Then one can listen to the music, chat with friends, or just enjoy the passing parade.

In the early editions of *Choose Mexico* we reported that the beauty and unspoiled antiquity of Oaxaca were beginning to attract more tourists, particularly those interested in exploring the Zapotec and Mixtec ruins nearby. At that time this mountain city still had only a small colony of North American residents. Most of those who had chosen to live there seemed to indicate that they liked it that way. One reason may be that food and housing prices have remained somewhat lower in Oaxaca than in many other parts of Mexico. We were told apartment rentals start at $200 a month, and our experience was that wonderful restaurants were very affordable. Another reason may be what a retired resident described as "freedom from pressures for conformity."

Today the number of full- or part-time foreign residents, mostly from the United States and Canada, has grown in number to what some there estimate to be 2,000 or more. It is hard to be precise, because Oaxaca seems to attract retirees who are more interested in experiencing Mexican life close up than in becoming part of a foreign enclave. Certainly there are opportunities to meet and socialize with fellow *norteamericanos*. One is at the lending library on Calle Alcala just a few blocks from the town center (which is said to have one of Mexico's best

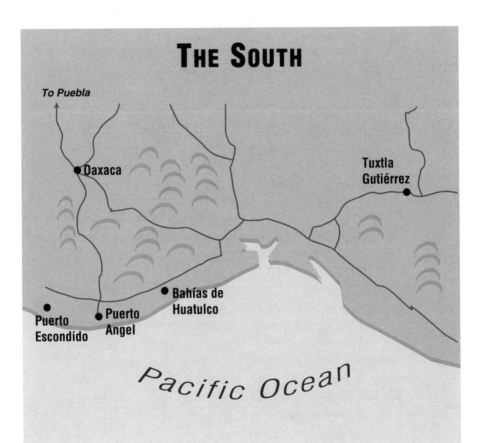

THE SOUTH

To Puebla

● Oaxaca

Tuxtla
Gutiérrez
●

● Bahías de
Huatulco

● Puerto
Angel

●
Puerto
Escondido

Pacific Ocean

collections of English-language books outside San Miguel de Allende). It is the place to go when you want to get together with fellow expatriates to get news from home, to exchange local gossip, and to obtain current information on such practical matters as where there is a particularly attractive house or apartment for rent at a reasonable price. We also found that there tends to be a daily early morning cluster of English-speaking residents and tourists in one of the outdoor cafes on the *zócalo*. One morning while we were there, more than sixty expatriates gathered for brunch in the sunny patio of a local restaurant to benefit community causes. Several language schools serve the many foreign residents who want to get beneath the surface of this magical city.

A glance at the English-language *Oaxaca Times* reveals a schedule of cultural activities, ranging from concerts to video showings of classical Mexican films to art exhibitions. There are ads for restaurants to suit all tastes and budgets.

Because Oaxaca offers reliably comfortable winter temperatures, it attracts many part-year residents from the United States and Canada. Year after year they desert the cold and damp of their home communities for the warmth and stimulation of Oaxaca for periods ranging from one to three months.

Many foreign residents, whether living in Oaxaca full- or part-time, seem to choose rooms, suites, or cottages on the grounds of the numerous small affordable hotels, scattered throughout the city. Some are able to negotiate attractive monthly rental rates in comfortable accommodations that are just a few blocks from the center of town.

Oaxaca is certainly an increasingly viable choice in the Mexico retirement sweepstakes and a wonderful place to visit, even if you have only a few weeks to spend in Mexico.

Cuernavaca

Cuernavaca is the matriarch of Mexico's "retirement" communities. Long before anyone had heard of Ajijic or San Miguel de Allende, Cuernavaca's superb climate and tranquil ambience held an irresistible appeal for retirees, seasonal visitors, and tourists. From the very early days, famous people were drawn here like a magnet. The Aztec king Montezuma adored Cuernavaca; he maintained a luxurious palace here.

Cortez, the conqueror of Mexico, liked the palace so well that he moved in and remodeled it to his taste. Archduke Maximilian and his wife Carlota had a mansion here, as did silver baron José Borda. Most of Mexico's presidents either lived in Cuernavaca or spent weekends there. Affluent residents of Mexico City feel obligated to have weekend homes here, and foreigners from all over the world choose Cuernavaca for second homes. Graham Greene loved to winter at his house in "the land of eternal spring," as do several other authors and artists who join less-famous expatriates in making Cuernavaca their home. All of these people can't be wrong. Cuernavaca is a special place.

The location, just an hour's drive via a superhighway to Mexico City, makes it convenient for residents here to visit the capital, enjoy an opera, have dinner, and make a quick return to Cuernavaca's clear air and balmy temperatures. The town sits on a mountain slope at an altitude about 2,500 feet lower than Mexico City; this explains its constant springlike climate. This also explains why so many of the capital's residents flee to Cuernavaca on winter days when temperatures in Mexico City are a dozen degrees cooler than Cuernavaca's semitropical ambience. Magnificent views of the western flank of Popocatépetl volcano can be seen on clear days.

Residents here seldom find it necessary to visit the megalopolis. Everything one could conceivably need can be found right here. Cuernavaca is proud of her own cultural events, theaters, concerts, and university research institutes. Residents can find everything from a Sam's Club to German delicatessens and all other accoutrements of the twenty-first century. As long-time resident Rhonda Tranks (originally from Australia) says, "You feel like you are living in an active and vibrant Mexican city, not just a foreign enclave. We often say, 'we are so close and yet so far from Mexico City'!"

The wealth that has poured into this lovely valley over the years is readily visible in its stately colonial mansions, palaces, churches, and private homes. Cuernavaca's quiet residential neighborhoods begin close to the city center and feature lovely homes with red-tiled roofs—trimmed in pastel (and sometimes vibrant) pinks, blues, and yellows—and landscaped with brilliant flowers and lush, semitropical vegetation. Houses are often surrounded by high walls to provide privacy for swimming pools and patios with luxuriant landscaping. Flowers are everywhere.

Although Cuernavaca's population has increased tremendously over the years, the town has managed to preserve much of its original charm. The downtown is centered on a colorful and bustling town plaza (it sprawls up the hill to the Palace of Cortez, which today is an outstanding historical and archeological museum). Adjoining the plaza are narrow streets of the original town, where you'll find artisans' shops, small retail stores, and street merchants selling woven leather *huaraches,* silver jewelry, antique furniture, embroidered blouses, and handicrafts of all descriptions. Excellent restaurants abound.

Because Cuernavaca lies on a gentle mountain slope, locating above or below the town provides several distinct microclimates. A cool mountain forest lies at the higher altitude above the city, and on the downward side, the climate is drier and warmer. In Cuernavaca itself, temperatures are mild year-round. The rainy season traditionally lasts from May through September, with heavy showers at night and delightfully clear and sunny days. The marvelous weather here makes outdoor recreation a year-round affair. A half-dozen golf courses, at least four of them eighteen-hole layouts, are open around Cuernavaca, and horseback riding and tennis are just two of the activities enjoyed throughout this area. Several spas with mineral and thermal waters, landscaped grounds, and camping areas are nearby, including Cuauda, Atotonilco, La Fundición, Las Estacas, Oaxtepec, and Temixco.

Living in Cuernavaca offers much more than golf and bridge. The area is incredibly intellectually stimulating, being rich in Mexican archeology and history. The region is saturated with pre-Hispanic, colonial, postcolonial, and revolutionary history. It boasts an extraordinary number of U.N. historical and cultural sites. The romantic revolutionary general Emiliano Zapata was from nearby Morelos.

Cuernavaca has an unusually large number of English-speaking residents. These are not only North American retirees, but also a large number of foreigners employed by several international companies located in the region. The town also hosts a large number of Americans who come here to study Spanish at Cuernavaca's highly regarded language schools. Students correctly feel that total immersion classes in Spanish, and staying in a Mexican home, are a great way to begin an investigation of Mexico as a place for retirement.

This large foreign community does something else for Cuernavaca:

It makes it a newcomer-friendly place where it's easy to blend into the rich Mexican environment. Several social organizations are in place here, one of the more important being the Newcomers Club of Cuernavaca. The group welcomes all English-speaking residents of the community, regardless of nationality, race, or creed, and provides information, social activities, and friendship to all. More than 150 families belong to the club, with activities ranging from book, film, and dance clubs to lectures, travel, and sports (tennis, golf, walking, hiking), as well as cooking classes, play-reading groups, and holiday festivities. Members contribute to the community through numerous philanthropic activities that take place year-round, including benefit dinners, luncheons, and, this year, a rodeo. Proceeds go to a children's hospital, an organization for the blind, and more. The club's Web site is at www.solucion.com/newcomers/.

One newcomer, Liisa Searfoss, came to Cuernavaca in 1998 from Princeton, New Jersey. She says, "We came here as strangers, but quickly found how easy it is to jump in and become part of this community. Within three months I found myself accepting the position of secretary of the Newcomers Club. The second year I took a staggering leap into the first vice president's slot. I can easily understand how there are those who come with a two-year 'trial time' to Cuernavaca only to realize twenty years later that it has become their home." (Searfoss later became president of the club.)

To help you settle in, the Newcomers Club has three "must-have" reference materials: (1) *The Newcomers Cuernavaca Survival Guide;* (2) *The Newcomers Directory of Recommended Services;* and (3) *The Newcomers Family Activity Guide.* Other local organizations cooperate in publishing *The Directory of Foreign Residents of the State of Morelos,* which lists hundreds of individuals and families. The book has several pages of associations and clubs, ranging from Alcoholics Anonymous and the American Legion to a home for orphaned children supported largely by U.S. contributions and volunteers. Also in the directory, together with numerous banks, beauty salons, delicatessens, and so on, are a number of veterinarians, a video club, and a washing machine repair service. A listing of physicians and dentists fills several pages.

Another expatriate group is the Guild House, meeting the second Wednesday of each month. The Guild House maintains a rather large library of English-language books, with a wide assortment of paperbacks and hardcovers for sale at very low prices. All Cuernavaca groups unite for a binational July Fourth celebration of both U.S. Independence Day and Mexican–American Friendship Day. Festivities include the trooping of the colors of both countries, the singing of their national anthems, and a feast that includes both hot dogs and *cochinito pibil.*

The Pacific Coast

We often hear people exclaim: "I'd never want to live in someplace like Acapulco or Puerto Vallarta! Much too tourist plagued. I want to live some place more authentic! Someplace more truly *Mexican!*"

Think about this for a moment. Why do so many tourists travel to Mexico's beach towns in the first place? They go there simply because these are wonderful places to visit! The scenery is lush and tropical, like a movie set. Balmy breezes caress your skin on palm-fringed beaches. Winter days are typically in the seventies, and summer highs are in the mid- to high-eighties; it's shirtsleeve weather year-round. Therefore, it's not surprising that the same folks who look forward to vacations here every year also think about Mexico's west coast when it comes time for retirement. As for being "authentic," will someone define the term? When folks think about retiring in the United States, are they more likely to consider an "authentic" town like Soapy Springs, Nebraska, or some "touristy" place like Palm Springs, California?

When you hear people talking about the great time they had on their Mexican vacation, chances are they visited Mexico's west coast. Termed the "Gold Coast" or the "Mexican Riviera" by tourist agencies and travel writers, this section of Mexico draws by far the most tourists every year. There are many good reasons.

First of all, because of the heavy influx of tourists, accommodations are plentiful, excellent restaurants are everywhere, and prices tend to be competitive. More important is the climate, especially for those who enjoy the warmth of the tropical beaches and the warm ocean waves. The climate here is great because seasonal temperatures and rainfall are moderated by the Pacific Ocean. The Pacific, with its deep, temperate body of water, maintains a steady year-round temperature in the coastal regions. This condition shields you from excessive summer heat, and

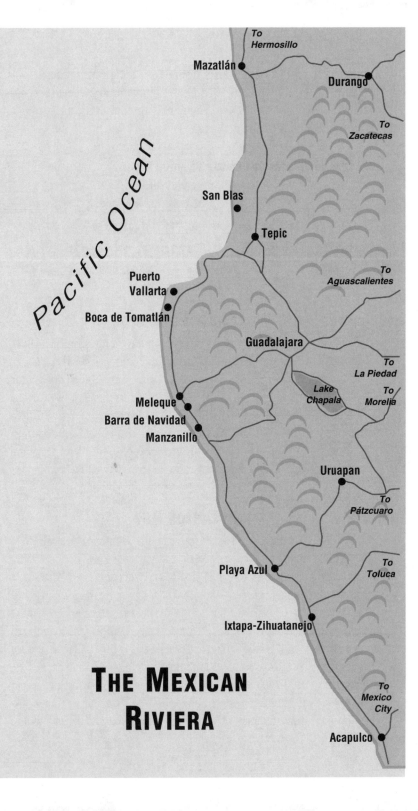

To Hermosillo

Mazatlán

Durango

To Zacatecas

Pacific Ocean

San Blas

Tepic

To Aguascalientes

Puerto Vallarta

Boca de Tomatlán

Guadalajara

To La Piedad

Lake Chapala

To Morelia

Meleque

Barra de Navidad

Manzanillo

Uruapan

To Pátzcuaro

Playa Azul

To Toluca

Ixtapa-Zihuatanejo

THE MEXICAN RIVIERA

To Mexico City

Acapulco

winter "northers" that blow down from Alaska are greatly moderated by the time they reach Mexico's Gold Coast. Temperatures change very little from month to month, with most rainfall coming in the summer. Winters are almost totally rain free.

Weather on the Mexican Riviera's Pacific Coast

	In degrees Fahrenheit											
	Jan.	Feb.	March	April	May	June	July	Aug.	Sept.	Oct.	Nov.	Dec.
DAILY HIGHS	88	88	88	88	90	91	91	90	90	90	90	88
DAILY LOWS	72	72	72	73	76	77	77	77	76	76	75	73
RAIN (inches)	—	—	—	—	1.5	10.4	9.0	10.5	15.0	6.5	2.0	0.5

West Coast's Desert

Not *all* of Mexico's west coast is touristy and tropical. Above Mazatlán, north of the Tropic of Cancer, the country is clearly a desert. Here the Baja California peninsula to the west across the Sea of Cortez blocks the breezes, moist from the cool Pacific currents that blow to the south and nourish the vegetation there. Also because the Sea of Cortez is relatively shallow, it soaks up the sun's heat and radiates this warmth landward. In turn the warm air holds its moisture, rather than dropping it as rain, thus creating a desert instead of a tropical landscape.

San Carlos Bay

On Mexico's west coast, the first place south of Arizona that attracts a considerable number of retirees is San Carlos Bay, located near the fairly uninteresting agricultural center of Guaymas. Originally San Carlos was a "discovery" of winter retirees—those RV addicts who wintered in nearby Kino Bay or Puerto Peñasco. But it quickly became exceedingly popular with conventional retirees as well. With a backdrop of rugged mountains, balmy winters, and gentle, protected beaches, San Carlos Bay is a place retirees come back to year after year to hold reunions with friends.

Visitors from Arizona, New Mexico, and Texas began staying longer and longer; then they started building homes, both modest and elaborate. The steadily increasing numbers of North Americans sparked an astounding expansion in construction. Today the area has the appearance of a true resort town. Locals estimate that more than a thousand homes in and around San Carlos belong to gringos. The RV parks are still evident, but they're dwarfed by conventional home developments and condominiums.

Several gated communities of rather elaborate homes occupy strategic positions on the shore of San Carlos Bay. These developments are popular with those who want to tie up their yachts and fishing boats at a dock in their backyard. Beachfront lots are plentiful for those who wish to build, even though prices aren't always exactly cheap, particularly in the town itself. During our last visit, we were fortunate to find four open houses being held the same afternoon in the main part of San Carlos. All four homes backed up against the beach. The views were spectacular, the interiors were luxurious, and the prices were exorbitant, ranging from $175,000 to $400,000. Farther north of town, beach and view homes were considerably less expensive, ranging from $50,000 upward.

Boating is part of the scene here. During the summer, while you do your retirement thing in cooler climes, a marina at San Carlos's largest RV park will store your boat. Several retiree organizations are quite active here, sponsoring Spanish classes, dancing, and art lessons for their members. North American residents also support an orphanage and buy school supplies for local children.

San Carlos Bay now has a dozen restaurants, several grocery stores, a drugstore, some small shopping malls, two marinas, and everything you might need for a winter's retirement. At least one Mexican bank has established a branch here. The downside here, as anywhere along the Sea of Cortez, is the scorching summer sunshine that sends most folks scurrying north for a couple of months of cooler weather. Some may protest that because most residents do not live here year-round, they shouldn't be considered "retired" in Mexico. However, those who retire in Montana and travel to Arizona for the winter are still considered Montana retirees, aren't they? Predictably, more and more are sticking it out, enjoying having San Carlos to themselves during the hot months.

Alamos: A Ghost Town Revived

South of Guaymas you'll pass through two more agricultural cities: Ciudad Obregon and Navajoa. Neither has much to propose for retirement living. However, we can highly recommend Alamos, a fascinating colonial town about a seven-hour drive from the Arizona border and about 35 miles east of Navajoa. There's even premier-class bus service direct from Nogales.

Spanish conquistador Francisco Coronado explored the area in 1531 on his expedition north. The Jesuits began constructing a mission here in 1613. One of Mexico's oldest silver-mining cities, Alamos started its boom more than four centuries ago, in early 1683, with the discovery of rich ore bodies. By the late 1700s it had grown into a prosperous city with a population of more than 30,000—for a while the richest silver producer in all of Mexico. Its many substantial buildings attest to its former grandeur.

But like many mining towns, Alamos's fortunes rose and fell with changes in the world economy. By the early twentieth century, the mines were pretty much worked out. The Mexican Revolution exploded about that time, and wealthy landowners fled as the revolutionaries confiscated their land. Pancho Villa's troops entered Alamos in 1915, but refrained from sacking it because of Villa's high regard for the colonial jewel. Alamos became a ghost town after the revolution, unpopulated for decades. Alamos is a living museum where little has changed over the centuries. Today nobody seems to remember where the original mine workings were located.

Somewhere back in the 1950s the town was "discovered" by a small group of North Americans: artists, sculptors, and writers. Recognizing the ghost town's inherent beauty, they bought—for less than a song—old homes and silver baron mansions and set to work restoring them. The project was so successful that the Mexican government declared the town to be a national monument, just as they did with San Miguel de Allende and Taxco. Modern buildings are forbidden, and remodeling must faithfully preserve the structure's original appearance. Today artists' studios and apartments are hidden away in these old colonial mansions, which once housed silver barons and wealthy merchants. Typical decor of these mansions includes Moorish arches, covered walkways decorated with intricately fashioned wrought-iron work, and graceful fountains in landscaped gardens.

The population is said to be approximately 6,000, but that must include everyone living in the area. The number of North Americans is difficult to pin down because they are constantly coming and going, but the average is about 250. You never get the feeling that the place is crowded. The number of expatriates in Alamos is small compared with some other gringo colonies discussed in this book, but the residents are just as loyal to their adopted home as those living in San Miguel or Ajijic.

Residents here are totally convinced they've found Mexico's ultimate retirement Mecca. Because summers are livable in this high-altitude desert, many live here year-round, others retire here just for the winter, and many others visit on a regular basis. The English-speaking community is very active and engages in several worthwhile community projects that boost the retirees' image with the local people. One fund-raising project is a regularly conducted house tour that permits tourists and residents to enjoy the restoration miracles performed on these centuries-old mansions. One holiday tradition is the Christmas Posadas, and another is the Children's Carnival, which are celebrated through the month of December, when part-time residents are often in town.

The Casa de los Tesoros, a remarkable hotel—claimed by some to be one of Mexico's finest—is located here. Several less expensive hotels are found on or near the main plaza. Three RV parks accommodate motorized retirees. Almost all of the RV folks are snowbirds who fly home for the summer. A few who own private airplanes literally do fly home, using the town's excellent paved 3,900-foot landing strip (1,346-foot elevation). For those with a desire to fish, the beaches of Huatabampito, on the Sea of Cortez, are about an hour and a half away by car. World-class bass fishing can be enjoyed at nearby Lake Mocuzari.

Mazatlán

Mazatlán is one of Mexico's premier beach resorts. It has long been popular as a place for tourism and escape from northern winters—especially for those snowbirds living in the western half of North America. Even though Mazatlán is the nearest west coast location with a climate where year-round retirement is practical, until the last few years a surprisingly small number of North Americans have settled in for retirement. This is changing rapidly, although Mazatlán will probably never gain a large enough foreign population to be considered a "gringo enclave." At least retirees who live here hope that never happens.

With a population of approximately 500,000 inhabitants, Mazatlán is located on a long, flat stretch of the Pacific beach at a point where warm currents from the Sea of Cortez rendezvous with cool, westerly waves from the open Pacific that brush past the tip of the Baja Peninsula. This bestows on the region comparatively mild temperatures and lower humidity than some of the more southerly resorts along Mexico's "Gold Coast." And Mazatlán's summers are dramatically cooler than anywhere to the north along the shores of the Sea of Cortez, where the desert coast is best described as baking hot in the summer, with occasional frost in the winter. Mazatlán is the first place south of the border that can be genuinely called "tropical." In fact that imaginary line (the Tropic of Cancer) that defines the tropics runs just north of the city limits.

Now that the four-lane *Maxipista* (superhighway toll road) zips down from Nogales to Mazatlán, it's entirely possible to make the drive in one long day, although we'd recommend breaking it up into two easy days' drive. It's also practical to take one of the inexpensive deluxe buses from the border, and many daily scheduled air flights serve Mazatlán. This makes it easy for your family and friends to visit from time to time and feel envious of your retirement situation. You really don't need to own an auto here, not with the excellent public transportation. Taxi fares used to be rather expensive, but lately they have become affordable; there's too much competition to justify exorbitant fares. You'll see a fleet of open-air taxis, which are cute but a bit more expensive. They are unique to Mazatlán and are called *pulmonias*. As a resident you would most likely have your own auto or use public transportation, but the taxis are there when you need them. By the way, Mazatlán has greatly improved its bus system, with modern equipment replacing the old, rickety buses that used to lumber along.

Mazatlán continues to develop; each year more condos, apartments, and homes spring up to accommodate the swelling population. Housing choices are plentiful in all price ranges, whether buying, renting, or building. The difference between Mazatlán and other, less popular beach towns is that you'll find few oceanfront homes for sale in the most popular beach areas. The land is too valuable. Mazatlán's precious beach properties have been preempted by large hotels and deluxe resorts. Yet just a few blocks from the beach, many lovely homes are available for rent or purchase. A number of RV parks accommodate winter retirees, with some parks perched right on the beach. Like most Mexican RV parks, they fill up in the winter and empty out in the summer.

An interesting development here is a new assisted-living complex. The Melville was designed for those retirees who would rather stay in Mexico than return home when health problems prevent them from living alone. The recently completed complex, consisting of nineteen living units, is located in the Olas Altas area of old Mazatlán.

Real estate here tends to hold its value. According to residents the 1994 downturn in the economy had little effect on prices. At first some homes—particularly properties owned by Mexican families—were placed on the market at reduced prices. However, as in most other retirement communities in Mexico, prices asked by North Americans remained fairly level. Because the demand for upscale homes didn't fall, sellers found little pressure to cut asking prices.

In addition to miles of sunny beaches, Mazatlán also boasts superb sports fishing and a busy commercial port. It deservedly calls itself the shrimp capital of the world. Here shrimpers from the warm waters of the Sea of Cortez routinely unload cargoes of unbelievably enormous prawns. Unfortunately most of these delicious crustaceans—some as large as lobsters—are destined for Japan (where price is no object), and U.S. residents seldom get a chance to sample them. However, you can often buy some if you meet the incoming boats and do some bargaining. Jumbo shrimp taste delicious sautéed with butter, minced garlic, and a pinch of chili powder. *¡Ay, qué rico!* (Don't forget to squeeze a lime on them, too!)

At first glance Mazatlán's crowded tourist section of town might seem to be a drawback. As it happens this is also the favorite area for expatriates to live—in enclaves just a few blocks off the main beach drag. Fortunately tourists keep to their beach streets and seem to be oblivious to the peaceful neighborhoods nearby. No one we interviewed in Mazatlán felt that tourists were a particular bother. As one woman put it, "They live in their little beach world, and we live in our world. The only time we meet is when we go to the tourists' restaurants." Incidentally, several excellent restaurants, with surprisingly good food at bargain prices, cater to tourists. Mazatlán's old downtown section is a real surprise, with narrow streets and a real Old Mexico look—a real contrast to the glitzy and modern tourist areas. Elderhostel has chosen Mazatlán as a place to give their cultural courses starting in 2001. This and the fact that the locals are rediscovering their downtown gives a new meaning to Mazatlán!

When we wrote our first edition of *Choose Mexico,* we reported that traffic wasn't as bad here as in places like Puerto Vallarta or Mexico City. (No place in the world is as bad as Mexico City!) Today we have to rescind that opinion because the population of automobiles has soared along with the population of humans, but the streets remain the same size. Despite the heavy traffic, though, Mazatlán drivers seem to be unusually calm and courteous. The sound of honking horns and the sight of shaking fists are almost nonexistent.

Because tourism is a major industry here, many people around Mazatlán speak English. You'll discover this early on in your first visit—when you're hounded by time-share salesmen, tour guides, and persistent fishing-trip operators. (We get rid of them by saying that our plane leaves in an hour.) Consequently, Mazatlán is a good place to ease into Mexican culture and practice your Spanish; you can feel confident that you can always lapse back into English for a word or two and you'll be understood. In fact, if you speak Spanish well, local people may react with pleased astonishment.

Mazatlán has a split personality. One world is a tourist playground, and the other world is that of foreign residents who have an intimate, close-knit society. Many of the activities revolve around volunteer projects. The American Legion, the Rotary Club, Friends of Mexico, and Hands across the Border coordinate some of these projects, and the Amigos de los Animales is busy saving wildlife. Newcomers will have no problem finding a circle of friends with like interests.

Mazatlán's sea-level altitude is easy on those with heart problems. Residents report that medical care and hospitals are excellent here, and they attest to an abundance of good, English-speaking doctors and dentists. A new medical facility, Sharp Hospital, offers all of the latest diagnostic and surgical equipment, with everything state of the art. Although Medicare isn't recognized here, some U.S. medical insurance plans cover expenses that occur outside the country, and permanent residents in Mazatlán carry local health insurance. Retirees here swear by the quality medical care they receive.

Mazatlán's weather is typical of the rest of Mexico's tropical coast. It's exceptionally pleasant from November until May. (These months make up the dry season, a time of little or no rain and balmy temperatures.) The season for rain starts in late May or June and lasts through September. Then the weather turns warm to hot, and the humidity climbs. This is the most beautiful time of the year in Mexico because the hills and fields are green and fresh looking. Yet because of the ocean, summer temperatures are quite pleasant, with highs in the mid-eighties. As in Florida, in the summertime you need to get up early and do your tennis, bicycling, or hiking before the weather gets too warm. A leisurely lunch is followed by a long nap and time for reading. Later in the afternoon you can resume outdoor activities, perhaps a swim in the surf, and be ready for a late supper, which is the norm here. Mazatlán boasts three first-rate golf courses. There's El Cid's twenty-seven-hole layout, Estrella del Mar's eighteen-hole beachfront course out by the airport, and a nine-hole public course.

What about crime in Mexican Riviera resort cities? Is it any worse than in other retirement areas in Mexico? Could it possibly be as dangerous as in Florida resort cities? (Hardly.) Below is a quote from Mazatlán residents Henry and Nadine Laxen on the subject of crime in their neighborhood. (Reprinted from their Web page, with permission. Visit their Web site at www.maztravel.com.)

"To give you a feel for the level of crime in Mazatlán, let me tell you about our local newspaper, the *Noroeste*. In their local crime coverage, which is printed every day, they often include pictures of the guys who stole a bicycle, and sometimes of the gun or knife that was confiscated. Finding someone with a gun is a big deal, and gets big coverage, with pictures not only of the villain, but of the firearm as well. Can you imagine the *Los Angeles Times* doing this? They would need to publish a one-hundred-page crime section daily if they were to include pictures of guys stealing bicycles.

"I can honestly say that Nadine and I feel much safer living here in Mazatlán than we have living almost anywhere . . . in the United States. Where we used to live in California, going down the hill to Safeway for some milk was a truly frightening experience. Here, we have walked in the heart of downtown at midnight on several occasions, and have never felt threatened in any way. In fact, even late at night you will still pass young men and girls strolling on the streets or in the parks, holding hands and making out."

Putting all these factors together, Mazatlán might be the ideal place for a three- or six-month experiment in Mexican living. With plentiful rentals, sunny beaches, and a resort atmosphere, what better place to spend a winter?

Puerto Vallarta

For years Puerto Vallarta was a sleepy village, isolated and cut off from the rest of Mexico—and happy to be so. The only road in was unpaved; visitors had to come by four-wheel-drive, boat, or a DC-3 that bounced to a landing on a dirt airstrip. When the paved road from Tepic finally broke through the tropical forest, Puerto Vallarta suddenly found itself thrust into the modern world of tourism. It also began to accumulate retirees and expatriates from the north, who formed the nucleus of today's foreign community.

Puerto Vallarta never stopped growing; today it is a thriving city of 250,000 inhabitants. Located on a long, narrow strip of land between the mountains and the sea, "PV," as its North American devotees call it, is less than a dozen blocks wide in many places. For this reason the main part of the old town center hasn't developed the usual beach resort facade, with high-rise glass-and-steel buildings. Instead hotel complexes have been forced every year to expand farther north and south, where high-rise condos and luxury hotels sprout like weeds. These are the places where tourists stay—in hotels where they pay top dollar and where it costs several dollars to take a taxi into town. This north-south expansion allows the original town to retain a slight sugges- tion of its old village atmosphere. Cobblestoned streets and centuries- old buildings add to the charm. The secret to affordable retirement in Puerto Vallarta is to find an apartment in the older section of town where local working people live and where permanently retired cou- ples greatly outnumber the well-heeled tourists. You'll find plenty of apartments available, particularly in the late spring, when the flighty snowbirds vacate the premises and begin their annual migration north. This is another town for testing out your tolerance of Mexico; if you find you don't care for living here, the worst that can happen is you will enjoy a long vacation at a seaside resort. The plus side is that liv- ing away from the beach is not only inexpensive, but the tourist crush isn't concentrated close to your neighborhood; it's spread out over a 20-mile stretch of beach.

Some of the more affordable housing is typically found on the hills behind town—usually 8 blocks or more from the beach. Construction here is older, but in addition to favorable rent, you enjoy the bonus of gorgeous ocean views and vistas of the town below. A nice two-bedroom apartment with a view can be found for as little as $500 a month through one of the many English-speaking real estate agencies, but you can usually find something on your own for much less. If you don't mind living a bit farther from the ocean, in an all-Mexican neighborhood, you can find an unfurnished apartment for as little as $300 a month. Of course you can pay much, much more for some of the gorgeous homes and villas that perch on oceanside cliffs or cling to the hillsides above the city.

For the ultimate in elegant living, visit the luxury development north of town, Nuevo Vallarta, one of the fanciest places we've encountered in Mexico. Some houses, set back on enormous landscaped plots, would cost several millions of dollars if they were in a similar posh U.S. location. But then other homes cost no more than you'd expect to pay for a bungalow in San Marcos, Florida, or Santa Barbara, California. (Those places aren't cheap, either.) Nuevo Vallarta is a breathtaking place, but it's not something for a couple looking for an inexpensive retirement. For an alternative location across the bay from Puerto Vallarta, look at the discussion of Yelapa (see a description in the "For the More Adventurous" section).

Many full-time American residents make their homes in Puerto Vallarta, but as in most tropical resorts, the expatriate population is somewhat impromptu. Many people stay for a few months, then either return home or move on to try some other Mexican location. We've seen estimates ranging from 2,000 to as high as 15,000 expatriates living in Puerto Vallarta. These estimates are difficult to verify. Because people come and go so frequently, it's difficult to distinguish between retirees and visitors who are on extended vacations. Suffice it to say there are many North Americans living here; you'll have no problem finding compatible neighbors.

Because of this large foreign population, two Puerto Vallarta hospitals cater to American and Canadian patients, and they maintain bilingual staffs. These are the Medassist Hospital and the CMQ Hospital. The Crita Movil Ambulance Service, with well-equipped vehicles, is on call twenty-four hours a day and reportedly has English-speaking drivers.

Time-Shares/Condominiums

When inspecting any beach city or town along Mexico's west coast, from Mazatlán to Acapulco, you'll surely be deluged by persistent time-share salespeople. They grab you by your shirtsleeve and insist that you accept a complimentary breakfast, lunch, cruise, or car rental. Should you take them up on the "free" offer, you can be sure of several hours of high-pressure sales tactics. These salespeople are experts, so keep your resistance up, or better yet, do as we learned to do when in Mazatlán: Just say, "Sorry, but my plane leaves in an hour."

Time-shares are sprouting on the beaches, and a few blocks back from the water both regular and time-share condos are popping up. Our view of time-sharing is that it should not have a place in anybody's retirement plans. When you pay big money for the right to stay in a condo for a couple of weeks each year, all you're doing is paying rent in advance for a condo you must share with twenty-five other people. It no more belongs to you than does the hotel apartment you rent for a vacation. Vacations are one thing, retirement is another. On the other hand, if you buy a condominium or house and rent it out when you don't plan on using it, that's a different story. You control all fifty-two weeks a year, and should you desire, you can retire full time to your condo. The key word is *control*.

We investigated one condo development in Puerto Vallarta, and we know of similar ones in Acapulco, Mazatlán, and other west coast locations. Understand that we're neither vouching for these condos nor encouraging anyone to invest, but the management rental plan sounded enticing. Prices of the condos we looked at ranged from $75,000 to $150,000 for two-bedroom units that were located on a desirable stretch of beach in a high-demand tourist area. For a percentage of the rent, a management team operates the participating units as a hotel, renting by the day or week to tourists. According to the sales force, the apartments rent for $75 per day in the low season and $125 a day during the high season. Management withholds the commission and deposits the balance of the rent money to your account.

On paper this sounds like a great idea, but developers have a way of making things sound a lot better than they are. So beware! It all hinges on the ability of management to keep the rentals full and to fulfill all their promises. Should the management have rental units, you can be sure your apartment will be rented only when there is an overflow. The bottom line here is be absolutely sure you know what you're doing when you buy this kind of condo, and *stay away* from time-shares.

Several public service organizations are supported by the U.S.-Canadian community. One, which was brought to our attention recently, is the America-Mexico Foundation. To raise funds, this group collects donations and holds benefits and auctions of donated goods. One major goal of the foundation is to provide scholarships for Mexican children who strive for an education but are impeded because of family financial problems. A spokesperson said, "As long as the children maintain B averages or better and sustain good behavior, the foundation will help them obtain their educational goals." The program now has 200 children enrolled. Address: America-Mexico Foundation, APDO 515, Puerto Vallarta, Jalisco, Mexico 48300, tel: (322) 3–1371.

Another organization is the International Friendship Club (IFC), which was started in 1987 by a small group of U.S. and Canadian expatriates. Their role is organizing the international community to provide services and collect and distribute funds in response to the humanitarian and educational needs of the community. Activities of the IFC include assisting local schools, hospitals, retirement homes, day-care centers, and playgrounds. The IFC also participates in the community-wide toy distribution to children on holidays. Members started the Cleft Palate Project, which is known all over Latin America, and have helped many youngsters get the necessary operation to correct this birth defect.

Following the example of San Miguel de Allende, Ajijic, and Guadalajara, Puerto Vallarta expatriates have started a library. This project will undoubtedly become the social and cultural center of the foreign community as well as further improve public relations by reaching out to the Mexican community. Those of you looking for volunteer work might seriously consider becoming part of a library-project team. This is an excellent way to become a part of the community and meet new friends as well as to contribute to a worthwhile endeavor.

South of Puerto Vallarta, about halfway between Puerto Vallarta and Boca de Tomatlán, Mismaloya is blossoming into a retirement community. A large hillside development is under way, with some homes tucked in forest settings and others with ocean views. The beach here became famous as the set for Richard Burton's movie *The Night of the Iguana*, but Mismaloya has undergone explosive development—perhaps too fast for its size. That's the downside of Mismaloya, the danger that it might become overwhelmed by large hotels and condos and become a bit too commercial.

Manzanillo

Manzanillo is one of Mexico's oldest cities. It was settled in the year 1522, shortly after Cortez overwhelmed the Aztecs at Tenotchtitlán (now Mexico City) during the Spanish conquest. Manzanillo became established as Mexico's major port on the west coast. From the beginning of Spain's occupation of Mexico, treasures from China and the Philippines passed through this calm bay. Located approximately 150 miles south of Puerto Vallarta (in the state of Colima), Manzanillo isn't exactly a tourist destination in the style of Mazatlán or Acapulco. Its main occupation is as a busy marine port and railway shipping terminal. Manzanillo's downtown is strictly commercial. Devoid of elegant restaurants and tourist shops, most of the city seems rather ordinary to us.

It seems unlikely that many foreign residents would choose to live in the city of Manzanillo; instead you'll find them along the coast north of Manzanillo. This is where the resorts, condos, and luxury residential communities draw tourists as well as retirees.

The number of foreigners here is small compared with the more successful resort towns along the Mexican Riviera. One reason may be that the beaches aren't as safe for swimming because of the undertow and riptides. It's no problem for experienced swimmers or surfers, but it does keep tourism down. This doesn't displease the expatriate community at all. The places where retirees make their homes are scattered along the beaches and slightly inland. The most impressive landmark hereabouts is a magnificent complex of whitewashed villas and bungalows known as Las Hadas, or "Home of the Fairies." The architecture captures the magic of a tale out of *The Arabian Nights*. One of the attractions here is the eighteen-hole Las Hadas Golf Course.

Manzanillo is clearly a magnet for sports fishermen, billing itself as "the sailfish capital of the world." (Seems like we've heard this claim in other Mexican resorts!) All in all the atmosphere here is more informal and relaxed than in Acapulco or Puerto Vallarta. Like most of the west coast, average monthly temperatures here are in the upper seventies and mid-eighties year-round. The rainy months from July through September bring some hot and steamy days. (Miami, in comparison, is hotter in the summer, colder in the winter, and far more difficult to escape from when the heat becomes uncomfortable.)

About 70 kilometers north of Manzanillo is one of the prettiest beach areas on the coast: the villages of La Manzanilla, Tenacatita, and Melaque. Strung along a horseshoe-shaped bay with pristine beaches, palms, and quiet residences, this has always been a favorite with the writers. Tenacatita and Melaque are the larger towns, with shopping and tourist facilities. La Manzanilla is a smaller village with about a thousand residents who subside on fishing from the Pacific Ocean. These places, especially La Manzanilla, have changed very little over the years, seemingly suspended in the Mexican past. The number of expatriates living here have been on the increase lately, with at least a couple of families operating hotels, fishing tours, and other tourist-related businesses.

Ixtapa-Zihuatanejo

Driving six hours south of Manzanillo, on a fairly good highway, you'll traverse the Costa Grande (the Big Coast). This is where the state of Guerrero angles 200 miles southeast from the Rio Balsas toward Acapulco. You'll travel through some interesting country, places that were unavailable to motorists until a new highway pushed through here about a decade ago. The pavement passes through quaint villages and past rustic coconut plantations, farmhouses, and crops of copra drying along the road shoulders. If you're looking for "authentic" Mexico, this is where you might want to visit.

The most popular retirement location you'll encounter along the Costa Grande is Zihuatanejo, a little more than halfway between Manzanillo and Acapulco. Local residents affectionately refer to the town as "Zihua." The Costa Grande and Zihuatanejo aren't exactly newcomers to the tourist scene. Their gorgeous beaches and steep cliffs circled by forested hills in the background were attracting crowds long before the Spanish arrived. Legend has it that in the 1400s, a Tarascan Indian king built a royal bathing resort on Las Gatas Beach in Zihuatanejo Bay. However, until a paved highway from Acapulco was cut through the mountains in the 1960s, Zihua languished as a sleepy fishing village in isolated splendor. The town woke up abruptly when developers began constructing a luxury resort on the beach at Ixtapa, a few miles north of Zihuatanejo. Before long, Zihua was being "discovered" by tourists and expatriates.

In many ways Zihuatanejo is like the Acapulco of forty years ago. It's evolving from a sleepy little village into a town, but mercifully it hasn't quite turned the corner to become a city. Most residents hope that it never will. Zihuatanejo's town square, the Plaza de Armas, overlooks the main beach, Playa Municipal, just beyond the palm-lined pedestrian walkway, Paseo del Pescador. At least this part hasn't changed since Zihuatanejo was still a village. In the downtown area shops and restaurants are within a few blocks' walking distance of the Plaza de Armas.

Our favorite beach here is Playa la Ropa, a crescent of white sand about a mile in length. The beach supposedly got its name, Playa la Ropa (the clothes beach), 200 years ago when clothing floated in from an offshore Chinese wreck. The beach is reached via the Paseo Costera, which passes some of the choice residential areas and offers great views of the nearly endless line of beaches around the bay.

Fortunately for those living in Zihuatanejo, the glamorous resort of nearby Ixtapa draws the glitzy tourist trade and crowds, thus keeping Zihuatanejo's prices within reason and its traffic flow relatively calm. Retiring here gives you the best of both worlds—quiet and affordable Zihuatanejo, with the glamour of Ixtapa just a few minutes away.

When bar-hopping in Zihuatanejo, you'll often find yacht captains and crews killing time between sailings. The harbor is popular with yachts cruising between California and Acapulco; the waterside bars never lack new faces. By the way, we always thought that retirement on a sailboat would be the ultimate. Many people do this, of course, and you'll find them in Mexican ports. However, the yachting people we've met report that getting to Mexico is a snap, but getting back north is tough because of currents and prevailing winds. The wealthy sail their boats south, then pay someone to make the slow trek back to California.

At times rentals are reportedly in short supply in Zihua because apartment and home building hasn't kept up with the increasing demand. Most newer construction is taking place away from the town center, especially on hills overlooking the bay. Small mountains ring the town, and the best building sites, with spectacular views of the bay, sit high on the slopes.

About 15 miles away in Zihua's sister city of Ixtapa, ten beaches invite bathers, surfers, and strollers along a dozen miles of creamy, azure coastline. Ixtapa is a luxurious beach resort with the sophistication of

Acapulco but on a smaller scale and with cleaner beaches. Playa de Palmar is the main beach; protective offshore shoals and rocks break some of the surf's energy, keeping the waves safe enough for swimming and body surfing.

Ixtapa's eighteen-hole, Robert Trent Jones–designed Campo de Golf is open to the public. The club has full facilities, including a pro shop, a swimming pool, tennis courts, and a restaurant. A second layout, the new eighteen-hole course at Marina Ixtapa, was rated by *Golf Digest* as one of the best in Mexico. Several Ixtapa hotels also have tennis courts available to the public.

Many condos going up here have time-share arrangements, and you know our opinion on that subject. Regular apartment buildings are available for rent, and an upscale housing development is under way. Therefore, Ixtapa is an alternative for those who prefer the luxury of a busy beach resort to the small-town environment of Zihuatanejo and who don't mind paying the price.

Continuing north along the coast on Highway 200 is the interesting village of Troncones. About 4.5 kilometers past the village of Buena Vista (32 kilometers north of the southern turnoff for Ixtapa), Troncones is to the left on a little-marked turnoff, then about 3 kilometers to the ocean. The area commonly referred to as "Troncones" is actually the 5 or more kilometers of beach from the village of Troncones to the village of La Majahua to the north. Years ago this lovely beach area was set aside by the government for tourist development, along with Ixtapa. Playa Troncones snoozed for a couple of decades, while Ixtapa became a world-class resort. Now, however, the village area is undergoing rapid growth along with the best beach, Playa Manzanillo, nearer Majahua. Until two years ago many of the more desirable locations were part of an *ejido* and therefore not available for sale. Fortunately this delayed development for so long that there is little danger it will ever become a high-density tourist area like Ixtapa. Its future seems destined as basically residential, a good place for retirement or peaceful vacations. Residential development has blossomed along the beach at Playa Manzanillo, with many tasteful private homes, although there is also a small hotel and a few bed-and-breakfasts. Nearby Ixtapa serves as a place for golf and boutiques.

Recently prices have risen dramatically. Building lots with 66-foot beach frontages are being offered in the $75,000 range. A new development with larger lots and lower prices is under way on a breezy hillside with ocean views. Growth here has been so positive that Troncones was featured in a front-page article in the *Wall Street Journal* as a model for development.

Troncones is still too small to have a formal retiree organization. The winter gringo community is probably about fifty, plus vacationers. One resident said, "The community is close-knit in the sense that pretty much everybody knows everybody. But it is an open community in the sense that it welcomes newcomers, since everybody here is a newcomer. The longest resident gringos have been here less than ten years."

Acapulco

Back in the 1950s Acapulco was one of the world's glamorous "jet-set" destinations. The epitome of tropical luxury, Acapulco became the playground of Hollywood and European celebrities. The beaches were incredible, so beautiful they seemed like movie settings of what tropical beaches should look like. Before the town grew into a city and crowded with tourists, it was common to see John Wayne, Hedy Lamar, Susan Hayward, and a gaggle of other famous personalities dining in restaurants, shopping in town, or playing in the surf. Nightlife rocked on into the early dawn, and frosted margaritas were served on the beach by tuxedoed waiters.

Years ago as an experiment in tourism development, the Mexican government launched an intense promotion of Acapulco as Mexico's top tourist destination. At that time it was the *only* upscale resort city in the entire country. Puerto Vallarta and Zijuatanejo were primitive villages isolated by mud roads, and Mazatlán was a grungy fishing port. Cancún and Huatulco hadn't been invented yet—they were still swamps and cane fields.

The experiment was a success. Hotels sprouted from nowhere. Apartments, condos, and luxury homes climbed the hillsides in search of the best views. Elegant multistory hotels and nightclubs lined the beaches like monuments to the gods of tourism. Restaurants and tourist facilities struggled to keep up with the affluent clientele. The winding two-lane road from Mexico City was replaced by a high-speed four-lane highway. Acapulco's population grew from approximately 25,000 to nearly two million inhabitants.

However, too much tourism success has a way of choking itself off. From the very beginning, Acapulco overbuilt. Competition between hotels and rental units became fierce, with price-cutting, bankruptcies, and unfinished buildings dotting the landscape. At that point the Mexican government decided to repeat the experiment elsewhere by promoting other Pacific beach towns: Puerto Vallarta, Mazatlán, and Hualtulco—as well as Caribbean locations such as Cancún and Cozumel. Acapulco stopped sponsoring ads directed at North American markets. The official emphasis shifted toward Mexican tourism, targeting middle- and working-class families from within Mexico. Direct international air service was curtailed; the city became neglected by foreign tourist agencies.

The result has been a bonanza for tourists and retirees who are looking for bargain accommodations. Hotels, apartments, and condos are forced to keep rents in line with the Mexican tourist's ability to pay. What once were luxury accommodations, available only to those who could pay top rates, are now priced within the pocketbook of all. Several of the more luxurious hotels have been converted into affordable condos and apartments. The bottom line is that among all of Mexico's resort locations, Acapulco offers the widest range of lower- to middle-priced housing in the country. You can find a hotel suite 2 blocks from the ocean going for as little as $35 a night. Acceptable rooms near the *zócalo* can be found for $20. Super-luxurious accommodations on Playa Condesa go for as little as $50 a night.

Competitive rents apply to apartments and houses as well. It turns out that during Acapulco's heyday as a jet-set resort, it was stylish to build on the steep hillsides for terrific views. The higher up, the more expensive the layout. Today Mexican tourists arrive by bus and prefer accommodations near the beach rather than on a steep hill that requires an automobile. Consequently, hillside rents have been forced downward to attract tenants. For less money than in Guadalajara, San Miguel de Allende, or other popular retirement locations, you can rent a spacious two-bedroom apartment with a view of the bay for as little as $300 a month, including utilities. These places are often on the market with an asking price of less than $40,000. Of course you're not on the beach, so you'll need a car or you'll face a long climb uphill to go home. Immediately after the devaluation of 1994, several condo and apartment projects fell into bankruptcy, with units selling at giveaway prices. The market has recovered somewhat, but there still are bargains to be found.

For a time—while the government was concentrating on promoting other vacation destinations—the infrastructure of Acapulco suffered from neglect. Streets were beginning to look dirty, and some public buildings looked shabby. But after a hurricane devastated parts of downtown Acapulco in 1997, a vigorous effort, combined with a substantial amount of resources, was made to refurbish the city. They've done a great job, with everything looking as spiffy as it ever did.

As mentioned earlier in this book, with the appearance of enormous buying complexes like WalMart, K-Mart, and Gigante, shopping patterns have changed in Mexico. In this respect Acapulco was already far ahead. It had large supermarkets and malls long before the rest of the country did. Our favorite was a gourmet supermarket near Hornos Beach—a place where we could find luxury delicatessen treats as well as staples. We always came away burdened with packages. This trend continues, with the full spectrum of U.S.-style shopping.

Restaurants are divided into two classes. You'll find luxurious, exquisitely designed restaurants that cater to affluent tourists, as well as restaurants for ordinary residents. The basic difference, aside from the decor, is that tourist places charge the maximum and don't have to worry about serving top-quality meals (because tourists in a large resort like Acapulco visit only once). Family-owned and -operated establishments must serve excellent food, or they'll go out of business.

Servants are more expensive here than elsewhere and may not be as loyal. This is because of the competition for help among the hotels and tourist businesses. You may find a great cook, only to have him or her discovered by a hotel restaurant and recruited away. Most North Americans aren't used to having servants anyway, so this shouldn't be any barrier to living in Acapulco.

Acapulco's public transportation system is excellent; it's easy to get around on the many city buses plying the streets. Taxis are also plentiful. Although many of those living here insist that an automobile is totally unnecessary, this author believes that Acapulco is one place in Mexico where a car comes in handy. It is, after all, a large city, with beaches and facilities spread all over. And again, with a car you have the ability to go up into the hills and find the best bargains in quality housing.

The exact number of expatriates living in Acapulco has never been determined: Suffice it to say there could be as many as 500. Several social and fraternal organizations serve this community, and they are great places to become known and make friends. Acapulco's American Legion Post 4 meets every second Thursday for breakfast at the Club de Yachts de Acapulco. Then there's the Friends of Acapulco club; it doesn't hold regularly scheduled meetings but does sponsor get-togethers and fund-raisers throughout the year. This organization focuses on helping poor and needy children in Acapulco.

The bottom line: If you're looking for a place in the tropics, even if only for the winter months, don't overlook Acapulco, even though you may have heard from tourists that the prices are high. Don't be put off by the notion that Acapulco is a tourist town; if it weren't a gorgeous paradise, tourists wouldn't go there in the first place.

Baja California

Baja California—a place with a reputation for mystery and romance—is a long peninsula that, for almost a thousand miles, juts south of the state of California. Both sides of the peninsula are lined with almost unexplored beaches. Baja is a world all its own. A wonderland of desert scenery, the peninsula is famous for secluded beaches, lost Jesuit missions, rugged mountains, and deep canyons. Separated from the mainland by the blue, blue waters of the Sea of Cortez (also called the Gulf of California), the peninsula has been isolated so long that it has evolved its own flora and fauna, distinct from anywhere else in the world. Zoologists and botanists pilgrimage here to enjoy themselves.

Baja's economy, similarly isolated from the mainland, has also evolved its own characteristics. With only one highway and one railroad connecting the peninsula with Mexico's mainland, all goods and merchandise must travel over these slow routes or else arrive by ship. This increases prices to the consumer. Much merchandise comes by truck from the United States, which also makes things more expensive. Therefore, it isn't surprising to find that prices and wages are higher here than on the mainland. Despite this Baja California is still Mexico, and

Baja Californians are the same friendly breed you find on the mainland.

For many people living in the western United States, Baja California is the only part of Mexico they know. This is particularly true of Californians. They fondly recall Baja's diverse attractions: long stretches of beach where enormous Pismo clams are there for the taking, moonlit grunion runs, camping, fishing, soaking up sunshine while drinking Tecate beer flavored with lemon and salt.

Baja is more than simply a place for tourists to let off steam. For uncounted numbers of West Coast residents, Baja has become a retiree's playground. In recognition of this movement, and to encourage retirement, the Mexican government relaxed the rules for property ownership in Baja, which used to be the strictest in the country. Now the land ownership laws are the same as elsewhere in Mexico.

One reason so many Californians retire in Baja California is that it's so conveniently nearby. For people retiring from southern California, having a home in Ensenada means being able to drive north to visit the grandchildren any time they choose. It means neighbors and friends they used to work with are much more likely to drop in for a weekend visit than if they had a similar residence in Puerto Vallarta or Lake Chapala. Some expatriates who own homes in the Rosarito Beach area actually commute to jobs in San Diego and vicinity.

Because most northern Baja California retirement spots are within a few hours of the border, it's no problem to run on up to San Diego or Calexico for shopping. "You'd be surprised how often I find I need a special tool or some nuts and bolts that I can't find here," said one man who is building a home in Ensenada. "In two hours, I'm in San Diego. I visit the hardware store while the wife stocks up on hard-to-find grocery items. Then it's back home after a milkshake-and-hamburger fix at some fast-food place."

Because it's convenient and close, Baja offers a way to sample Mexico's graciousness and economical living without investing excessive time or money in the adventure. Baja is an excellent place for preretirement planning—an opportunity to see whether you actually like Mexico and its people. Baja is a place from which to move into the Mexican culture gradually, yet be close to Hollywood and Disneyland, if that somehow makes you feel more secure. If you like what you see, you might decide to investigate a different type of Mexican retirement on the mainland.

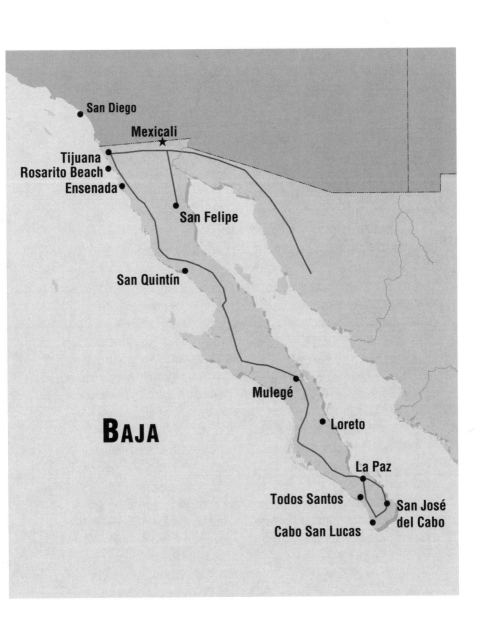

San Diego

Mexicali

Tijuana
Rosarito Beach
Ensenada

San Felipe

San Quintín

Mulegé

Loreto

BAJA

La Paz

Todos Santos

San José
del Cabo

Cabo San Lucas

As we pointed out earlier, because Baja is isolated from Mexico proper, you'll find prices and wages higher and Yankee influence more apparent. Yet for the novice these differences aren't so obvious, because prices and wages are so much less than back home that they seem downright ridiculous. In Ensenada, for example, a maid will come in to clean your house and do your laundry for $8.00 to $10.00 a day. On the mainland the wage might be $5.00 a day. (This would be a generous wage, because $4.00 a day is normally the minimum wage.) Maybe your Mexican neighbors can hire help a little cheaper, but anyone who would complain about paying these wages or even more (after all, you are comparatively wealthy) shouldn't even consider living in Mexico.

Free Zone

The northern part of Baja is known as the *zona libre* (free zone). The government deliberately keeps this area quite relaxed as far as immigration and customs are concerned. You don't need tourist papers or an automobile permit to enter, only automobile insurance. You can usually cross the border without even saying "hello" to Mexican customs and immigration officials. Don't misunderstand: This doesn't give you any rights of residency or any legal status at all. By law your stay is limited to seventy-two hours, although the law is seldom enforced—unless you're a troublemaker. Because there is no way to prove when a tourist actually crossed the border, many Californians spend days, weeks, even months at their weekend getaways.

By no means are we encouraging you to break Mexican immigration laws by staying longer than the seventy-two-hour limit—we're merely reporting on the present practices. If you plan on staying for a while, we recommend that you follow the entirely reasonable rules of the Mexican government. There are several ways to do this, all covered in the section on legal matters (see pages 54–56). It used to be that getting a tourist visa was simple; you just asked for your card and it was yours. The rules on tourist visas have been undergoing a series of changes lately. They are explained in detail on page 54, but briefly the present rule is: After receiving your tourist card at the border, you must validate it at a local bank by paying a fee of approximately $15. The fee can vary, depending on the rules in force at the time.

Gringo investment in real estate in the *zona libre* is impressive. Everywhere you turn, particularly along the beaches, you'll find single homes, condos, and luxury gated developments. But please let us encourage you to check with a locally recommended lawyer before laying out money for that oceanfront Baja property. Several scandals and horror stories have muddied the water here, with people buying homes from sellers who didn't own the properties.

The Mediterranean Coast

The long string of beach communities stretching some 70 miles between Rosarito Beach, Ensenada, and Punta Banda is probably the fastest-growing retirement region in Mexico. Since residency restrictions have been loosened with multiple-entry FM-3 residency and property ownership liberalized, a flood of gringos have taken advantage of the close-to–San Diego locations. Not all are retired, either; some regularly commute to jobs or businesses in the San Diego area, whereas others work for U.S. companies facilities in Baja California. The recent addition of a "commuter lane" across the border makes a commuting trip even easier. New home construction is at an all-time high. At least 25,000 North Americans (possibly a lot more) have homes here, either weekend places or permanent residences.

When asked why they chose this region for residence, all those interviewed listed weather as a major consideration. "It has a balmy Mediterranean kind of climate," points out one retiree. "It rarely gets over eighty degrees and almost never below fifty degrees at night. We have a San Diego climate with a Mexican environment." Another resident said, "I live in the most expensive neighborhood in Ensenada, yet I don't have air conditioning, nor do I know anyone who does." Few houses have heating systems, either, because the ocean keeps winter weather from dropping to extremes. For all but the most luxurious homes, an electric heater or a fireplace suffices for most of the year, although the coldest January days can be frosty. Continual breezes from the cool Pacific Ocean moderate temperatures along the coast, but a few miles inland, temperatures are anything but "Mediterranean." (See for yourself on the temperature chart.)

Weather in the Baja California/Rosarita Beach/Ensenada area

	Jan.	Mar.	Apr.	May	Jul.	Aug.	Oct.	Dec.
	In degrees Fahrenheit							
DAILY HIGHS	66	68	70	72	75	77	75	66
DAILY LOWS	48	50	55	57	63	66	57	50

Rosarito Beach

Here in the *zona libre,* just a few miles from the California border, Rosarito Beach is a very popular place for retirement, second homes, and vacation retreats. A four-lane highway takes you back to convenient shopping on the U.S. side of the border in short order. Rosarito Beach has a population of more than 80,000, with estimates of 5,000 or more North Americans, mostly Californians, living here.

The town abounds with small ranch-style homes, crowded together and landscaped like suburban neighborhoods across the border—but with a taco flavor. Although many sections of town are typical Baja-grungy, you'll also find several upscale, gated communities reminiscent of southern California developments. Folks who live here claim that the beach is one of the finest in Baja.

The retirees here have formed a club called the United Society of Baja California, complete with a monthly newspaper filled with local news and listings of rentals and property available in the Rosarito Beach area. This place is for those who need to be within easy driving distance of San Diego. It's Mexico, of course, but less Mexico-like than the rest of Baja.

As you travel farther south, you'll encounter numerous attractive gringo communities perched along the ocean cliffs, San Antonio Shores being one of the largest. These are mostly gated or restricted access developments and almost exclusively inhabited by gringos. Most homes are used as weekend getaways, but many are lived in full time. The architecture tends toward tasteful Old Spanish homes, with red tile roofs and adobelike walls. Along with the upscale communities between Rosarito and Ensenada, you'll find a few areas distinguished by cheap, slapjack construction, more on the order of fishing camps. In fact, that's exactly what some places are: fishing camps. The better developments have security guards and limited access to outsiders.

Ensenada

Ensenada is located a little more than one hour south of Tijuana by four-lane divided toll highway. Duty-free shopping, very low prescription drug prices, nice beaches nearby, and friendly people make Ensenada and surrounding communities very popular for retirement and weekend homes. In Spanish the word *ensenada* means bay, or cove. The cove was discovered in 1542 by Sebastián Vizcaíno, who was so impressed with its beauty that he named it Ensenada de Todos los Santos (All Saints' Bay). Over the years it has grown from a sleepy fishing village to a bustling city of more than 300,000 inhabitants, and it likes to call itself Cenicienta del Pacifico (Cinderella of the Pacific). Fishing and tourism are still big industries, but the momentum of industry and shipping business has grown impressively. Ensenada's ship harbor is the third largest seaport in Baja. Education is another big source of jobs in Ensenada; the city has campuses of the University of Baja California, the National University of Mexico's Institute of Astronomy and Physics, a private medical school, and several private research centers.

Although Ensenada gets plenty of tourists, it's basically a genuine Mexican city. You'll find all the services you would expect from a city, from shopping malls to excellent hospitals and fine restaurants. A few gringos live in the city proper, but the majority live in one of the communities on the northern and southern beaches. Ensenada is their commercial center, with residences in a wide variety of locations, from elegant gated communities to ramshackle fishing camps. Many elegant homes are perched on hills overlooking the ocean, some on cliffs overlooking the surf below.

The actual number of gringos living here is difficult to ascertain—so many are continually coming and going. But there's no question that several thousand *norteamericanos* permanently make their homes near Ensenada, and that thousands more are part-time residents. Ensenada, by the way, has three language schools where you can immerse yourself in Spanish. This may be the nearest place to the border where you can get total immersion in Spanish learning, small classes, a native Spanish teacher, and living quarters with a non–English-speaking family.

Ensenada has several motels with small apartment units that rent by the month. Staying in one of these is an excellent way to try out the area and see whether this might be your dream retirement place. The town itself is full of house rentals at rock-bottom prices (provided you don't insist on having English-speaking neighbors). One man we interviewed, a widower from Tacoma, told of his living in a working-class neighborhood, paying an embarrassingly low rent, saying that his neighbors are very friendly and keep an eye on his house while he is away. (We didn't check the neighborhood, so we can't guarantee that his flowery descriptions are accurate.)

Living expenses in Ensenada are somewhat higher than on the mainland, but this is to be expected anywhere in Baja California. The region is isolated from the rest of Mexico, and much of the economy is connected to California. Local residents complain that utilities are constantly on the increase and that telephone service is substandard. Of course, these complaints can be heard all over Mexico.

Punta Banda and La Bufadora

About 13 miles south of Ensenada, along the shore and at the end of Bahía Todos Santos, are several small retirement communities. The main ones are Punta Banda and La Bufadora, although the entire area past Ejido Cantu is usually referred to as Punta Banda. The name La Bufadora refers to an interesting "blowhole" in an oceanside cliff, where impressive spouts of water are created by the pounding waves.

Punta Banda started out as a collection of the most rustic and innovative homes you can imagine. Early residents began living in travel trailers or motor homes, which evolved into permanent structures in an interesting way. Typically a residence began with something like a 20-foot travel trailer. The first year the owners would lay out a patio and put up a picket fence to spiffy things up. Because a 20-footer is somewhat cramped for living space, the next year they built on a living room so they could spread out a little, and perhaps added a storage room. Then, as the grandkids started coming to visit, they added on a bedroom or two. By this time the old travel trailer was beginning to fall apart, so they pulled it out and replaced it with a kitchen. In its final stage the compound rambles all over the place and has no relationship to the original conception of an RV lot. Today many conventional—and sometimes elaborate—homes have been added to the housing selections.

Punta Banda and La Bufadora began rather modestly a couple of decades ago, but today you'll find plenty of services, including restaurants, a large building supply store, small grocery stores, a fresh fruit/vegetable stand, and even an insurance agent and a post office! Recently an arts and crafts store opened, displaying the work of local craftsmen and offering supplies for "do-it-yourselfers."

The total number of residents in Punta Banda and La Bufadora is approximately 1,000 permanent gringo residents, 1,000 Mexican residents, and another 2,000 or more temporary gringo residents. They've developed an unusually active social structure. Among the most important clubs is a one called Sociedad de Amigos de Punta Banda, which has several hundred members. They've also organized a volunteer fire department. Among the several civic and social clubs, there's an active local theater group that gives performances at the Gertrude Perlman Theater, an ad hoc theater in nearby La Jolla Camp (on the road to La Bufadora).

Of course we caution everyone to be very careful about purchasing leases in the restricted maritime zone, but extra prudence is due here. The problem began with certain leases granted to several gringos on *ejido* land. At the time this was illegal, but the government took action to make it okay. Then thirty years later—after some really nice homes had been built—the Mexican Supreme Court ruled that it was illegal after all and that the land belonged to the original owners who had it before the land was made into *ejidos*. To date the government has been quite reluctant to enforce this ruling, and negotiations with the U.S. government are under way. Our understanding is that the problem is confined to a place called Punta Estero, about 3 miles from Punta Banda. But we've cautioned over and over: Beware of *ejido* lands!

This problem has produced much negative publicity, leaves many land owners feeling nervous, and has had an effect on tourism in the region. Everyone hopes that it will be resolved soon.

A few miles south of Punta Banda the *zona libre* ends. From here onward you need tourist papers. (Be sure you get your papers stamped here, because the next place to do it is in La Paz.) This is where the *real* Baja starts, according to four-wheel-drive enthusiasts and true desert lovers. Here rolling hills and rugged clifflike mountains are sparsely covered with strange, one-of-a-kind plants, like the majestic cardon cactus (similar to the saguaro cactus on the mainland), squat barrel cactus, and spiked plants of all types. This is the only place on earth where you'll see things like the weird-looking cirio trees—commonly called bojuum trees—which grow like upside-down carrots, or thick-trunked elephant trees, which bleed a blood-colored sap when punctured with a knife. Smoke trees, salt pines, and cacti of all descriptions add to the inventory of desert wonders. Several small communities, with occasional North Americans in residence, string along the paved highway. Some interesting places, like the wine-growing valleys around Santo Tomas and San Vincente, might be suitable for gringos who can get by without speaking English every day.

San Felipe

On the Sea of Cortez side of the peninsula (but still in the *zona libre* part of Baja), the town of San Felipe has mushroomed in just a few years from a small fishing village into a major center for vacationers and retirees. The attraction here is miles of sandy beaches washed with warm gulf waters—a scenic desert setting with a mysterious panorama of the towering peaks of the Sierra San Pedro Martir in the distance.

San Felipe has always been a favorite with RV retirees and snowbirds, those who customarily winter in Tucson or Yuma. They discovered that by driving 120 miles south of the border on a good paved road, they can enjoy a pleasant winter retirement on Mexico's Sea of Cortez. RVers found it a great place to wake up in the morning and look out over the sea, shimmering and blue-green, with fishing and shrimp boats crisscrossing in the early haze.

Fishing, by the way, is why many journey to San Felipe in the first place. It's fabulous, with huge sea bass and enormous red snappers elbowing each other aside to gobble up your bait. And San Felipe is conveniently located close to the California border. Family and friends can visit for the weekend without a major transportation problem. The present two-lane road is currently being widened into four lanes.

The town has changed tremendously over the last thirty years, when we first started spending winter months in the beachside RV parks. The sand and dirt streets are now paved, and the long main street is a bustling commercial artery that parallels the beach, loaded with good restaurants and thriving businesses. San Felipe boasts several banks and supermarkets that are expanding rapidly to meet the demands of the growing retirement population. This is no longer the exclusive domain of the home-on-wheels crowd and weekend fishermen. Conventional housing and year-round retirement living are taking over.

San Felipe is undergoing a construction boom. Retirement residences are popping up everywhere, with housing styles ranging from fish-camp rustic to Mediterranean deluxe. Although many North Americans own property in town, most lease or build homes away from San Felipe's center, on individual beach- or ocean-view lots or in one of the many tasteful developments. Rentals are not plentiful, but real estate people in town can often find something for you.

Between 20,000 and 22,000 Mexican citizens live here today, joined by an additional 7,000 Americans and Canadians who have either part- or full-time living arrangements during the cooler months. Some of the more heat-proof northerners (about 700 of them) stick it out all year, but most flee north for the summer months. Summers here, unlike those on the Baja peninsula's Pacific side, are fierce. Temperatures often top 110 degrees Fahrenheit. At that level you needn't mention low humidity; it's just plain hot!

To be fair we must admit that summer in San Felipe is only a little warmer than that in Phoenix or Las Vegas. The pleasant fall, winter, and spring make up for cruel summers by providing gloriously sunny days, perfect for enjoying the desert-sea environment. You can be pretty sure it won't rain on your picnic here; sometimes a year or two can go by without a drop. But when it does rain, as anywhere in Baja, the desert suddenly bursts into a symphony of lush green and brilliant flowers. This spectacle is an emotional experience that makes waiting worthwhile.

The ambience here is Mexico–Baja California, but because of the high numbers of North Americans in residence or visiting, most folks aren't exposed to Mexican culture to any extent unless they choose to get involved with natives. Almost all your neighbors will be from the United States or Canada. Many prefer it this way. One retired lady said, "I didn't come here to learn a new language or study a new culture. I simply want to kick back and enjoy my winter retirement." However, those who care to will find every opportunity to practice Spanish and make Mexican friends.

Kay and Bill Gabbard live year-round in a San Felipe development called Club de Pesca (a combination of houses and RVs fronting on the beach). Bill says, "One of the things I like about living here is that it is family oriented. It's great fun to watch kids playing as they explore the beach and tide pools. Personally, I would not want to live in a place where kids are excluded, nor would I want to be in a self-contained American community."

Labor costs are higher here than in Ensenada because of the booming economy. Still, by stateside measures, wages are very low. Kay Gabbard says: "We do not have a lot of property around our house, so we just have a man come in twice a week to sweep, rake, clean up, and water the plants. I pay him $20 per month. Of course, he works at our development, so some of this is part of his job, and he does it during work hours. We have a lady come in one morning a week. She cleans the patio, carport, and house and charges $15 for a little over two hours of work. This seems a little high, but she does a good job and can be trusted when we are not at home. Local women who do housework like that can actually make much more than their husbands." For folks who don't want to hire their own housekeepers, a new housecleaning service has recently opened.

As in most expatriate communities, volunteer organizations are the centerpiece of social activity. Cocktail parties, luncheons, and breakfasts are all excuses to get together and plan cooperative action and make new friends in the process. This is a great way to become acquainted with the community while undertaking worthwhile projects.

One of the most active groups is Las Amigas, an organization of Mexican, American, and Canadian women who help local schools improve the quality of education. They also provide needy families with clothing and food. Fund-raising events turn out to be fun events for the entire community; Las Amigas sponsors entertainment such as casino nights, dances, chili cook-offs, dinner theater melodrama, and parties celebrating everything from St. Patrick's Day to Halloween. Several Las Amigas–sponsored students are presently attending universities, pursuing degrees in architecture, education, medicine, and nuclear physics.

Another social group is the San Felipe Players, a group of actors, writers, set builders, and lovers of live theater. They enjoy bringing the magic of the stage to San Felipe. And there's the San Felipe Association of Retired Persons, an informal, apolitical, nonprofit organization open to all San Felipe residents and visitors. Volunteer projects aren't limited to social organizations. Kay Gabbard's pet project is the San Felipe Book Buddies, an outreach project dedicated to getting quality picture books and reading materials to the town's schoolkids. Classrooms have government-supplied textbooks, but no children's literature in Spanish. The Book Buddies Web site is www.inet-toolbox.com/bookbuddies.

To sum it up, living in San Felipe makes for a different kind of Mexican retirement, one that is basically part-time and an alternative to the usual Padre Island, Brownsville–McAllen, or Lake Havasu kind of winter escape.

Baja California Sur

The peninsula is broken into two political entities, north and south, with the territory of Baja California Sur only recently elevated to statehood. The first time John Howells visited Baja California Sur was in 1963, on a four-wheel-drive camping adventure. In those days driving the unpaved trails of Baja was a true safari, with many hard days of bouncing through clouds of dust and climbing rocky ledges from the top to bottom of the peninsula. Baja fans formed a sort of cult in those days, with adventurers who actually made it all the way to La Paz or Cabo San Lucas being awarded the highest honors. During the journey John reports asking himself many times, "Why am I doing this?" His wife asked the same question, although in a much more intense manner. An overnight ferry from La Paz to the mainland avoided a return trip and probably saved a marriage.

Today a fairly good asphalt highway links the northern and southern parts of Baja; driving is a snap. A long expanse of almost uninhabited country separates the population centers of the north from the south. The drive is long, but worth it; it's liberally endowed with spectacular and unforgettable scenery. Scattered along the way are some tiny settlements, an occasional town, and always-friendly, helpful people. Sometimes residents seem quite shy, but if you practice your Spanish with them, you'll find they warm up very quickly.

The people in the lower parts of Baja interact with Americans differently than do Mexicans who live nearer the border, and for good reason.

Here they see a different type of American tourist. Those "ugly Americans" in search of boisterous weekends, gaudy souvenirs, cheap thrills, and hell-raising usually don't stray very far from Tijuana or Mexicali. Tourists who bother to travel this far are different; they obviously appreciate Mexico and the fascinating Baja scenery, or they wouldn't be here. The local people sense this, and they treat you accordingly. They haven't met the other kind of gringos.

As in other parts of Mexico, you'll see the Green Angels (Angeles Verdes) as they patrol for motorists in trouble. At last report, the Green Angels' funding has been reduced somewhat, but the workers try to cover their routes at least once every day. They carry a truckload of spare parts and gasoline. The drivers are excellent mechanics and speak some English, and the services are free (except for parts and gasoline, all available at cost). The trucks are all equipped with two-way radios, so they can be reached either by CB or by calling the hot-line number, 520–6123.

Incidentally, along this stretch of highway are some of the most innovative automobile mechanics in the world. Just because there are few or no parts for repairs doesn't stop them. They perform miracles by recycling parts from old hulks, reworking them, and fitting them into automobiles that aren't even closely related. Still, don't let this lull you into venturing into the open country of Baja without a vehicle in good repair, and don't forget to keep an eye on the gasoline gauge.

The highway is paved and, although pockmarked in places, is in fairly good shape. Signs posted along the way proclaim that the highway was not intended to be a "high-speed" highway and caution you to drive carefully. Good advice. Many stretches have no shoulders, so wide vehicles, such as RVs and travel trailers, should use special caution. At times every other vehicle seems to be an RV. Fortunately traffic along the highway is usually light and relatively tension free.

It isn't until you get as far south as La Paz that you begin to encounter North Americans in any considerable number. From here to the tip of the Baja Peninsula, the weather undergoes a subtle change. The cool water of the Pacific Ocean pushes its way into the Sea of Cortez, moderating the temperature a bit. Summers are tolerable from La Paz south to Los Cabos, at land's end, and expatriates aren't forced to evacuate every May. Here, when it rains, it rains in summer rather than in winter, as is the case up north. Therefore year-round living is feasible.

Make no mistake—this is still desert country. Rainfall is scanty, with as long as two years between storms. Then it comes in torrential downpours that turn the arroyos into raging rivers. By the way, be very careful when driving in one of the infrequent rain storms—*anywhere* in Baja. Slight dips in the road can quickly become deep, swirling currents of water. It's best to wait for someone else to splash through before trying to ford what looks like a shallow rush of water crossing the highway. Okay, so it only comes halfway up on the ducks—wait anyway.

La Paz: The Pearl of Baja

When early Spanish explorers discovered the sheltered bay of La Paz off the Sea of Cortez in the mid-1500s, they also discovered an astonishing wealth of pearl oysters in the warm sea waters. This led to the founding of the town of La Paz. Centuries of harvesting the valuable crop have eliminated pearls as an industry, although today an occasional oyster will yield a small treasure.

Over the years La Paz has grown to be the largest city in Baja California Sur, with close to 200,000 inhabitants. An unusually clean city with all services and enjoyable winter temperatures, it's not surprising that La Paz attracts a large number of North American residents. Approximately 1,500 of them choose to live here year-round, and at least double that number come here on a seasonal basis. Because the bay is so well protected, hundreds of yachts are always in attendance, with an estimated 400 yacht owners living full-time on their vessels. Several well-kept trailer parks draw seasonal visitors. Some RV enthusiasts claim this is absolutely the best place in Baja for winter retirement.

Although tourism and retirement are important to the economy, they have a relatively small impact on the overall scheme of things. La Paz gives you the feeling of a substantial, prosperous Mexican city—without the helter-skelter of some Baja locations. It's prosperous and bustling, with tourism and retirement incidental to everyday commerce. La Paz has an attractive downtown, nice shopping centers, and excellent non-tourist restaurants scattered throughout the city. The inviting *Malecón,* or walkway, runs alongside the broad street that curves about the picturesque bay. It's popular with early-morning joggers as well as strollers throughout the day and evening. Most tourist shops, restaurants, and tour agencies are found along a 6-block stretch of the *Malecón.*

The harbor and marina form the focal point of the city for retirees. A good place to meet fellow expatriates is by the marina at the Dock Cafe, where gringos convene for informal breakfasts every morning and for dinner and music in the evening. Throughout the winter a seagoing-oriented group, the Club Cruceros, meets on the third Tuesday of each month at Los Arcos Hotel. Meetings are open to everyone (whether you own a yacht or not), and the club maintains a trading library at its clubhouse at Marina La Paz. The clubhouse hosts informal social gatherings, where friends meet and discuss current events, lie about the fish they almost caught, and debate the best places to find lobsters.

La Paz lives up to its name (the word *paz* means "peace") in that it is quiet and safe. During the authors' last visit in fall of 2000, we looked at the local newspaper's "police page" to see what kinds of crimes were being reported. Two stories made large headlines. One reported that two youths had been arrested for drinking and driving at excessive speeds. The other major story told of another youth who ran through a red light and crashed into another automobile. One driver was slightly injured. Would these crimes be reported in your local newspaper? That's not to say that La Paz doesn't suffer the petty theft normal in other Mexican retirement locations, but local residents insist that violent offenses are rare and they feel personal safety is exceptionally high.

Several agreeable neighborhoods in the town of La Paz are quite suitable for retirement. Most are in mixed Mexican–North American areas rather than gringo enclaves. Housing costs can range from very affordable to exorbitant, all in the same neighborhood. The bulk of the expatriates seem to gravitate toward neighborhoods on the southern edge of La Paz, where well-to-do Mexican families and gringos cluster. There don't seem to be many, if any, exclusive enclaves of foreign residents who keep to themselves. Most residents prefer to be integrated throughout the city, enjoying the cultural experience of having Spanish-speaking neighbors.

The local expatriate community is well regarded by its neighbors because of its participation in local affairs. With the Club Cruceros leading the way, the community holds fund-raising events to collect money for children in need of medical and other help. Every December they host a bazaar, with an auction, food stands, and entertainment. The proceeds are used for Christmas gifts and school supplies for the kids.

Los Cabos

One of the biggest explosions of development and population increase is under way on the lower end of the peninsula, an area known as Los Cabos. Consisting of the area between Cabo San Lucas and San José del Cabo—once widely separated, now almost twin cities—the Los Cabos area is sprouting hotels, condos, and housing developments. Some folks come because of Los Cabos's classic desert scenery and balmy climate, but most have designs on the game fish, so abundant just off the coast. Others love the area's four excellent golf courses. Sometimes dubbed the Pebble Beach of Baja, Cabo San Lucas boasts two championship courses, and San José del Cabo claims two famous courses.

An international airport sits halfway between the towns, making it convenient for friends and family to visit those ensconced in their retirement homes. Frequent flights from Los Angeles, San Francisco, Portland, Vancouver, and other West Coast cities make getting here a snap (only three hours from San Francisco), so residents here can expect frequent visitors. Every flight seems to carry a full load of enthusiastic tourists looking forward to fishing, surfing, and just plain loafing in the sunshine. Because of the dry desert climate, there is abundant sunshine. The total rainfall is less than 5 inches a year. Most of it falls in August and September, making the landscape unexpectedly green at that time of year.

Because of its popularity, housing prices in the Cabos area can be shocking. We've seen condos, which would barely fetch $100,000 in Mazatlán, selling for more than $200,000. Most houses on the beach, or with good ocean views, command prices that would be expensive even in California or Florida. Prices go up daily, and North Americans seem to be buying condos and houses as fast as the Mexicans can build them. So much construction is going on that skilled workers have to be imported from the mainland to keep up with the demand. To give you an idea of how big the market is, the Mexican immigration offices here released the figure of 4,500 foreigners living full-time or most of the time in the Los Cabos area.

Why the boom? We really don't understand it at all. Although Baja is wonderful, after a while you may get homesick for some green plants, forests, and wildflowers, instead of sand and cactus. (And the parts of Baja that we like best are the rustic, undeveloped places where gringos are still novelties.) Yet when interviewed, most North American residents insist this is the best place in all of Mexico to retire. "I wouldn't even consider living on the mainland," is the typical reply. "We love Baja, and we wouldn't care if it costs *more* to live here than it does back home!" They point to the astonishingly blue ocean, the rugged cliffs with surf frothing against the rocky shore, and the crystal-clear skies. "Where else in the world could I have a view like this from my living room?" To quote a cliché, it's all in the eye of the beholder.

This economic boom has had an effect upon the cultural atmosphere of Baja. With higher prices and practically a dollar economy, wages have naturally risen for the natives, and employment is at an all-time high. Construction workers earn from $150 to $200 a month, as opposed to $90 or less on the mainland. However, even though workers earn big money for Mexico, prices are so high in tourist facilities that Mexicans seldom patronize them. Nice restaurants and bars are exclusively gringo. After all, a worker making $12.00 a day can't really afford to hoist many $2.00 beers with the gringos. Here, there are *three* economic realities—one for tourists, one for gringo residents, and one for Mexicans.

San José del Cabo

In our first edition we hinted that San José del Cabo was Baja's "well-kept secret." Today it's undergoing an even more vigorous boom than Cabo San Lucas. Some secret! About 30 miles north of Cabo San Lucas, San José del Cabo was our favorite town in all of the peninsula; at that time, it was totally unspoiled, like something out of a Hollywood movie set. In an early edition we described San José del Cabo as "an old town with sparkling white houses, dressed in flowers, neat as an old maid's bedroom."

Not surprisingly San José del Cabo was "discovered" (we hope not because of our book), and retirees began moving in. They bought empty buildings, some centuries old, converted them into plush homes, then waited breathlessly for new condo developments to become available. Restaurants opened on side streets, competing with one another to bring in gringo customers.

Although the town has tripled in size since we reported on it in the original version of *Choose Mexico,* this growth was mostly outward. The center of town has fortunately escaped "renewal" and modernization. It looks pretty much as it must have a century and a half ago, with the landscaped squares and grassy parks intact and the old-fashioned flavor of Mexico.

The town's main street is a landscaped boulevard with restored nineteenth-century buildings housing boutiques, restaurants, and shops. The boulevard provides a promenade for tourists and residents as they enjoy the peace and quiet of San José del Cabo. The central square is a place where folks gather in the evening to chat and make new friends—as is traditional in old-fashioned Mexican towns—instead of seeking out discos as they might in Cabo San Lucas. Plans are afoot to close the main thoroughfare to motor traffic, thus turning it into a pedestrian mall and an even more user-friendly place. Yet for those who crave nightlife, loud music, and overpriced drinks, Cabo San Lucas is only half an hour's drive away.

The expatriate population is substantial, probably close to 2,000, and retirees have considerable economic influence over the town. Restaurants compete for their business and turn out some surprisingly good menus. Local stores stock everything a foreigner might desire.

The southern edge of town is where the most development has taken place, although a nice section known as Chamizal sits above the town and is still expanding. If the boom continues, numerous condominium complexes and individual homes threaten to spread all the way to Cabo San Lucas. The builders deserve credit for the tasteful designs, with Spanish colonial styles prevalent.

Time-share developments are fewer here than in the Cabo San Lucas area, with most new construction either condos or private homes. We have friends here who own both condos and private homes, and they seem to have no problem renting them out when they are back in the States. Of course in the summer months, when it really becomes hot here, renters are scarce, but not totally absent.

The cost of living here is, like most of Baja California, higher than average. On the other hand, most of San José del Cabo's residents and visitors are affluent enough that higher costs are not relevant. The upscale housing in the area attests to this. This is not to say that there aren't some economically priced neighborhoods—and in fact some gringos prefer to live in some of the small villages not far from the town center, where rents are almost gifts.

Cabo San Lucas

The name *Cabo San Lucas* seems to have a magical quality for many people, and they're convinced that "Cabo" is the ultimate place in all of Baja California. We have never understood its fascination for many North Americans. To us Cabo San Lucas is a large, sprawling place, without a real "downtown" section—unless you count a concentration of souvenir shops and incredibly loud gringo bars. (For some reason gringo tourists feel an obligation, when patronizing Cabo bars, to pour tequila down their gullets, shout at the top of their voices, and do all the other things that they can't do back home without going to jail.)

This is a new town, with few buildings more than thirty years old, so it isn't surprising that Cabo doesn't maintain the traditional Spanish-Mexican architecture found in San José del Cabo. Most construction doesn't bother pretending to be anything other than new, utilitarian, and no-nonsense.

Nevertheless, countless North Americans have fallen in love with Cabo and seem to be standing in line to buy the next new house or condo. Tourists fly down from everywhere in the United States and Canada for the incredible sailfish and marlin sportfishing and are happy to pay $900 a week for a one-bedroom apartment that would cost $900 for *two months* on the mainland. Several developments offer luxury homes and condos starting at $250,000. That's for a small one—who knows how much for a "big" one? We've heard rumors that a million bucks isn't out of range. Of course there are affordable homes and condos with great views of the ocean. But *affordable* is a relative term here. What you'd pay for a modest little home would buy something breathtaking on Mexico's mainland.

Despite our puzzlement as to why people are fighting to buy property here, the fact is that many of those who love Baja wouldn't consider living anywhere else. There's something special about the desert that attracts some people but repels others. Of course the fishing there is marvelous, and for many Baja residents, that is reason enough to love Baja.

You needn't live in Cabo San Lucas or San José del Cabo to enjoy the best of this southernmost part of Baja. Take a look at our section on retirement sites for the more adventurous to learn about small towns, villages, and beach hangouts in the Los Cabos area.

At the risk of making enemies of some Baja lovers, we have to question the inflated prices in the lower tip of the peninsula. Is it worth the extra investment to live in Baja Sur? Obviously the answer to the question by many who live in Cabo San Lucas and its environs is a resounding "yes." Indeed there's a sense of romance, beauty, and mystery about the Baja desert that isn't to be found elsewhere. There's a certain crispness in the dry air and the breezes off the sea that makes it a special place. The way nature balances life and environment with delicate perfection reveals some deeply miraculous secrets of the universe. Again, the only answer seems to be found within yourself. You have to go and "try it before you buy it."

About 40 miles north of Cabo San Lucas, the small town of Todos Santos is in the process of becoming a much bigger town. The boom is being fueled largely by foreigners buying up old homes and constructing new ones. Until the paved highway reached Todos Santos back in 1986, the town was isolated from the rest of Baja. A highly prosperous sugar cane center back in the nineteenth century, Todos Santos was abandoned when the market suddenly collapsed, making it a virtual ghost town. The small town center contains many fascinating old buildings that have been renovated for use as stores, galleries, and restaurants. This provides a quiet atmosphere of historic old Mexico, contrasting sharply with Cabo San Lucas's modern glitter and hustle. The nearby tall smokestack of an old sugar mill stands as a reminder of Todos Santos's historic past.

With an abundant water supply flowing underground from a nearby mountain range, Todos Santos is in an unusual position for Baja California. There's enough surplus water to irrigate orchards of avocados, mangoes, and papayas, as well to supply an anticipated tourist and retirement boom. Within reason, of course. Persistent and credible rumors circulate to the effect that a large luxury development is on the way. Besides a four-figure number of condos and luxury homes, plans include an eighteen-hole golf course. According to those "in the know," the developers have promised to install a water and sewage system for the entire town, promising to use reclaimed water for the golf course (to lessen fears that water shortages will ensue if the planned golf course becomes a reality).

The first time we visited here, about ten years ago, only a handful of North Americans had homes here. Most of them returned to the United

States or Canada for the summer. But during our last visit, we were astounded at the growth, with many new homes popping up alongside restored old adobes. Local people estimate that 300 people live here year-round and perhaps a thousand spend a good part of the year in Todos Santos. Despite the increased population, this is a quiet, laid-back place. During the siesta hour the streets are all but deserted.

Because of its proximity to the Pacific Ocean, Santo Tomas is considerably cooler than locations on the Sea of Cortez side of the peninsula; thus, it's more livable year-round. But curiously the town is not on the beach, but several kilometers inland. Miles of beautiful, yet deserted, beaches stretch south to Cabo San Lucas and north for hundreds of miles, with just a few homes and small hotels scattered sparsely along the way. One reason for residents ignoring beachfront properties could be the frequent warnings against swimming or even wading in the surf; riptides and undertow are common.

Driving in Baja

Baja roads are average for Mexico—which says a lot for Baja because until a few years ago, most roads were dirt trails liberally spotted with 2-foot-deep potholes filled with powder dust. Some of us maintain that it was better that way, but then, others probably didn't have four-wheel-drive vehicles or enjoy riding around with red bandanas over their face to cut the dust.

Shirley Miller, in her travel article, "Baja Alone" (from *Mexico West Newsletter*), describes her trip driving alone from California to the tip of Baja and back. She reports, "Well, all I can say is that a woman alone driving the Baja highway from Tijuana to Cabo San Lucas is safer than she would be driving into downtown Los Angeles. Nary a problem with gasoline, my trusty 1980 Chevy pickup, the roads, or anything else, for that matter." Her only caution is that one should bring plenty of cassette tapes, because reception on the car radio fades rapidly as you get farther away from civilization.

FOR THE MORE ADVENTUROUS

The vast majority of North Americans who choose retirement or long-term living in Mexico will join one of the well-established English-speaking colonies in places like Guadalajara, San Miguel de Allende, and Cuernavaca. This makes good sense; they know they'll find a welcoming community of expatriates and friendly neighbors to help them get settled in their new surroundings. They'll find excellent medical facilities with English-speaking doctors and nurses. Transition into a new culture is infinitely easier when you're surrounded by people who speak your language and who, themselves, have had to adapt.

However, not everybody requires the nurturing ambience of a large gringo society. Some might prefer to blend totally into the landscape of a Mexican village or a small town where English is a foreign language. These people are more interested in adventures than comforts. This is particularly true of some of those newly entering the age of retirement: the advance guard of the "baby boomer" generation who are already in their fifties and rapidly moving on.

With early retirement incentives and downsizing in today's business world, many younger folks are being cut loose into the world of leisure time and retirement, whether they like it or not. This new wave of retirees (voluntary and otherwise) were just becoming adults during the Vietnam War era, and they tend to view the world differently from those who matured in Korean War times or earlier. The new retirees were the "younger generation" of the 1960s. Before they settled down to becoming successful yuppies, these baby boomers (now graying at the temples) preferred roughing it when they traveled. They enjoyed backpacking and international travel on a shoestring. Rustic accommodations were just fine—part of the adventure. For many of them the luxury of Puerto Vallarta or the picture-book glamour of San Miguel de Allende could be a bit bourgeois and "older generation" for their taste.

For these adventurous souls—as well as any others too free spirited to march to the conventional drumbeat—we'll now take a look at some alternative living situations in Mexico. But before you start packing, you ought to think about how you will fit into some of these lifestyles.

Some places described here are small towns or villages with just a few expatriates in residence. In the larger towns and cities mentioned, only a handful of gringos make their homes. If you don't need a wide circle of friends and acquaintances, that's not a bad situation. It's fascinating how a tremendous level of camaraderie develops among gringos who reside in places where the English-speaking population is small. It doesn't take long before you know every expatriate in town, even those who live in the boondocks and only visit the village to shop occasionally. On the other hand, in a large city with many expatriates, you're always a stranger to those outside your immediate circle of friends.

An important item that younger retirees seldom consider is medical care. Typically one doesn't begin to worry about hospital quality and doctors until one's health begins to falter. Therefore, along with descriptions of these alternative retirement possibilities comes a recommendation to check out the health-care situation. (If you're in good health and consider yourself made of iron, you'll probably ignore this advice.) Small-town clinics can be *very* rustic, and village doctors are often newly graduated medical students fulfilling their required assignment of one year of public service. (They're stationed in the village because no regular doctor is willing to work there.)

Before deciding to live in a place where *nobody* speaks English, however, you need to examine your requirements for social interaction. Yes, living life in a totally Spanish-speaking environment sounds fascinating. But unless you speak the language, you may feel uncomfortable when you can't communicate with your neighbors beyond exchanging greetings or asking a storekeeper the price of an item. As mentioned earlier in the book, you don't "pick up" a language simply by being exposed to it. Sometimes it's essential to be near other English speakers, people to turn to in emergencies. Therefore, the places mentioned in this section have at least some English speakers, but whether they will have a critical mass large enough to suit you is left to your personal investigation. If you really want to immerse yourself in the culture, you can do that anywhere in Mexico; no law says you have to associate with gringos just because they are there.

Don't think that the places mentioned in this section are the only choices for off-the-beaten-path retirement. Mexico is full of options. The towns discussed in the following section are either the better-known ones or those we're personally acquainted with and enjoy visiting.

Guanajuato

Many people consider Guanajuato to be Mexico's most beautiful and romantic of the colonial cities. Certainly its architectural splendor, physical setting, and pervasively European look and feel place it in the running for that title. Its location, on the slopes of a canyon, makes for narrow streets and numerous stairways. Rather than having a single central plaza, or *zócalo*, like most Mexican towns, it has a number of small parks, each with its own special character. The main plaza is the scene of Sunday band concerts and is a place to socialize and meet other expatriates.

The University of Guanajuato, with a 250-year history and a modern campus, is considered one of Mexico's best. Inside and out, the Juarez Theater displays nineteenth-century opulence but annually plays host to the Cervantes Festival, which showcases the international cultural treasures of the twenty-first century.

For reasons we do not fully understand, Guanajuato, unlike nearby San Miguel de Allende, does not have many foreign retirees. The number has always been difficult to pin down. Perhaps one reason is that this community is often the choice of people who do not want to be surrounded by large numbers of their compatriots and who do not publicize their presence there. However, we do know that more than thirty U.S. and Canadian residents did meet recently to discuss their common interests. We believe that it is safe to assume that there are at least one-hundred North Americans settled in that community and that their numbers will grow, particularly if the number of foreigners in San Miguel continues to grow and people who want a more Mexican setting begin to look elsewhere.

Close to the Southwest Border

Several readers have asked about retirement places on the west coast that are closer to the border than Mazatlán. We wish we could locate an idyllic place for you, but it isn't all that easy. From the border south to Hermosillo, we've found few places where Americans might want to live. This is desert country without the desert attractions we expect in places like Palm Springs or Phoenix. Also many Mexican desert towns exist on a marginal economy and can have very rustic living conditions.

The closest nice-looking place in western Mexico is Hermosillo, about a three-and-a-half-hour drive south of Nogales. Modern, clean, and prosperous, Hermosillo is one of our favorite stopovers on our way south. The downtown is pleasant, with traditional parks and squares, and people seem friendly. The weather here is similar to Phoenix's, although probably with even less humidity. As you may surmise, summers are hot. Hermosillo's prosperity comes from agriculture; it's the center of a rich farming region. A number of gringos live here, most of them engaged in agriculture in some way or another.

Saltillo, a town not far from the Texas border, is another example of a modern city where you could try a traditional Mexican lifestyle. Because of the university and an active student population of gringos studying Spanish, there is a contingent of North Americans residing there, so you won't be totally on your own. Because the city sits at a high elevation, summers are delightful. The downtown section, with its many good restaurants, is clean and modern. You'll find any type of residential area you might care for, ranging from luxurious to moderate to modest.

Yelapa: A Tropical Paradise

Some people dream of living in a tropical village, where there are no automobiles or electricity and where pigs and chickens run loose in the streets. Those of you who've vacationed in Puerto Vallarta have probably taken the cruise boat to Yelapa, about an hour's sail from PV. The beach is a delightful medley of tropical sand, sun, and music, with a few tequila sunrises thrown in. Typically the visitor has lunch in one of the palm-thatched *palapa* restaurants, strolls the narrow streets of Yelapa's small village, and returns to Puerto Vallarta on the boat, with the band playing and margaritas flowing.

These visitors miss the "real" Yelapa, much to the delight of the "real" Yelapa residents. Yelapa is as different from modern, urban Puerto Vallarta as different can be. The village features dirt streets and tropically rustic homes. It's a place where electricity is a new innovation, and communication with the mainland is mostly via cell phones. Yelapa's semi-isolation is the delight of residents who know that a short boat ride away is "civilization" should they wish to go out for a night on the town or buy a new microwave.

Thea and Roger, who've lived there off and on since 1981, said, "There are probably a hundred of us gringos living here at any given time. Not so many that we don't recognize almost everyone as we do our shopping in the one grocery store." They also pointed out that the kinds of retirees living here permanently are truly unusual people: "Writers, artists, musicians, philosophers, we have 'em all."

However, it isn't all sweet music and tropical breezes. Several drawbacks prevent more people from moving to Yelapa. For one thing, you can't own the land your house is built on. This land is officially part of the Indian reservation, so title belongs to the tribe, the municipality, or to somebody other than the residents. Nobody is completely sure. So when gringos "buy" a house or build one, they're always aware of their tentative position.

Another drawback is the difficulty in getting back and forth to the mainland; the only way is by water. Until recently the only public transportation was by the tourist steamers, but today there are five "water taxis" that carry passengers for about $7.00 each way. Some residents resent this innovation, for that may mean even more visitors.

San Blas

For a tropical village (small town, actually) that's "unspoiled" and truly Mexican—yet not as unspoiled as Yelapa—you might consider San Blas. Reputedly a pirate hangout during the days of the Manila galleons, the town tries to maintain a "buccaneer" motif. Actually the town was founded as a naval base to *chase* pirates and as a place to outfit expeditions for the colonization of the west coast. Ships sailing out of San Blas established colonies as far north as Alaska. Yes, Alaska. The city of Valdez, Alaska, was named for the Spanish captain Valdez, who sailed out of San Blas to plant a royal colony there. Enough history.

As a tropical village San Blas is a jewel. It's a subdued place of a few thousand inhabitants, where often you'll see a mama pig herding her litter of piglets along the sandy streets. (Most streets are unpaved.) Many local people live in thatched-roof houses. Some buildings along the square date back to the time when the king's sailors used San Blas's main street for shore leave.

For some reason or other, this part of the coast always seems to be green and lush while the rest of the west suffers from lack of rainfall during the winter season. Even during the severe drought of 1988, this stretch of beach looked marvelously tropical and verdant.

Housing and food are as inexpensive in San Blas as anywhere in Mexico, according to the year-round, English-speaking residents we interviewed. One person, who was in the process of finding a place for the summer, told us that he had his choice of half a dozen houses for very low rents. (Costs vary widely depending upon the season.) Summers here are hot and exceptionally humid—the kind of weather that makes you understand the custom of an afternoon siesta. One serious drawback to year-round living in San Blas is the seasonal appearance of "no-see-ums," tiny, almost invisible gnats that delight on feeding on any victim not liberally doused with insect repellent. The town has never been able to battle the little critters successfully. For this reason you can have San Blas almost to yourself during the summers.

Matachén and Playa los Cocos are about a ten-minute drive from San Blas and are very rustic but picturesque villages. The view of the mountains and Matachén Bay are marvelous. Then, if you follow the road that skirts the ocean, you come to a village called Santa Cruz, which is also worth investigating. We've met several people who regularly haul fishing boats there and spend several months with the surf lapping at their beachfront site.

North of San Blas are a string of picturesque beach villages. The people here are friendly, and the villages are small. Most have a few American residents. A particularly inviting village is San Francisco, about an hour north of Puerto Vallarta. It is growing quickly, but prices of homes are still at bargain levels.

Boca de Tomatlán

Not very far south of Puerto Vallarta is one of west coast Mexico's prettiest rustic villages. Boca de Tomatlán is the picture of tropical paradise as it clings to the sloping canyon walls where the Tomatlán River empties into the Pacific. The mouth of the river has a shifting sandbar, which turns the river into a small lake at high tide. The steep walls of the canyon's mouth tame the surf by forming a small bay where boats can anchor and children can float on inner tubes. Add tropical vegetation, and you have an idyllic scene.

Despite Boca de Tomatlán's easy access, very few gringos make their homes there. As best we can tell, there are only two or three North American families who own property here, and they stay here only part time. A few years ago, before the movie actor and director John Huston died, you could occasionally see him sampling the delicious freshwater lobsters and quaffing a cold beer in one of Boca's tiny restaurants. Huston had a house on the beach just around the opening of the river. It could be reached only by boat.

In an earlier edition of *Choose Mexico*, we predicted that Boca de Tomatlán would be the next boom area for retirement, but we were mistaken. It's still on the list of possibilities, however.

Puerto Escondido

With the completion of a paved highway south from Acapulco, Mexico's southwestern corner, known as the Costa Chica, is now accessible. The highway passes through some fascinating places, many of which could make outstanding retirement spots for those who don't need English-speaking neighbors. In one area the inhabitants are descendants of black slaves who have lived in isolation here and have preserved some of their old customs from Africa. Another stretch of highway takes you through the only place in Mexico we know of where women still dress every day in pre-Columbian costume: beautifully woven skirts of cochineal-dyed material.

Back in the 1960s Puerto Escondido was "discovered" by the surfing and backpacking student set. Its beaches rank among the finest on Mexico's west coast, and it is known as one of the premier surfing spots in all of Mexico. People come here for the huge waves that come rolling in as high as a house, then curl over to form a tube in which surfers can defy death. The waves here give the term *high-rollers* a new meaning. If you're brave enough, you can body surf along the beach with the highest waves, but most people our age tend to go to the southern portion of the beach to catch gentler rollers.

We find Puerto Escondido to be one of the most beautiful and welcoming beach communities on Mexico's west coast. Thankfully the big developers and tourist promoters haven't discovered the place. Puerto Escondido has escaped the dramatic changes that over the past decade have altered the faces of less pretty beach areas.

The main street that follows the beach is lined with very pleasant and affordable small hotels and restaurants. While "PE" or "Puerto" (as residents call it) attracts its fair share of tourists, they rarely overcrowd the town. For a few months in winter, many longer-term visitors from the United States and Canada enjoy total relaxation in the sun. But for some reason Puerto keeps few year-round expatriate residents. According to locals, only about fifty North Americans live here more or less permanently—most of them work for or operate businesses. The majority of residents are semipermanent. Some migrate back and forth between Oaxaca and Puerto Escondido, as if they can't quite make up their minds. Because of the marvelous waves here, you'll usually find a contingent of aging surfers trying to recapture those glorious days of the 1960s. When you used to say: "Don't trust anyone over thirty," it must be tough to be approaching age sixty!

Surfers of all ages, backpackers, and conservative tourists all combine to lend a special air to PE. One woman I interviewed described Puerto Escondido as having a combination "Haight-Ashbury and Gilligan's Island" ambience.

Most construction in Escondido has been focused on tourism—hotels and time-share condos—so there aren't many apartments and houses for rent. However, just north of town several elegant subdivisions are being laid out near the Posada Real. The Zicatela Beach strip has developed, and a number of houses have been built along the main highway south of town. Again, most of these are for time-share, vacation, and second homes. Residents usually don't think of these areas as part of PE.

To sum up, Puerto Escondido could be a place to investigate for relocation in Mexico, particularly if you are into tropical beaches and monster waves. There are enough fellow North Americans to supply social needs, and developers haven't quite pushed prices out of reach or squelched the quality of life.

Puerto Angel and Huatulco

Puerto Angel is another place we predicted would become a hot spot for tourism and retirement. The area beaches are so beautiful and varied and the panorama is so gorgeous, we were convinced it couldn't miss.

We envisioned cruise ships docking here and spiffy condos and view homes going up on the steep hillsides that overlook one of the most gorgeous bays we've ever seen. Well, we were wrong again. Puerto Angel remains the charming, unsophisticated village it was fifteen years ago. There are still only a couple of main streets and remarkably few tourist businesses. Until recently the town didn't have a single curio shop—not even a place that sold postcards. There are some moderately priced hotels and some excellent restaurants specializing in the fresh fish and lobster that are brought in daily by local fishermen. But Puerto Angel is still a very quiet and restful place, with most beach activity taking place away from the village.

If you follow a dirt road a few miles west of Puerto Angel, you'll find the small village of Zipolite, with its mile-long beach of warm, white sand. A strip of tiny restaurants and bars compete for the tourist business, which isn't terribly crushing because of the beach's isolation. This is a ruler-straight beach that faces the open ocean, so riptides and currents make it rather dangerous for all but experienced swimmers. But the biggest attraction here, particularly for the younger set, is that Zipolite Beach is "clothing optional." Technically nude bathing is against the law, but local cops seldom enforce this law. Several beaches in this area enjoy the same laxness—something unusual in Mexico.

Huatulco, about 35 kilometers from Puerto Angel, is where we should have predicted a tourist boom. But at the time Huatulco was little more than a shabby village situated on a nice, sandy bay. When the Mexican government decided to construct a spiffy resort here, they went to work with a vengeance. Before long there was an airport, a Club Med, and four large hotels, including a Sheraton. All of this expansion happened rather rapidly. Then suddenly things slowed to a crawl. Apparently tourism wasn't keeping pace with the expansion of facilities.

The original idea was to make the resort into an "authentic Mexican village," but the large luxury hotels destroyed this possibility. Those who've visited Huatulco as tourists rave about how wonderful their stays were, but who knows how it will be for those wishing to live there for longer? There are several condos in place, presumably time-shares, but regular housing may be in short supply.

Taxco: The Forgotten Silver Queen

This colonial gem, nestled in the mountains just three-and-a-half hours southwest of Mexico City, has been the favorite of John Howells since he was a teenager. In those days, when the family lived in Mexico City, they spent one or two weekends a month in Taxco. Although it's grown from a small town to a city, the main part of town hasn't changed a bit; it still looks like 1948.

Taxco is another must-visit place—a scenic delight of genuine colonial architecture (few modern reproductions here), with narrow, cobblestoned streets rising sharply toward the main plaza. If Walt Disney had wanted to design a sixteenth-century mining town, it probably would have looked just like Taxco.

Like San Miguel de Allende, Taxco owes much of its current fame and popularity with foreigners to an American. In this case it was William Spratling, an Alabama-born architect and college professor. He came for a visit in 1929, fell in love with the place, and decided to stay. In 1931 he started the process of resurrecting Taxco's long-dormant silver industry. Today his efforts can be seen in the town's highly successful silver commerce.

Back in the eighteenth century, Taxco's wealth was based on the silver mines that had been worked since the time of Cortez. Today, the economy is based on silver far more than on tourism; the town has about 200 shops, mostly family operated, where silver is handcrafted into jewelry and flatware. Many of today's best silversmiths are the grandchildren of Spratling's apprentices.

Why hasn't Taxco become a popular retirement center? Perhaps it is a consequence of progress. At one time the only practical way to get from Mexico City to Acapulco was by highway, and you had to pass through Taxco. The drive used to take twelve hours, so Taxco was the logical stopover place between Mexico City and Acapulco. Many visitors were so fascinated by the town that they couldn't resist joining the artists already in residence and making Taxco their home. Before long several hundred expatriates owned or rented homes here, and a thousand or more stayed for lesser periods of time.

Taxco was on its way to becoming as popular with retirees as San Miguel de Allende. Then progress came in the form of a high-speed toll road, which bypassed the town and drastically cut the number of tourists who are exposed to Taxco. Now most people drive or fly directly between Acapulco and Mexico City. Consequently those who might have considered retirement in Taxco don't get the chance to look it over. Most tourists today are Mexican, European, and Japanese. Just one factor that could account for Taxco's comparatively scanty retired population: Its steep streets might intimidate older, less vigorous retirees and send them toward more level colonial towns. But with people taking retirement at much earlier ages today, we might expect to see additions to the numbers of retirees, both in town and on small ranches that sit in tropical splendor toward the base of the mountains.

Xalapa

As a place for gringos to congregate, Xalapa may be Mexico's best-kept secret. This would appear to be true if you count the small number of expatriates who have "discovered" the town and who have decided to live here. Some estimate that about 200 English-speaking foreigners live here, augmented by 150 or so Americans who study at the University of Veracruz. The university and its student population have a strong cultural influence on Xalapa, with art galleries, the Ballet Folklórico, outstanding anthropology and science museums, and the first-rate Xalapa Symphony Orchestra. The town proudly bills itself as the "Athens of Veracruz."

Xalapa is a beautiful city nestled on the side of a steep hillside and surrounded by lush coffee plantations, banana groves, flower gardens, and tall pine trees. The town is encircled by the black volcanic peaks of the Sierra Madre Oriental in the distance and enhanced by breathtaking views of Mexico's tallest mountain, the snow-covered Pico de Orizaba. The surrounding region is sprinkled with a number of interesting small towns, many of them great places to retire if you like to be near a larger city but enjoy the intimacy of a village. Tourists haven't discovered Xalapa either; they naively bypass the region by speeding along the superhighway directly to Veracruz or on their way to the Yucatán. Tourists don't know what they are missing, although the English-speaking residents here don't seem to miss the tourists.

When considering Xalapa as a place to live, expect higher-than-average rainfall and a greener-than-average landscape. In the winter a light but persistent winter rain known as the *chipichipi* nurtures the plant life, and in the summer, frequent evening mists create a natural greenhouse environment. Plush with bougainvillea, gardenias, roses, and flowers of all descriptions, Xalapa deserves its reputation as the "Flower Garden of Mexico."

Although a bustling city of more than 300,000, as well as the capital of the state of Veracruz, Xalapa doesn't seem that large at all. It artfully manages to combine its role as a modern commercial center for coffee and fruit growers with the charm of its antique colonial heritage. The old downtown section preserves its cobblestone streets, neoclassical architecture—with antique doorways and wrought-iron balconies—and buildings painted in bright pastels and primary colors. In addition to good downtown shopping, there's a brand-new Costco store just outside of downtown, in the Las Animas area. You'll even find gyms and fitness/aerobic centers, good Internet services, and just about anything else you might need to ease into retirement here.

The name *Xalapa* comes from the Aztec (Nahuatl) language and means "water springs in the sand." Don't be puzzled if you see Xalapa (pronounced ha-LA-pa) spelled "Jalapa" on your road map or travel guide. In archaic Spanish the x and the j sounds were practically identical and used interchangeably. *Mexico* was often spelled *Mejico,* and *Xalapa* was spelled *Jalapa.* (*Xalapa* was the original form, and locals want to return to that spelling.) By the way, those hot chile peppers we know as jalapeños are so named because they originated here.

Those hot peppers contrast with Xalapa's pleasant, cool climate. Perched at an altitude of approximately 4,500 feet, Xalapa enjoys year-round spring weather. The town has been a traditional weekend haven for residents of the hot and steamy port city of Veracruz, only a couple of hours' drive from this cool mountain setting. Had Xalapa been closer to Mexico City, it would surely have rivaled Cuernavaca as a place for weekend homes and tourism. The climate and ambience are similar, except that Cuernavaca gets much less rain. This writer recalls several pleasant visits to the region when he was a youngster and his sister's fiancé lived in Jalapa (would that make him a jalapeño?). We loved it then, and during our last visit a few years ago we were relieved to find that population growth hadn't diminished the city's charm.

Alan Cogan, who lives in the Lake Chapala region, agrees with my assessment. He had this comment about a recent trip to Xalapa: "Of the six cities my wife and I visited—Morelia, Cholula, Puebla, Xalapa, Veracruz, and Queretaro—Xalapa is, for us, the hands-down winner. If we were ever to leave our lakeside home for another destination in Mexico, that's where it would be."

An investigation of Xalapa isn't complete without a visit with Roy Dudley, a thirty-year resident of the "city of flowers." Roy, a professional photographer, is also Xalapa's biggest booster. He came to Xalapa three decades ago to finish his bachelor's degree in Spanish at the Universidad Veracruzana and has lived here ever since. Roy loves to point out the advantages of living here and offers tours and retirement seminars in addition to operating his photography studio. He lives in the center of downtown with his wife and children and says, "We rarely use our car since taxis only cost around a dollar! Why hassle finding a parking place when a taxi will drop you off right where you want to go? And for 'walkaholics,' like me, who love to explore new sights and sounds on foot, Xalapa is wonderful, with narrow and often steep streets. Xalapa is the place to make lasting friends where you can meet for a delicious cup of *capuchino* or *Americano* at the myriad cafes and restaurants this city has to offer." If you are considering moving to Xalapa, be sure to contact Roy about his retirement seminar, which includes a tour of the region's cultural and scenic marvels. E-mail him at roydudley@xalapa.net or visit his Web site at www.xalapa.net/roy.htm.

Baja California Off-the-Beaten-Path

Driving the highway south of Ensenada, below the *zona libre*, treats you to some spectacular desert landscapes. Occasionally, but not often, you'll encounter a North American or two living in one of the small villages along the highway. Two of the most striking towns, San Ignacio and Mulegé (two of the prettiest places in Baja), have a few North Americans living there, and we suspect these places will become more popular with gringos in the near future.

San Ignacio was founded in the seventeenth century by Jesuit missionaries who discovered that the high water table around San Ignacio naturally irrigated the soil. Even before the church and mission were completed, groves of oranges and lemons, grapevines, and date palms were thrusting roots into the damp soil. The Jesuits were expelled from Baja more than two centuries ago, but dates, citrus, and grapes survived fabulously. Today they grow like weeds, sometimes like a jungle. Not only here, but farther south in Mulegé as well, the trees and vines grow lushly. You will understand the meaning of *oasis* if you ever visit these two towns.

Before the paved highway, Mulegé was a favorite destination for off-road adventurers. They looked forward to the shade of tall date palms, tropical flowers in profusion, and the cool waters of one of Baja's few real rivers. An old town—dating from the 1600s, with buildings that defy centuries of weathering—Mulegé was in itself fascinating. But even more interesting was the fact that before the new highway, it was a penal colony. On a hill overlooking the town sits a large pastel-colored building: the territorial prison. Convicts who were judged to be nonviolent and who could be trusted to be part of society (yet legally couldn't) were exiled to places like Mulegé to serve out their sentences. This was not only a very humane practice but wonderfully practical. Instead of placing a prisoner into a cage with the taxpayers spending $40,000 a year to keep him there (U.S. style), Mexico sent nondangerous prisoners into "exile." (They may still do this—I'm not sure.) The convict's family then joined him, and together they somehow managed to earn a living. (Remember Mexican taxpayers are very much against pampering convicts by paying room and board for them.) The family either found jobs or started a business, much the same as if they were still on the mainland. The children went to school, the parents worked, and the family lived normal lives as responsible members of the community. The prison on the hill was reserved for someone who occasionally misbehaved, perhaps appearing intoxicated in public or quarreling with neighbors. If a convict misbehaved too often, he was shipped back to the mainland and tossed into a regular prison. As you can imagine, few people ever misbehaved. If you were looking for a crime-free environment, you couldn't have found any safer place than Mulegé!

However, in the interests of tourism, the government closed the "prison" (which rarely held prisoners in the first place). Today the children and grandchildren of convicts might be the owners of the stores or restaurants in town. These days serious crime is almost nonexistent; Mulegé is no different from almost any small town in Mexico.

A river—slow-moving and tropical, fringed with bamboo, tall trees, and massive date palms—runs through town and down to the gulf. A half-dozen trailer parks face the river. These parks are very popular with winter retirees. Although we're getting farther south, where cooler currents from the Pacific Ocean temper the warm Gulf water, the summers here are still not particularly livable. Even so, some people talk of plans for a 300-unit condo and a marina on the river.

Just south of town is a development called Villas de Mulegé. Houses there can be built to your specifications. Without electricity, this development features solar energy. Because approximately 98 percent of Mulegé days are sunny, this doesn't seem to be such a bad idea. Our guess is that before long, the town is in line for development.

Loreto

The desert-by-the-sea town of Loreto is the oldest permanent Spanish settlement in Baja. It was founded in 1697 when the missionary Juan Maria Salvatierra and his band of loyal followers established a mission and a fishing village. The location on a bay of the Sea of Cortez was selected because it was protected by the Isla del Carmen that sits offshore. About seventy years later, in 1769, Father Junípero Serra set forth from Loreto on his famous undertaking to establish a chain of seventeen Jesuit missions—stretching as far north as San Francisco, California.

For years Loreto languished as a sleepy village, hosting infrequent gringo tourists who flew there in private or chartered planes for a few days of fishing adventures. Then when the paved highway made its way south from the border, making automobile travel practical, Loreto's future began to look better. It looks even better today, with direct air service from Los Angeles to the new airport at nearby Nopolo Cove making it relatively easy to get here. The town is in the early stages of a potentially big tourist development, encouraged and sponsored by the Mexican government's tourism ministry. Other ambitious facilities are under way here, particularly at Puerto Escondido (not to be confused with the mainland's west coast town of the same name), 16 kilometers to the south. The big attraction here, of course, is still fishing, but lately more and more people are considering full- or part-time retirement in Loreto. With more and more North Americans coming every day, this area is growing from a sleepy fishing resort into a bustling complex. An eighteen-hole golf course and eight professional tennis courts are some recent additions to the recreation scene. Some local boosters believe that when all of the projected facilities in the area are completed—including a European-style village somewhat like Manzanillo's Las Hadas, with red-tiled roofs and sparkling white walls—Loreto will be as popular as anywhere on the mainland. A new Cancún, they say.

A new Cancún? Maybe; maybe not. Again, the problem with all of the Sea of Cortez side of Baja California Sur is the fierce summer heat. As soon as the temperatures begin climbing in May, the gringos begin packing, not to return until October or November. Another problem is the water supply; some say it isn't adequate to support a large population. So Loreto will not likely become a new Cancún but will remain Loreto. There's nothing wrong with that.

Bahía de Palmas

On your way south, about halfway between La Paz and Cabo San Lucas, is an interesting, fast-growing North American colony, spread along the Bahía de Palmas. This colony is on the Sea of Cortez side of the peninsula (although it's just about open ocean at this point), so the weather is more civilized. Some fancy homes, as well as some ordinary places and RV lots, have been built next to the beaches. Homes aren't cheap around here, with a few selling for prices as high as $200,000. Nothing is crowded, and if you're looking for isolated beaches, beautiful ocean water, and quiet, then you've found it.

Los Barriles and Buena Vista are the larger communities along the bay. But neither is really large enough to be called even a village. From here on southward runs a dirt and gravel road that follows the coast (and some really spectacular scenery) all the way to San José del Cabo. Very,

very few people live here, but you'll find RVs and gringo houses scattered along the way, taking advantage of the view.

Because of the way the wind blows across the bay, this area is reputed to have the best windsurfing anywhere. It seems that high-velocity thermal winds swoop down from the high inland mountains, sending winds of 20 to 25 knots to really speed the windsurfers along! (Better know what you're doing, though.) Several really nice hotels in the area cater to the windsurfers as well as tourists who want someplace different to visit.

Just south of here is a place called Santiago, one of the most interesting towns in Baja Sur. It sits in a broad canyon that is continuously watered by volcanic springs and not affected by drought and low rainfall. The result is a lush oasis of trees, tropical plants, and flowers. Some of the streets are lined with flowering trees with brilliant red blossoms that look almost surrealistic. The Palomar Hotel there has one of the best chefs in Baja, and it's worth a detour just to taste one of his soups. But according to local people, not one North American resident has ever chosen to live here. We don't understand this.

The Yucatán

The Yucatán is historically, geographically, and culturally separate from the rest of Mexico. In fact the Yucatecans do not think of themselves as Mexican. The region enjoys a distinct Caribbean flavor tempered by an ancient Maya culture. People here speak Spanish with a distinct accent, and many natives speak a Mayan dialect exclusively. Their homeland, closer to Miami than to Mexico City (only an hour and forty minutes by air), has become familiar to great numbers of North Americans who are drawn by the peninsula's resorts and ruins. Because the Yucatán is easily accessible from the east coast of the United States and Canada, it is one of the most popular travel destinations in Mexico. Some visitors, particularly those who get to know the inhabitants, decide to make the Yucatán their retirement home.

The huge peninsula juts far to the north, bounded by the Gulf of Mexico on the west and by the Caribbean on the east coast. The interior features tropical jungles and colonial cities, mysterious archeological sites, rustic villages, and modern cities. Nowhere else will you find such an exotic blend of elements. Parts of the Yucatán catch extremely heavy rainfall, whereas other areas are exceptionally dry. It's a land of perpetual summer, with temperatures in the high eighties and low nineties the year-round.

Weather in the Yucatán

| | In degrees Fahrenheit | | | |
	Jan.	April	July	Oct.
DAILY HIGHS	82	92	91	86
DAILY LOWS	64	70	73	67

Although the Gulf of Mexico coast of the Yucatán is somewhat boring, the Caribbean coast from Cancún south has some of the most delightful beaches in the world. Long stretches of sand and coral are fringed by low jungles and an occasional coconut plantation or vegetable farm. Numerous peaceful bays are perfect for snorkeling, diving, and boating, with an abundance of coral reefs easily enjoyed, even by novices. Overuse and development have threatened some coral reefs, but many towns, like Puerto Morelos and Akumal, are taking vigorous steps to correct the problem of water consumption and sewage treatment.

Although much of the beachfront land is tantalizing as a site for that dream home, be warned against potential legal pitfalls. Often people who "own" this land don't realize that they are living on their property only because "possession" is that well-known percentage of the law. When they try to sell, they discover that their family land belongs to someone else. When they move, the legal owners will swoop in and take possession. Don't let this discourage you, however: Property is always available, but do find a reliable lawyer. Away from the beaches land ownership is more available and more reliable but, alas, less desirable.

Mérida

Mérida is a most unusual Mexican city. Residents call Mérida the "Paris of the West" because of its charming, tree-lined boulevards, lovely colonial mansions, and spectacular estates of the henequen barons of the 1800s. Mérida is widely known as the "White City," partly because its buildings are mostly of limestone construction, but also because of its

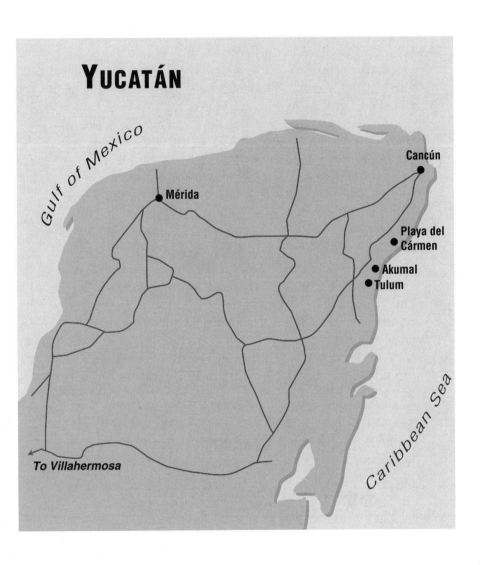

cleanliness. Streets, plazas, and parks are cleaned twice daily. Residents also claim that Mérida has the lowest crime rate per capita in Mexico.

Over the years the city has managed to maintain much of its colonial charm, and if it weren't for unmuffled motorcycles and trucks, it could be described as a sleepy paradise. One problem here is the summer weather. Located 33 kilometers from the Gulf of Mexico, without tempering Caribbean breezes to help cool things off, Mérida can get hot during the summer. Fortunately it doesn't have oppressive humidity, and temperatures rarely rise above the low nineties.

Yet the North Americans who live here love it. After the publication of an earlier edition of *Choose Mexico*, we received an enthusiastic letter from a college administrator from Texas who had just bought a new, three-bedroom, two-and-a-half-bath, two-floor townhouse in Mérida. The purchase price (complete with full-time security) was $23,000, but it cost another $6,400 to add a carport, balcony, patio, water heater, stove, refrigerator, ceiling fans, cabinets, and shelving. Furnishing the house—kitchen, bedrooms, living room, and dining room—with custom-made furniture and original art brought the total close to $34,000. Our correspondent can't say enough about how delighted he is to live in the Yucatán with all its human and ecological riches. He does say, however, that there are few North Americans in his neighborhood and he is not unhappy about it.

If you do not need the companionship of other North Americans and want to experience one of Mexico's most attractive areas, you might consider Mérida.

Cancún

While Acapulco was enjoying the title of "Jet-set Capital of the Americas," Cancún could barely claim the title of a backwater village. Dirt trails connected Cancún to the rest of the world, and airplanes larger than a two-motor DC-3 were unknown hereabouts. Then when the Mexico Ministry of Tourism decided to shift the tourist emphasis away from Acapulco to places like Puerto Vallarta and Mazatlán, developers began looking at Cancún. By an astounding coincidence some high-ranking politicians, including the president of Mexico, just happened to own many acres of land along the beach, so the decision to turn the location into Mexico's most popular tourist destination wasn't a difficult one to make. Of course the year-round summer weather, the amazingly blue waters, and the soft-sand beaches fringed with coconut palms helped the decision too.

Today Cancún is one of the hemisphere's most popular beach resorts. Some three million tourists visit anually. Luxury hotels and condo developments line the beach. Prices in the tourist areas bear a much closer resemblance to those elsewhere in the Caribbean than to those in most of Mexico. Condos are being marketed aggressively, but before you sign up for one—in Cancún, Acapulco, Lake Tahoe, or any resort town—figure out what your weekly and daily costs will be. A popular ploy is to sell condos on a two- or three-week time-share basis. This is for tourists, not for anyone who seriously wants to live in Mexico.

If you choose to live in Cancún, look at one of the many small houses being built in or near the downtown area. They are far less expensive than the beachfront hotel area and look very comfortable. Other nice residential areas are found in the small towns surrounding Cancún.

Puerto Morelos is one example of a place near enough to Cancún to enjoy all the tourist benefits, yet far enough away to feel like you are living in Mexico and not Miami. Located just twenty minutes south of Cancún on the Maya Riviera, Puerto Morelos is a haven of peace and solitude, an authentic fishing village on the Caribbean coast. An American retired couple owns Cabanas Puerto Morelos—the village's only room accommodations, which consist of three one-bedroom, one-bath units with kitchenettes. They describe the village this way: "The road into town leads directly to the *zócalo,* a gathering place at day's end. Children's games, gossip, and music are daily events in this tree-shaded town park, and impromptu guitar music frequently fills the air. Brightly painted cement benches and lovers' chairs that face one another are spread throughout the square. Several intimate restaurants, markets, a pharmacy, and gift shops surround the *zócalo.*"

Local people are convinced that Puerto Morelos will retain its small village atmosphere and avoid the overdevelopment taking place along the coast. They point out that the government has declared the reef area and the mangroves behind the village to be ecological preserves. This means that development will be very limited.

The Yucatán's East Coast

A booming area for retirement is the east coast of the peninsula, from Cancún down to Tulúm. A great four-lane highway leads south, passing through or near a dozen beach towns, each with a small population of North American expatriates happily living there. Some call this region the "Mayan Riviera" but local residents object to this description, partly because it clearly lacks the sophistication of a true riviera, and partly because they hope it will always stay that way. Pristine beaches, quiet jungles, and clean air are why they live here, and they shudder every time a multinational company buys another beach to erect a mega-resort.

Along the length of the highway, numerous side roads—often 2 or 3 kilometers long—lead to beach communities too small to be called villages. The largest town here is Playa del Carmen, where condominium and home building is booming. It sits about 75 kilometers south of Cancún. From there the island of Cozumel is just a short trip by auto ferry. Both places are attracting Americans and Canadians for retirement living. Playa del Carmen is *the* place for heavy-duty shopping, with a supermarket the size of a large Safeway and a wide selection of goods. Three banks serve the town, each with a *cajero automatico* (automatic teller machine).

Akumal, about 110 kilometers south of Cancún, is undergoing an extraordinary wave of development, partly as a result of incoming gringos. Building is said to be "going wild." New developments are spawning from the Akumal boom, with Akumal Sur and Aventuras Akumal under way. Nearby Puerto Aventuras is a planned community with a marina, great shopping, and a bilingual school. The bay is particularly lovely for swimming.

Besides the great weather, one of the attractions of the Akumal area is exotic snorkeling lagoons with underwater caves and spectacular varieties of small and large fish. Local retirees become involved with volunteer efforts to preserve these miraculous *lagunas*. They work with the Centro Ecologico Akumal to help preserve the pristine water quality and to educate tourists to help them have an ecologically aware vacation in the Yucatán.

Business Opportunities

Until recently going into business in Mexico was all but out of the question for most people. The government erected so many barriers that we used to claim that the easiest way to go into business was to marry a Mexican. One of the regulations: Unless you qualified as a long-term *inmigrado* or had a spouse who was a citizen, you needed a Mexican partner who would own 51 percent of your business. Then along came the North American Free Trade Agreement (NAFTA), and things began to change.

NAFTA affects expatriates living in Mexico in two ways. First of all, prices of most imported goods are dramatically lower; you can now afford to purchase the brands you did back home. Second, it's much easier to go into business in Mexico. Beginning in 1994 as an implementation of NAFTA, Mexico's Foreign Investment Law (FIL) abolished most restrictions on foreign investment. Today foreign investors are permitted to own 100 percent of any Mexican business, corporation, or partnership, except for a few restricted enterprises.

Aside from the obstacle course you expect when dealing with government bureaucracy, going into business in Mexico is a lot easier today. Many restrictions have been lifted, but it's still not totally wide open. Don't confuse *investment* in a business and *working* in your business. Technically you still need FM-2 status to actually work in your own business, although many small-business people find ways around this restriction. Besides, with labor so inexpensive, why work? Just manage.

Mexico no longer requires citizenship or permanent residency for professionals (dentists, doctors, engineers, etc.), either. The catch here is that right now Mexico isn't required to recognize foreign professional licenses. To open a practice, however, you'll probably need a license. Under NAFTA, the government is committed to providing a procedure under which foreigners may obtain validation of their credentials. Check with your professional colleagues for details.

We interviewed a number of expatriates who've gone into business in Mexico, and we asked for their insights and advice about entering the Mexican world of business. The one theme everyone mentioned was the importance of developing a personal relationship with associates, clients, and customers. As one businessman in Ajijic pointed out, "If you're not willing to take time to engage in some pleasantries before starting your business meetings, you can be sure it will cost you." You see, Mexicans believe in pleasure *before* business. Exchanging pleasantries, talking about their families, and maybe commenting on the weather are considered polite before jumping into the reason for the meeting. Keep your meetings easygoing and relaxed, and if the meeting is at your office or home, be a gracious host.

Like most Latin Americans Mexicans are uncomfortable with direct confrontation, so when dealing with Mexican associates or employees, it's important not to pull rank, raise your voice, or use sarcastic comments. To them dignity and the appearance of integrity are most important. In this vein a Mexican businessperson will try to avoid giving you a direct no and thus avoid risking your displeasure or appearing to be rude. Pinning someone down to a final agreement usually involves a number of smaller agreements. However, even when your Mexican partner or client isn't in agreement, he or she might avoid saying "no" by saying "maybe" or offering some other vague reply. This is called *dar largas*, "beating around the bush," and is why getting your final agreement in writing is important. You need to recognize the difference between a "polite yes" and a "genuine yes."

To successfully function in a different culture requires patience and insight into the system. You cannot assume that everything works the same way in Mexico as it does in Canada or the United States. For one thing, you must be prepared for a great deal more government interference in your business. One bit of advice given by expatriate entrepreneurs: "Before you get too deep into the business, be sure you have a good lawyer and accountant." One woman told us that she was informed that her workers needed to belong to a union. When she explained that there was no union available for the type of work her employees were doing, she was urged to "start one for them."

South of the border the employer-employee relationship is often on a more personal level. To Mexicans North American management can seem rude, uncaring, and demeaning. Workers here hate to be considered just another payroll number, ready to be sacrificed at any moment. Latin American concepts of time also create tension in business and employee relations. In Mexico time is something relative. When your supplier promises a delivery *mañana*, he doesn't necessarily mean tomorrow. *Mañana* translates as "sometime in the near future." Time is not the sacred, all-important mechanism we North Americans consider it to be. In our value system being late for an appointment is considered insulting; being late for work is a good reason for discharging an employee. In Mexico being late for an appointment is almost anticipated, and the more important a person is, the more tardy he or she can be expected to be. (Why this is so is something that's always eluded us.) Mostly your employees will try to be punctual, but if something interferes with getting to work on time, they don't see this as any big deal.

The time-proven key to success for those entering business in Mexico: Do something that you already know something about. Martin Parker, for example, retired to Ajijic not planning on going back to work. Because of his background in insurance, however, he received an offer from Sanborn's Mexico Insurance Service Co. to become a local agent. Because his wife already had her FM-2 papers, they decided to take on the job and became the first North Americans in Mexico to be licensed as insurance agents. "If you're a thinking person," Martin says, "and you find your niche, you can make it in business here." He outlined several stories of fellow expatriates who achieved success in Mexican real estate.

One example is Judy King, who sells real estate in the Guadalajara area. She is one of the partners who make up Re/Max Fenix. She says, "When I first came to Mexico, moving here was the farthest thing from my mind. I was on a vacation, pure and simple. But, on the third day, even in the center of Guadalajara, I suddenly felt like I had come home, even not speaking Spanish. From that moment on, it was like I was just watching my life go by, as opportunities fell from the sky into my lap."

She first took a position in a small local real estate company (there were no franchise companies in those days). Eventually she switched to larger offices and finally, with several associates, received her own franchise—Re/Max Fenix. "This area of Mexico is the only one that has a local real estate board that requires training and testing to work in the system," Judy says. "That's important, because I personally feel that selling real estate in Mexico involves a lot more than showing houses. More like an Adult Ed course, teaching newcomers the how-to's and where-to's of living in a foreign country."

When asked to compare business conditions here with the United States, Judy replied, "Businesspeople here are different from those back home. The book *Distant Neighbors* sums it up by saying: 'The Mexican reveres yesterday, lives for today and believes tomorrow will take care of itself.' This attitude is seen so clearly in business. I believe this attitude leads to a lack of interest in the concept of cause and effect. The best example I know happened a few years ago when very few American products were available in grocery stores. One morning a case of snack crackers arrived. The first four delighted shoppers each purchased three boxes, eliminating the supply. When the manager was asked when he would have more, he snorted and said, 'There won't be any more, they're too hard to keep in stock!'"

Judy King reiterated the oft-given advice about knowing what you are doing before considering going into business. She says, "So often I meet newcomers who act as if they're in one of those old Mickey Rooney movies. They exclaim, '*Hey, I know...we can start a business! We'll export pots to the U.S.! It will be really fun, just like shopping, and we will make a lot of money!*' These poor folks have no idea what they are getting into!" (Judy's e-mail is: judyking@laguna.com.mx.)

When David and Dona McLaughlin of Saskatchewan, Canada, were researching their move to Mexico, they found scanty resources on the Internet to answer questions about living, working, or starting a business in Mexico. Few travel books provided the answers either. David says, "Using the Internet for research made us realize its potential to assist others who were seeking the same answers. So, when we moved to Mexico in 1995 from Canada, our idea came along on a 3.5-inch floppy disc." A popular free monthly electronic magazine, *Mexico Connect* became Mexico's first on-line magazine.

The endeavor was a success from its inception. Today it is much more than a forum for retirees and travelers; *Mexico Connect* is a virtual treasure trove of information about Mexico, an encyclopedic resource of more than 10,000 articles, documents, and photographs. You'll find everything from history and current events to Mexican cooking and travel hints. Art and culture, political commentary, and up-to-date legal advice are offered in addition to the invaluable bulletin boards where topics about living and travel in Mexico are discussed in great detail. (You can check it out at www.mexconnect.com.)

More than twenty-five years ago, as a college student backpacking the country, Stan Gotlieb fell in love with Oaxaca. When he decided he'd had enough of the rat race and the weather in Minnesota, it seemed only natural to settle in Oaxaca. After getting an unexpected payment for letters he had sent a friend who publishes a newspaper, he began writing in a serious way as a method of supporting himself. Another friend suggested he start publishing his monthly *Letters from Mexico* on the World Wide Web, launching him on a career as a "man on the scene" in Oaxaca. Later he introduced an e-mail-only subscription newsletter, providing twenty issues a year for a $25 subscription fee. To supplement his writing income, he gives twice-weekly newcomer seminars to orient folks on the ins and outs of living in Oaxaca. He says, "I don't live in Mexico to work; I work in Mexico in order to live here." (For a sample copy of his newsletter, and all of the *Letters from Mexico* so far, visit Stan's Web site at www.realoaxaca.com.)

Another success story is Dennis Setera, a computer repairman who found a niche that needed filling and employed his special skills to start a business. During a trade mission visit to Guadalajara, Dennis realized that computer technology in Mexico lagged far behind the latest developments in the United States. Businesses here use a lot of outdated but perfectly usable equipment that is constantly in need of maintenance and repair to keep it functioning. He imported some inexpensive, last-generation equipment for repairing hard disks and other computer hardware and went into business. With virtually no competition, Dennis finds business booming. He reports his biggest difficulty is negotiating with Mexican businesspeople. "They act as though they hate to make a decision," he says. "And just when you think the deal is off, they suddenly stop stalling and want to close the deal immediately."

Many people dream about a small hotel or a bed-and-breakfast as their retirement business project. This is a business for which experience isn't absolutely necessary; the important ingredients are capital and elbow grease. Ernie Gorrie and his wife, Glenna Jones, found their opportunity in Troncones, a small beach village near Ixtapa. Starting very small, the building was designed to be expanded to fit future demand. It is now a flourishing bed-and-breakfast.

How do they find guests from all over the United States and Canada to vacation at their House of Tropical Dreams? At first it was tough. Once they tried distributing 4,000 brochures at a travel show, with no results. Then they hit on the idea of Internet. Ernie says, "About 90 percent of our guests learned about us from our Web page. We get about one hundred inquiries a week from our Web page (at www.mexonline.com/dreams.htm). Of course, they don't all make reservations, but at least our presence is known. Once we get another couple of years behind us and expand our base of happy vacationers, we'll be OK."

A prevalent practice in Mexico, when dealing with officials, is the *mordida,* or bribe. If you want something done in a hurry, a handout often does the trick. However, one businessman we interviewed said this: "Do it right the first time or it may come back to haunt you. We made sure that our contractor had all of the permits paperwork done for construction. We paid the insurance and social security fees for the workers. Some others built without it. But five years from now, some inspector could demand to see the paperwork. If you don't have it, you could pay not only the fees, but fines and interest (currently at about 40 percent in Mexico) as well. I'd rather pay a bit more at the beginning and know that I'm legal."

Pam Pastore, a Yankee from Connecticut, fell in love with the Baja California community of San Felipe. Too young to "retire," she decided to look for some kind of business opportunity. She took a survey of what local residents felt was lacking. Pam reports, "One of the many answers I got over and over was the need for a good housecleaning service. I thought, I can surely do that." It turns out that she had started Maid Marion, a housecleaning service in Connecticut, some twenty years ago, and she understood the concept of working in teams for maximum efficiency.

The vast majority of foreign residents live in San Felipe part-time, and many do not want full-time help they have to lay off at the end of the season. Also many people do not want to have a housemaid hanging around all day; they would prefer to have a team come in once or twice a week, spend an hour or two blitzing the place, and be done with it. "I immediately went to work getting my corporation started, my accountant set up, and my working FM-3. I trained a team of girls and we began to work. After only six months, Maid Marion employees are working three days a week for weekly maintenance clients and two days for big cleans such as new construction, and we're very busy with closing or opening cleans for private residences. By the way, I do not speak Spanish very well, but we manage fine." For more information you can reach Pam at the Maid Marion office, 700 Calzado Chetumal, San Felipe, Baja California, Mexico. Phone from the States is 011–526–577–1338. The local San Felipe number is 577–1338. You can also reach Pam by e-mail at bajanana@canela.sanfelipe.com.mx.

MEXICO ON THE INTERNET

The experience of living in Mexico has been radically changed by a revolution that started about a decade ago and is continuing today—we are referring, of course, to the digital revolution. As profoundly as the computer, e-mail, and the World Wide Web have affected the lives of Americans living in the United States, its impact is even greater on those living in Mexico.

The Mexican postal system is slow and inefficient. A letter to or from the United States is likely to take a week or two to arrive. This means an average wait of about twenty days to get an answer to a letter mailed home. Long-distance calls to or from locations outside of Mexico are outrageously expensive. Most people reserve them for special occasions or urgent business only.

Today, however, it is possible to keep in touch with loved ones on a daily—or even hourly—basis at minimal expense. You don't even need to own a computer. Internet cafes are everywhere, and the fees can be as low as $2.00 an hour. If all you need to do is check your e-mail and write some brief replies, fifteen minutes will often do it, and it will cost you a mere half buck. Most retirees in Mexico, however, find it more convenient to use their own computers and pay a small monthly fee for an Internet connection so they can communicate from home. A laptop is just fine for this purpose and can be brought into Mexico without a customs charge. Duty on a desktop computer will be charged at its depreciated value—not very much, if you have an older one.

But e-mail is far from the only use of the Internet. Up-to-the-minute news, stock prices, and weather reports are also available. You can pay bills, transfer money between your bank accounts, buy or sell just about everything imaginable, and make investments, all without leaving your Mexican retirement home.

The Internet is also useful for learning more about the country before you go there. Mexico Connect (www.mexconnect.com) has numerous features, links to other useful sites, and bulletin boards where current and prospective residents trade questions and answers, tips, and observations. Many popular communities are represented by Web sites with color photographs, real estate listings, detailed information about facilities, and other useful facts too numerous to describe. We have found it invaluable in our research for this edition of *Choose Mexico*.

If you aren't computer literate, it's time to learn. Adult education courses on using the Internet, some of them specifically for seniors, are available almost everywhere, but chances are your kids and grandchildren can teach you everything you need to know to get started.

QUESTIONS AND ANSWERS

Retirement in Mexico is an ever-changing process. Each time we revise *Choose Mexico,* we update it to reflect changes in laws and contemporary conditions. We've received many letters from readers asking for more information about living in Mexico. It's impossible to answer every letter, so we cannot always provide a detailed reply. Often while reading letters from readers, we discover areas of information that we overlooked and/or didn't stress enough in the previous editions. We've covered some of those topics in the main text of this edition, but we feel it may be helpful to reiterate them and to provide answers to some of the more frequently asked questions.

QUESTION: What does it cost to live in Mexico?

ANSWER: Although this is one of the most frequently asked questions, it can only be answered with another question: What does it cost you to live in the United States (or Canada)?

If you ask me that question, I will give one answer. If you ask my doctor, she will give another, and if you ask the person who bags my groceries in the supermarket, he will give still another. Obviously different people have different lifestyles, different expectations, and different ideas about what is a necessity and what is a luxury.

We have spoken to people in Mexico living on incomes ranging from several hundred to several thousand dollars a month. They all seem to be content with the way they are living.

What we can tell you from our examination of rents, food prices, health-care costs, and other expenses all over Mexico is that—at the time of writing—you can live on about two-thirds of what it costs you in the United States. This is not true of every location in the country. In the Los Cabos area of Baja, for instance, prices are just about the same as north of the border. In some of the more isolated spots, they are lower.

Do not go to Mexico expecting to live royally on an income insufficient to mantain a decent standard of living in the United States. There is no safety net in Mexico, and your fellow expatriates are unlikely to help. In fact, do not go to Mexico because it is cheap. Nothing is a bargain, unless it is what you want. Go to Mexico because you want to share in the richness of life there and be happy that if you can afford to live well in the United States or Canada, you can afford to live better there.

QUESTION: What is involved in driving my automobile into Mexico?

ANSWER: If you are on a tourist visa (FM-T), you are entitled to bring a vehicle into Mexico for 180 days. You will need:

1. The original certificate of title
2. An affidavit from the lien holder authorizing the temporary importation of the car (if the vehicle is financed)
3. A valid state registration and current license plates
4. A valid state driver's license
5. A VISA, MasterCard, or American Express card in the driver's name (This card will be used to post a bond to ensure that the car will be returned to the United States. Also, a small fee will be charged to the card for the car permit.)

Be aware that the Mexican government may begin to enforce the 180-day importation rule, and you could be refused reentry after a short return to the border. A car with foreign plates remains legal as long as its owner maintains the immigration status that he or she had when the car entered the country. This means 180 days for tourists. For those who apply for a one-year FM-3 visa, the automobile is legal in Mexico as long as the visa is renewed every year.

If your vehicle does not have Mexican license plates, never allow anyone else to drive it except your children, parents, and siblings, who must be able to document their relationship to the owner of the car if they are stopped by police. Failure to observe this rule can be a serious offense. It's a good idea to keep copies of identification papers in the automobile at all times.

QUESTION: I read in the newspaper that Mexico is undergoing inflation. If prices keep rising in Mexico, won't that make retirement too expensive?

ANSWER: Inflation is always under way in Mexico. Rising costs gradually climb upward until things reaches the point where the dollar and peso are out of balance. When this happens some prices can be almost as high as in the United States. Then a dramatic devaluation of the peso takes place, sending the cost of living to incredibly low levels. This repeating cycle has happened a half dozen times over the last fifty years.

At the time of publication of this edition of *Choose Mexico,* the authors believe that Mexico is due for another devaluation. Only time will tell whether the new government under President Fox will allow the peso to go into a free fall, as in the past, or whether he will gradually bring the peso-dollar exchange rates into balance. In any event, even though prices in pesos rise, the value of the dollar rises too (albeit not as fast as it should), so the actual cost of living rises at a slower rate than it might appear.

QUESTION: What are the age limits and income requirements for retirement in Mexico?

ANSWER: Nowdays it's relatively easy to qualify, and there's no longer a "fifty-five-and-older" requirement. At the present time the FM-3 *rentista* status is available to anyone who can show a monthly income of about $1,000 and $500 for each dependent. If you own property in Mexico, the amount of income required is reduced by one-half. All you need to do is present bank statements for the last three months showing you have deposited at least this amount each month.

QUESTION: Can I bring a firearm into Mexico?

ANSWER: This is probably the most serious question answered in this section. Don't even *think* about bringing guns into Mexico without permission. Mexican jails are always holding prisoners who crossed the border, forgetting they had a handgun in the glove compartment or the trunk! Unlike the United States, where a cavalier attitude is taken about firearms, in Mexico this is an extremely serious offense.

The best advice we can give concerning guns is: *If you feel you can't travel without a weapon, then do not travel in Mexico!* Shotguns are just about the only firearms permitted across the border, and the red tape involved is incredible. Besides proof of citizenship, you need a character reference in duplicate from your police department; the serial numbers, calibers, and makes of your guns; up to fourteen passport-size photos; and several days of running around to various Mexican government offices. Fees, stamps, and papers will cost about $120, plus *mordidas* and a doozy of a headache.

QUESTION: How is the fishing in Mexico?

ANSWER: Fishing in Baja and along the Pacific Coast varies from good to fantastic. The Gulf of Mexico also has a great reputation for fishing, and the Caribbean from Isla Mujeres to the Guatemalan border is well known for snorkeling and scuba diving as well as angling. Licenses are usually provided by the people who rent you the boat or can be purchased in town. Inland communities sometimes have lakes and streams nearby where freshwater species abound. Bringing your fishing tackle into Mexico is not a problem.

QUESTION: Newspaper stories report that crime in Mexico is becoming a big problem. Is Mexico still safe for retirement?

ANSWER: There's no doubt that crime rates have risen in Mexico, but the relevant question is: From what level have they risen and to what level? Folks living in traditional retirement areas and smaller towns report little if any difference in personal safety, and most say they feel much safer than in many parts of the United States. The news reports almost always deal with crime in Mexico City. Because there are no reliable statistics on the increase in crime in this enormous metropolis, it's difficult to measure just how much crime has risen. But there's no question that there is no more crime in Mexico City now than there was a few years ago, and as you would expect, there's more crime in large cities than in the provinces. If you were to read about all of the crimes reported in cities such as Chicago or Atlanta, you would probably want to steer clear of those places too.

A resident of Guadalajara has this to say about personal safety: "I travel almost every week to Mexico City. I take the normal precautions. Never, and I mean *never,* have I had the hint of a problem. I know, of course, that this limited experience does not mean there are no crime problems in the big city. The simple message is: Take your precautions, follow the rules, and you will enjoy your stay. You will be more secure there than in many other big cities in the United States."

QUESTION: I'm looking at a beach property in Mexico. Is buying property safe? Can the government suddenly decide to take it away?

ANSWER: Land that changes hands legally is perfectly safe. The key word here is "legally." We have never heard of a single case where non-*ejido* property held by a non-Mexican in a legal bank trust *(fideicomiso)* has been taken from the non-Mexican. Problems arise when someone buys *ejido* land without going through the process of obtaining the *fideicomiso.* It's important to have a competent lawyer handle the transaction. He will make sure the property is free and clear by checking the Land Registry Office and will obtain a no-lien certificate and tax statement from

Hacienda (treasury department). Your lawyer also must check for outstanding water bills, municipal taxes, or other encumberances.

QUESTION: Can I get a job in Mexico?

ANSWER: It's not altogether out of the question, but probably not, at least until you have achieved *inmigrado* status (at least five years).

Unless you are an *inmigrado*, it is illegal to work in Mexico without a work permit, which is obtained from the Department of Immigration (with its central office in Mexico City and some branch offices elsewhere around the republic). These permits aren't easy to obtain. Unless you can do some kind of work that no Mexican citizen can perform, you aren't likely to get permission. The restrictions have relaxed somewhat over the years, particularly in real-estate sales and promotion, teaching English, and some other fields.

If you are caught working without a permit, you take a big risk. According to the director of immigration in Baja California Sur (Lic. Gabriel Cuervo), "Working without papers in Mexico is a crime and could come with a generous jail sentence of eighteen months or deportation." Another point is that if you do obtain papers, they are good only for the employer specified. Should you decide to change employers, you need to apply for another permit. If you don't, you face the same serious charges as if you didn't have papers in the first place.

Finally, wages are so low in Mexico that you would have to have some kind of special talent that no Mexicans possess to demand any kind of decent salary. Real estate and condo salesmen working on commission may do well, however, depending upon their ability and their luck. Too often employers in Mexico believe that the minimum wage and maximum wage are identical. And with wages presently below $5.00 a day, you probably wouldn't want to work anyway.

QUESTION: Can I bring my pets with me?

ANSWER: Dogs and cats can be brought into Mexico if they are healthy and have received the required immunizations and you have a veterinarian's certificate to prove it. Ask your vet for a U.S. Interstate and International Certificate of Health and have it dated within seventy-two hours of crossing the border. To bring a pet back into the United States, you'll need another health certificate and a rabies certificate not more than thirty days old from a Mexican veterinarian.

QUESTION: How about moving my furniture there?

ANSWER: You can legally move your furniture and other household goods to Mexico once you have resident status. You cannot do so when you first enter Mexico as a tourist. Whether it pays to transport your property there, rather than selling and replacing it with new purchases in Mexico, is something you will have to decide for yourself when you have been there for a while. You may be surprised at the bargains on furniture that are available to you in Mexico.

QUESTION: Do American appliances work on Mexican electrical current?

ANSWER: Yes, the current is the same as in the United States. No adapters are needed, and anything that works at home will work there (although we have heard reports that electric clocks do not keep good time). However, you'll find that occasional intermittent voltage fluctuations can eat your electrical appliances, so be sure to have spike (surge) protectors for your plug-ins, especially your computer equipment. Telephone lines aren't grounded, so remember to unplug them during thunderstorms or use a surge protector that has phone jacks.

QUESTION: Can I have my Social Security check automatically deposited in my Mexican bank account?

ANSWER: At the present time Social Security checks cannot be deposited into a foreign bank account. Most expatriates maintain an account with U.S. banks that have connections with their Mexican bank. Then they simply transfer the money as they need it by calling a Mexican toll-free number.

QUESTION: What income taxes do retirees in Mexico have to pay?

ANSWER: If they receive income from the United States, they have to continue filing returns and paying taxes there. They do not pay any taxes to Mexico on their U.S. income. As we have stated before, most retirees cannot be employed in Mexico in the first place, so the only taxable income they are likely to have there is interest on their deposits in Mexican banks. The tax is withheld before the interest is paid.

QUESTION: Is my Medicare health insurance good in Mexico?

ANSWER: Not yet. Although there's substantial discussion and lobbying to change Medicare coverage someday, nothing has happened. So at the moment its coverage doesn't extend to Mexico. But the good news is that you can join the Mexican Social Security plan for about $250 a year. You must pass a physical by a certified IMSS doctor. You could be rejected if you have some preexisting illness or dangerous health condition. For those without insurance physician and hospital bills are usually low, with office visits often $20 to $25 and operations sometimes costing less than the airfare to go home to have the procedure done. Hospitals cost $40–$80 a day. Some retiree organizations offer group insurance for members; the Chapala Society, for instance, provides coverage, even for emergency health care when traveling in the United States or Canada.

QUESTION: How do we apply for our *inmigrante* status?

ANSWER: You can either apply for the FM-3 at the Mexican consulate nearest to your home in the United States or Canada, or you can apply when you arrive in Mexico. It's best to get everything done before you move, partly because you avoid a small fee, but more importantly, you can do all of the paperwork at home: by mail, FedEx, or UPS. You can also apply for your duty-free importation permit of personal and household goods at the same time. This application must be made at a Mexican consulate located in the United States. You'll need a *menaje de casa* (a detailed inventory, in Spanish, of everything you intend to bring, including item, make, model, and serial number), which would be difficult to do while living in Mexico. There's a fee of about $115 for the import permit; unless you have a lot of goods, it may not be worth the trouble to bother, and you may simply prefer to pay duty on your imports.

To obtain your one-year FM-3 status, you will need a valid passport and four copies of a letter in Spanish addressed to the proper immigration authority with your full name, address, and a request to obtain the FM-3. Make sure all of the following are enclosed with each copy:

- Proof of income; that is, bank statements for the last three months showing deposits
- A doctor's certificate declaring that you have no communicable diseases, including HIV
- A certificate from the your local police attesting to your good conduct
- Eight passport-size photographs (two per letter)
- Cash or a money order for $53 (confirm the amount; these rates are variable)

- If divorced, a certified copy of your divorce decree; if married, a certified copy of your marriage license

Remember that your FM-3 isn't valid until you've had it officially registered with immigration within thirty days of your entry into the country.

QUESTION: Isn't Mexican automobile liability insurance very expensive?

ANSWER: It is if you buy it by the day. It costs about $7.00 a day to cover your car for a short stay. But just as in the United States, it becomes far less costly when you insure for a longer period of time. The annual liability premium for an older car is about $150. If you bring in an expensive new car from the United States and want collision as well as liability insurance on it, you may well have to pay more than you do in the United States, unless you join a club with insurance benefits.

QUESTION: What will my legal status be?

ANSWER: This question is answered in great detail in our "Successful Retirement" section. The most important thing to understand is that becoming a legal resident of Mexico does not impair your U.S. or Canadian citizenship in any way.

QUESTION: Are there schools for English-speaking children and adolescents?

ANSWER: Every large city in Mexico (and some smaller ones, too) has at least one bilingual school to which many American (as well as some Mexican) families send their children. Because this is primarily a book for retirees, we do not list these schools, but we advise readers with young children to visit the community they are thinking of moving to and check personally.

QUESTION: What happens if I die while I am in Mexico?

ANSWER: Your spouse or friends can get a certificate from the local authorities that allows your remains to be flown back to your home country, if that is what you wish. It's not a problem.

QUESTION: Are U.S. television programs shown in Mexico?

ANSWER: Yes, just about anywhere with a satellite antenna. They are becoming increasingly popular in Mexico. Cable TV is readily available in and near the larger cities, with English-language stations included.

Video-rental stores are everywhere, stocked with the latest Hollywood films.

QUESTION: Can you recommend a real estate broker who can help me buy or rent a house or apartment in Mexico?

ANSWER: We don't feel that dealing with a real estate broker long distance is a wise way to shop for a home in Mexico. Also the ownership and personnel of real estate firms can change during the life of a book. As we discussed at greater length in the chapter on housing, we strongly urge you to visit a community before you make any commitments. It is also a good idea to study the real estate listings in English-language newspapers of the communities you are considering (see the appendix for names and addresses). These papers will have the names of real estate brokers of whom you may want to make preliminary inquiries. However, don't be discouraged by high asking prices, because you can almost always do much better on the spot. Bargains seldom make the newspaper ads; they are snapped up immediately.

QUESTION: Is it difficult to make friends in Mexico?

ANSWER: Jennifer Rose, who lives in Morelia, says: "For North Americans it's fairly easy to make friends when joining most established gringo communities. You'll be treated by the local community much differently once you've laid down roots here than being a tourist. As a new resident, you will be treated as a novelty, a breath of fresh air, welcomed as someone new joining the community. As far as the expat community's concerned, most are unwilling to make an emotional investment in developing friendships with transients. However, every community is different. Some factions bring out the Welcome Wagon, while others can be as chary of newcomers as fifth-generation Maine.

"As for Mexican friends, don't expect to make a great number of them at once. Understand that Mexico is a very stratified society. No matter how democratic you may consider yourself, inviting the bricklayer and the bank president to a dinner party is going to make both feel very uncomfortable. Expect different levels of friendship. There's the 'drinks but not dinner,' the 'Let's meet at a restaurant,' and the 'inner circle.'"

WILL YOU LOVE IT?

Most foreigners either love Mexico or hate it. This phenomenon is so well known that just about every guidebook to the country, after listing the numerous reasons for the author's deep affection for the land and its people, finds it necessary to warn that "Mexico is not everybody's cup of tea." (Someone should offer a prize for an alternative to that cliche—"cup of tequila" would not qualify.) No doubt the principal reason for these strong feelings is that Mexico, like many of its favorite foods, is highly spiced. Nothing is muted—neither the colors nor the sounds. Mexico does not sneak up on you. It confronts you immediately and totally.

The shock is particularly intense for the North American who has gone right next door to find himself in a country vastly different from his or her own. Mexico quickly shatters the illusion that foreignness is a function of distance.

Are Mexico's differences from the United States and Canada good or bad? We know our answer to that question, but we don't know yours. Even if we knew you very well, we are not at all sure that we could predict which it would be. Yes, there are some people whose reaction to the country we could confidently guess. Most of them are so rigid, impatient, or demanding that we cannot imagine them tolerating the inefficiencies and delays of Mexican life. We're proud that after a number of months in Mexico, we have learned to sit in a restaurant for twenty minutes before the waiter takes our orders and for another twenty until the food arrives, without any knotting of our insides. (We're doubly proud that we can even do it back in the United States.) We are not, however, sufficiently unreasonable to expect or demand that everyone master this trick. Would you be outraged or amused by the fact that each time postage for an airmail letter to the United States goes up, it is many months before stamps are available for the new amount or that often envelopes and packages have to be mailed with wall-to-wall small denomination stamps because no larger ones are available? Trivial? Of course, but if your answer is "outraged" or even if you would merely find that situation annoying, it's quite possible that Mexico is not for you.

There are just too many little things like that, which, if you let them, could add up to constant annoyance.

Somewhat more serious are the seemingly arbitrary and unpredictable shortages that plague Mexico for months at a time. Unlike the United States, where many brands of almost every product are available, Mexico usually has only one brand, and anything that interrupts its manufacturer's operations cuts off the supply altogether. Mexicans and longtime foreign residents there learn to deal with these shortages in a variety of ways. Approached in the right spirit, obtaining the seemingly unobtainable becomes a game. Of course it may not be the kind you enjoy playing.

Most North Americans are deeply offended by the sight of people spitting in the street. In the days when spittoons were a ubiquitous feature of the American domestic landscape, the aesthetic aversion to that practice was probably much weaker. However, a very effective antispitting campaign by the Tuberculosis Association succeeded in sensitizing our grandparents, and we continue to view it with an intense distaste that Mexicans do not seem to share. To be comfortable in Mexico, you do not have to enjoy the sight, but it does help to be able to ignore it.

Drinking only bottled or boiled water is a nuisance. How much more convenient it is to place your glass under any tap and enjoy, without any trace of concern, the clear liquid that pours out. It is also pleasant to pick up a piece of fruit in the market and eat it as you find it or, if you're fastidious, after running some cold water over it. After you have returned from Mexico, it usually takes some time before you are able to resume those practices without a moment of hesitation. Water in Mexico is not safe, and while there, you must learn to avoid everything uncooked with which it may have come in contact. Are these inconveniences serious enough to spoil your enjoyment of the country, or are they somewhat like the necessity to retrain your reflexes before you can drive or even cross streets safely in England? You may not know what your reaction will be until you have been in Mexico for a while. Part of the initial strain is fear that you will forget and inadvertently expose yourself to danger. That worry soon fades as the required new behaviors become second nature.

Many North Americans are appalled by what they see as the pervasive corruption of Mexican political life. Indeed it's true that few

Mexican presidents have left office without arranging for themselves and their friends to live in luxury for the rest of their lives. However, to see this as contrasting sharply with universal probity north of the border requires that one forget the sleaze factor that has figured so prominently in the history of just about every U.S. presidential administration in our time. Of course every scandal on the federal level has many counterparts in our statehouses. Less visible but far more widespread are the abuses of power routinely encountered in the world of commerce. It is all too easy to jump from the unquestionable fact that U.S. or Canadian customs inspectors are much less likely to take bribes than their Mexican counterparts to the dubious conclusion that North Americans are honest and Mexicans are crooked. It's not even a question of degree but rather of different culturally approved manifestations of what, sadly, appears to be a universal weakness. However, most North Americans do need some time to become comfortable with the idea of "tipping" minor public officials.

One certainly does not have to approve of the Mexican government to be happy living there. North Americans have fallen in love with the country under regimes that have covered the full spectrum from right to left, and often their affection has been very much in spite of the ideology and behavior of the party in power. Even today Mexico is full of Americans who deplore everything about the government's foreign and domestic policies, would love to see them become carbon copies of ours, but would not think of moving back to the United States where they could enjoy the originals. Very few, by any means, are too poor to afford the higher prices in their homeland, so there must be something else about Mexico that holds them.

This brief recitation of some things North Americans find to dislike about Mexico is far from exhaustive. It does, however, include many of the most frequently heard complaints. For those who allow them to, they constitute ample reason for choosing other places in which to spend time. For many others—the authors included—they are part of the price one must pay for sharing in the riches of Mexican life.

Uppermost among those riches are the people of Mexico. If we have repeated this observation too frequently throughout this book, it's because we know that although anyone who has spent much time in Mexico will agree, those who have never been there may not be easily convinced.

Of course there are other attractions. One is the climate. At any given time the weather may not be perfect everywhere in Mexico, but chances are that it is someplace, and usually not too far from where you are. The residents of Mexico City discovered at least five centuries ago that when, as occasionally happens, the winters there are a bit too nippy, it's easy to find temperatures a dozen degrees warmer in nearby Cuernavaca. In Guadalajara they know that in January, descending to the Pacific Coast (only a few hours away) takes you from the fifties to the balmy eighties. In San Miguel, Morelia, and dozens of other cities and towns of the Central Plateau, spring is "eternal." If you live in a climate that is bearable year-round, it may be hard to understand the thirst for warmth and sunshine that historically—for Northern Europeans from England to Russia—has made Italy an earthly paradise and that draws flocks of sun-starved Scandinavians to Spain every winter. Unless you have gasped for air in a New York, Washington, or Houston summer, the annual exodus to the mountains and the beaches may seem inexplicable. If, on the other hand, you suffer either extreme heat or cold in the course of a year, it may not be necessary for us to tell you much more about why the Mexican climate draws so many refugees from the extremes of U.S. winters and summers. Yes, parts of Mexico can be hot, but the bulk of the population lives in, and visitors flock to, places where altitude or sea breezes provide year-round moderation.

It's difficult to avoid sounding crass when discussing how reasonable living in Mexico can be. Compulsive bargain hunting is an illness and, many would say, one of the least attractive characteristics of North Americans abroad. Perhaps, though, retirees who are trying to make limited incomes provide the comfort they have been encouraged to expect as the reward for a lifetime of work can be viewed a little differently than tourists seeking cheap vacations. In Mexico we observed North Americans who would be barely making it at home living comfortably. This gave us renewed optimism about our own futures and colors our perceptions of Mexico as a place to retire. Certainly we would not advise anyone to move there for the low prices alone. Nothing is a bargain if you don't enjoy it. Nevertheless, the stretch that the low prices give to a modest income must be counted as one of the major advantages of Mexico as a place to visit or live.

In the end, although we hope that these observations may help you make some guesses about whether you will love or hate the Mexican experience, you will not know for sure until you've tried it. If you go there expecting to find a replica of life in the United States or Canada, but with palm trees and *mariachis* in the background, you'll be disappointed. Some things that you value highly are not considered important there. On the other hand, you may learn to appreciate some qualities—such as patience, courtesy, and simplicity—that our culture often slights. Even if you decide, after you have seen it for yourself, that you can't love Mexico as we do, we doubt that you will regret having tried.

Appendix

English-Language Newspapers in Mexico

Atención San Miguel (San Miguel de Allende weekly)
Apdo 119
San Miguel de Allende
GTO, Mexico

El Ojo del Lago (Lake Chapala area weekly)
P.O. Box 279
Chapala, Jalisco
45900 Mexico

Guadalajara Reporter (news of the Guadalajara area)
9051-C Siempre Viva Road, Suite 5–452
San Diego, CA 92173-3628
www.guadalajarareporter.com

The News (a daily, sold throughout Mexico)
Balderas 87—Third Floor
D.F. 06050, Mexico

Oaxaca Times (free weekly)
307 Macedonio Alcalá
Oaxaca
Oax 68000, Mexico

Newsletters

AIM (Adventures in Mexico)
Apdo 31–70
45050 Guadalajara
JAL, Mexico

Cuernavaca Calling
Apdo 4–587
Cuernavaca
C.P. 62431, Mexico

Mexican Living and Travel Update
6301 Squaw Valley Road
Pahrump, NV 89041

Mexico Travel—Monthly Report
P.O. Box 1498
Imperial Beach, CA 91933-1498
Phone and fax (619) 429–6566

Other Resources

California Commerce Bank
2029 Century Park East
Los Angeles, CA 90067
Guadalajara information number: 25–32–58.

Mexico Connect
www.mexconnect.com

Citizens Emergency Center—U.S. State Department—Situation reports on any destination around the world; locates travelers abroad to deliver emergency messages. Phone (202) 647–5225. Available: 8:15 A.M. to 5:00 P.M. weekdays, 9:00 A.M. to 3:00 P.M. Saturdays (Eastern Standard Time).

Mexican Consulates in the United States and Canada

U.S. Consulates

Alberquerque: 401 Fifth Street, NW, Alburquerque, NM 87102
(505) 247–2147 (phone) or (505) 842–9490 (fax)
Atlanta: 2600 Apple Valley Road, Atlanta, GA 30319
(404) 266–2233 (phone) or (404) 266–2309 (fax)

Austin: 200 East Sixth Street, Suite 200, Austin, TX 78701
(512) 478–2866 (phone) or (512) 478–8008 (fax)
Boston: 20 Park Plaza, Suite 506, Boston, MA 02116
(617) 426–4181 (phone) or (617) 695–1957 (fax)
Brownsville: 724 East Elizabeth Street, Brownsville, TX 78520
(210) 542–2051 (phone) or (210) 542–7267 (fax)
Calexico: 331 West Second Street, Calexico, CA 92231
(760) 357–3863 (phone) or (760) 357–6284 (fax)
Chicago: 300 North Michigan Avenue, Chicago, IL 60601
(312) 855–1380 (phone) or (312) 855–9257 (fax)
Corpus Christi: 8800 North Shoreline, Corpus Christi, TX 78410
(512) 882–3375 (phone) or (512) 882–9234 (fax)
Dallas: 8855 Stemmons Freeway, Dallas, TX 75247
(214) 630–7341 (phone) or (214) 630–3511 (fax)
Del Rio: 300 East Losoya, Del Rio, TX 78840
(830) 774–5031 (phone) or (830) 774–6497 (fax)
Denver: 48 Steele Street, Denver, CO 80206
(303) 331–1867 (phone) or (303) 830–2655 (fax)
Detroit: 600 Renaissance Street, Suite 1510, Detroit, MI 48243
(313) 567–7713 (phone) or (313) 567–7543 (fax)
Douglas: 541 Tenth Street, Douglas, AZ 85607
(520) 364–3107 (phone) or (520) 364–1379 (fax)
Eagle Pass: 140 North Adams Street, Eagle Pass, TX 78852
(830) 773–9255 (phone) or (830) 773–9397 (fax)
El Paso: 910 East San Antonio Street, El Paso, TX 79901
(915) 533–3644 (phone) or (915) 532–7163 (fax)
Fresno: 830 Van Ness Avenue, Fresno, CA 93721
(209) 233–3065 (phone) or (209) 233–5638 and (209) 233–6165 (fax)
Houston: 4507 San Jacinto, Houston, TX 77004
(713) 271–6800 (phone) or (713) 271–3201 (fax)
Laredo: 1612 Farragut Street, Laredo, TX 78040
(956) 723–6369 (phone) or (956) 723–1741 (fax)
Los Angeles: 2401 West Sixth Street, Los Angeles, CA 90057
(213) 351–6800 (phone) or (213) 351–6844 (fax)
McAllen: 600 South Broadway Street, McAllen, TX 78040
(956) 686–0243 (phone) or (956) 686–4901 (fax)

Miami: 1200 North West Seventy-eighth Avenue, Suite 200, Miami, FL 33126
(305) 716–4977 (phone) or (305) 593–2758 (fax)
Midland: 511 West Ohio Street, Midland, TX 79701
(915) 687–2334 (phone) or (915) 687–3952 (fax)
New Orleans: 1140 WTC Building, 2 Canal Street, New Orleans, LA 70115
(504) 522–3596 (phone) or (504) 525–2332 (fax)
New York: 27 East Thirty-ninth Street, New York, NY 10016
(212) 217–6400 (phone) or (212) 689–0456 (fax)
Nogales: 480 North Grand Avenue, Nogales, AZ 85621
(520) 287–2521 (phone) or (520) 287–3175 (fax)
Orlando: 823 East Colonial Drive, Orlando, FL 32803
(407) 894–0514 (phone) or (407) 895–6140 (fax)
Oxnard: 201 East Fourth Street, Oxnard, CA 93030
(805) 483–4684 (phone) or (805) 385–3527 (fax)
Philadelphia: 111 South Independence Mall East, Philadelphia, PA 19106
(215) 992–4262 (phone) or (215) 923–7281 (fax)
Phoenix: 1990 West Camel Back Road, Phoenix, AZ 85015
(602) 242–7398 (phone) or (602) 242–2957 (fax)
Portland: 1234 Southwest Morrison, Portland, OR 97205
(503) 274–1442 (phone) or (503) 274–1540 (fax)
Sacramento: 716 J Street, Sacramento, CA 95827
(916) 441–3287 (phone) or (916) 363–0625 (fax)
Saint Louis: 1015 Locust Street, Saint Louis, MO 63101
(314) 436–3065 (phone) or (314) 436–2695 (fax)
Salt Lake City: 458 East 200 South, Salt Lake City, UT 84111
(801) 521–8502 (phone) or (801) 521–0534 (fax)
San Antonio: 127 Navarro Street, San Antonio, TX 78205
(210) 227–1085 (phone) or (210) 227–1817 (fax)
San Bernardino: 532 North "D" Street, San Bernardino, CA 92401
(909) 384–8113 (phone) or (909) 889–8285 (fax)
San Diego: 1549 India Street, San Diego, CA 92101
(619) 241–8414 (phone) or (619) 241–8420 (fax)
San Francisco: 870 Market Street, San Francisco, CA 94102
(415) 392–5554 (phone) or (415) 392–3233 (fax)

San Jose: 380 North First Street, San Jose, CA 95112
(408) 298–5581 (phone) or (408) 294–4506 (fax)
Santa Ana: 828 North Broadway, Santa Ana, CA 92701–3424
(714) 835–3069 (phone) or (714) 835–3472 (fax)
Seattle: 2132 Third Avenue, Seattle, WA 98121
(206) 448–3526 (phone) or (206) 448–4771 (fax)
Tucson: 553 South Stone Avenue, Tucson, AZ 85701
(520) 882–5595 (phone) or (520) 882–8959 (fax)
Washington, D.C.: 2827 Sixteenth Street, NW, Washington, DC 20009
(202) 736–1000 (phone) or (202) 797–8458 (fax)
San Juan: IBM Building, Avenida Muñoz Rivera 654, San Juan, Puerto Rico 00918
(787) 764–0258 (phone) or (787) 250–0042 (fax)

Canadian Consulates

Montréal: 2055 Rue Peel, Bureau 1000, Montreal, QC H3A 1V4
(514) 288–2502 (phone) or (514) 288–8287 (fax)
Toronto: Commerce Court West, 199 Bay Street, Toronto, ON M5L 1E9
(416) 368–2875 (phone) or (416) 368–8342 (fax)
Vancouver: 810-1130 West Pender Street, Vancouver, BC V6E 4A4
(604) 684–3547 (phone) or (604) 684–2485 (fax)

INDEX